PAULO FREIRE

PEDAGOGY OF HOPE

Reliving *Pedagogy of the Oppressed*

With Notes by Ana Maria Araújo Freire

Translated by Robert R. Barr

continuum

NEW YORK • LONDON

2004
The Continuum International Publishing Group Inc
15 East 26 Street, New York, NY 10010

Printed in the United States of America

Library of Congress Cataloging-in-Publication Data

Freire, Paulo, 1921-
      [Pedagogía da esperança. English]
      Pedagogy of hope : reliving Pedagogy of the oppressed / Paulo
Freire ; notes by Ana Maria Araújo Freire ; translated by Robert R.
Barr
           p.   cm.
      Translation of: Pedagogía da esperança.
   Includes bibliographical references
   ISBN 0-8264-0590-8   ISBN 0-8264-0843-5
      1. Freire, Paulo, 1921-   . 2. Education—Philosophy.   3. Popular
education—Philosophy.   4. Education—Social aspects—Latin America.
5. Education—Social aspects—Brazil. 6. Freire, Paulo, 1921-
Pedagogía do oprimido. I. Freire, Ana Maria Araújo, 1933-
II. Freire, Paulo, 1921-   Pedagogía do oprimido.   English.
III. Title.
LB880.F732P432   1994
370'.1—dc20   93-44911
                                                                       CIP

For Ana Maria, Nita,
who gave me back a taste for life:
when life seemed so long to me,
so nearly hopeless . . .
I looked at her!

                        Paulo

In memory of Armando Neves Freire,
excellent brother, fine friend

                        Paulo

For
Stela
Bruno
Silvia
Temistocles
and Reinilda
With a brotherly embrace

                        Paulo

For Genove Araújo,
hopeful as a teenager, at ninety—
whom I can never pay what I owe,
lovingly,

                        Paulo

For
Zé de Melo and Dora
for reasons beyond counting
with an embrace from their friend

                        Paulo

Opening Words

We are surrounded by a pragmatic discourse that would have us adapt to the facts of reality. *Dreams*, and *utopia*, are called not only useless, but positively impeding. (After all, they are an intrinsic part of any educational practice with the power to unmask the dominant lies.) It may seem strange, then, that I should write a book called *Pedagogy of Hope: Reliving Pedagogy of the Oppressed*.

But for me, on the contrary, the educational practice of a progressive option will never be anything but an adventure in unveiling. It will always be an experiment in bringing out the truth. Because this is the way I have always thought, there are those who dispute whether or not I am an educator. It happened recently in a meeting at UNESCO in Paris—I have been told by someone who was there. Latin American representatives refused to ascribe me the standing of educator. At least I was not an educator as far as they were concerned. And they criticized me for what seemed to them to be my exaggerated "politicization."

They failed to perceive that, in denying me the status of educator for being "too political," they were being as political as I. Of course, on opposite sides of the fence. "Neutral" they were not, nor could ever be.

On the other hand, there must be countless individuals who think the way a friend of mine, a university professor, thinks. He came looking for me. In astonishment, he asked, "But Paul . . . a *Pedagogy of Hope* in the shameless hellhole of corruption like the one strangling us in Brazil today?"

The fact is that the "democratization" of the shamelessness and corruption that is gaining the upper hand in our country, contempt for the common good, and crimes that go unpunished, have only broadened and deepened as the nation has begun to rise up in protest. Even young adults and teenagers crowd into the streets, criticizing, calling for honesty and candor. The people cry out against all the crass evidence of public corruption. The public squares are filled once more. There is a hope, however timid, on the street corners, a hope in each and every one of us. It is as if most of the nation had been taken by an uncontainable need to vomit at the sight of all this shamefulness.

On the other hand—while I certainly cannot ignore hopelessness as a concrete entity, nor turn a blind eye to the historical, economic, and social reasons that explain that hopelessness—I do not understand human existence, and the struggle needed to improve it, apart from hope and dream. Hope is an ontological need. Hopelessness is but hope that has lost its bearings, and become a distortion of that ontological need.

When it becomes a program, hopelessness paralyzes us, immobilizes us. We succumb to fatalism, and then it becomes impossible to muster the strength we absolutely need for a fierce struggle that will re-create the world.

I am hopeful, not out of mere stubbornness, but out of an existential, concrete imperative.

I do not mean that, because I am hopeful, I attribute to this hope of mine the power to transform reality all by itself, so that I set out for the fray without taking account of concrete, material data, declaring, "My hope is enough!" No, my hope is necessary, but it is not enough. Alone, it does not win. But without it, my struggle will be weak and wobbly. We need critical hope the way a fish needs unpolluted water.

The idea that hope alone will transform the world, and action undertaken in that kind of naïveté, is an excellent route to hopelessness, pessimism, and fatalism. But the attempt to do without hope, in the struggle to improve the world, as if that struggle could be reduced to calculated acts alone, or a purely scientific approach, is a frivolous illusion. To attempt to do without hope, which is based on the need for truth as an ethical quality of the struggle, is tantamount to denying that struggle one of its mainstays. The essential thing, as I maintain later on, is this: hope, as an ontological need, demands an anchoring in practice. As an ontological need, hope needs practice in order to become historical concreteness. That is why there is no hope in sheer hopefulness. The hoped-for is not attained by dint of raw hoping. Just to hope is to hope in vain.

Without a minimum of hope, we cannot so much as start the struggle. But without the struggle, hope, as an ontological need, dissipates, loses its bearings, and turns into hopelessness. And hopelessness can become tragic despair. Hence the need for a kind of education in hope. Hope, as it happens, is so important for our existence, individual and social, that we must take every care not to experience it in a mistaken form, and thereby allow it to slip toward hopelessness and despair. Hopelessness and despair are both the consequence and the cause of inaction or immobilism.

In limited situations, beyond which lies "untested feasibility" alone[1]—sometimes perceivable, sometimes not—we find the why of both positions: the hopeful one and the hopeless one.

One of the tasks of the progressive educator, through a serious, correct political analysis, is to unveil opportunities for hope, no matter what the obstacles may be. After all, without hope there is little we can do. It will be hard to struggle on, and when we fight as hopeless or despairing persons, our struggle will be suicidal. We shall be beside ourselves, drop our weapons, and throw ourselves into sheer hand-to-hand, purely vindictive, combat. Of course, the element of punishment, penalty, correction—the punitive element in the struggle we wage in our hope, in our conviction of its ethical and historical rightness—belongs to the pedagogical nature of the political process of which struggle is an expression. It would not be equitable that injustices, abuses, extortion, illicit profits, influence peddling, the use of offices and positions for the satisfaction of personal interests—all of these things that make up the reason for which, with justifiable anger, we now struggle in Brazil—should go uncorrected, just as it would not be right for any of those who would be judged guilty not to be severely punished, within the limits of the law.

It will not do—it is not a valid argument—simply to admit that none of this is a "privilege" of the Third World, as we sometimes hear it suggested. Yes, the First World has indeed always been an example of scandals of every sort, always a model of wickedness, of exploitation. We need only think of colonialism—of the massacres of invaded, subjugated, colonized peoples; of the wars of this century, of shameful, cheapening racial discrimination, and the rapine that colonialism has perpetrated. No, we have no monopoly on the dishonorable. But we can no longer connive with the scandals that wound us in our remotest depths.

What cynicism—just to take one example among dozens—that certain politicians should seek to conceal their doings from their constituents (who have an absolute right to know what is done in Congress and why), and defend, with puritanical airs, in the name of democracy, some right to hide out in a "secret ballot" during a presidential vote of confidence! Why hide, unless there is at least some minimal risk to one's physical well-being? Why is concealment solemnly dubbed the "purity," "honorableness," "unassailability" of the president? Let these politicians have the dignity to assume responsibility for their option. Let them come right out with their defense of the indefensible.

Pedagogy of Hope is that kind of book. It is written in rage and love, without which there is no hope. It is meant as a defense of tolerance—not to be confused with connivance—and radicalness. It is meant as a criticism of sectarianism. It attempts to explain and defend progressive postmodernity and it will reject conservative, neoliberal postmodernity.

The first step I shall take will be to analyze or speak of the *fabric,* the texture, the very strands, of the infancy, youth, and budding maturity in which *Pedagogy of the Oppressed,* which I "revisit" in this book, came to be proclaimed, first in oral form and then in writing.

Some of these strands, these threads, will end with my exile, into which I go with a soul steeped in history—the cultural marks, memories, feelings, and sentiments, doubts, dreams that never got off the drawing board but were never abandoned—and longings, of my world, my sky, the tepid waters of the Atlantic, the "improper language of the people, the correct language of the people."* I ar-

---

*Manuel Bandeira, "Evocação do Recife," in *Poesias*, 6th ed. (Rio de Janeiro: José Olympio, 1955), p. 191.

rived in exile, and reached the memory I bore in my soul of so many intertwined threads; there I came to be marked and stamped by new facts, new knowledge, and these wove new experiences, as in a tapestry.

Pedagogy of the Oppressed emerges from all of this, and I shall speak now of that book—of how I learned while I wrote it, and indeed, of how, while first speaking of this pedagogy, I was learning to write the book.

Then, in a second step in this present book, I shall return to *Pedagogy of the Oppressed*. I shall discuss some of its stages, and analyze certain criticisms leveled against it in the 1970s.

In the third and final step in this book, I shall speak at length of the threads and the fabrics whose essence, as it were, was *Pedagogy of the Oppressed* itself. Here I shall practically relive—and basically, shall actually be reliving—and as I do so, rethink, certain special moments in my journeys through the four corners of the earth, to which I was carried by *Pedagogy of the Oppressed*. Perhaps, however, I should make it clear to readers that, in taking myself back to *Pedagogy of the Oppressed*, and in speaking today of the tapestry of my experience in the 1970s, I do not intend to wallow in nostalgia. Instead, my reencounter with *Pedagogy of the Oppressed* will have the tone of one who speaks not of what has been, but of what is.

The facts, the debates, the discussions, the projects, the experiments, the dialogues in which I shared in the 1970s, all bearing on *Pedagogy of the Oppressed*, seem to me to be as current as do others to which I shall refer, of the 1980s and today.

I should now like, in these opening words, to thank a group of friends, in Brazil and abroad, with whom, even before beginning to work on this *Pedagogy of Hope*, I held conversations about this project, and from whom I received such important encouragement:

Ana Maria Freire, Madalena Freire Weffort, Maria de Fátima Freire Dowbor, Lutgardes Freire, Ladislau Dowbor, Celso Beisiegel, Ana Maria Saul, Moacir Gadotti, Antonio Chizzotti, Adriano Nogueira, Márcio Campos, Carlos Arguelo, Eduardo Sebastiani Ferreira, Adão J. Cardoso, Henry Giroux, Donaldo Macedo, Peter Park, Peter McLaren, Ira Shor, Stanley Aronowitz, Raúl Magaña, João Batista F. Pinto, Michael Apple, Madeleine Groumet, Martin Carnoy, Carlos Torres, Eduardo Hasche, Alma Flor Ada, Joaquim Freire, Susanne Mebes, Cristina Freire Heiniger, and Alberto Heiniger.

I should also like to express my thanks to my wife, Ana Maria Freire, for the excellent notes appended here, which clarify and anchor important elements in my text. Superscripts in the text refer to her numbered endnotes at the back of the book. Asterisks, on the other hand, refer to footnotes at the bottom of the page.

I am likewise aware of my indebtedness to Suzie Hartmann Lontra, who so patiently and devotedly proofread the typescript with me.

Nor must I omit to express my gratitude to Werner Mark Linz, for the enthusiasm with which he has always discussed this project with me, whether face-to-face or in our correspondence—that same enthusiasm with which, twenty-four years ago, he read the manuscript of *Pedagogy of the Oppressed* and published it.

Finally, to Marcus Gasparian, one of the finest and most sensitive publishers in Brazil today, I send a brotherly embrace and a "Thank you very much" for the taste with which he constantly discussed with me what would come to be *Pedagogy of Hope: Reliving Pedagogy of the Oppressed.*

Paulo Freire
São Paulo
January 1994

CHAPTER

1

I n 1947 I was teaching Portuguese at Colégio Oswaldo Cruz,[2] the same school where I had completed my secondary education and, also, as a special favor of the school's director, Dr. Aluizio Pessoa de Araújo,[3] my preparatory course for law school.[4] It was at that time that I received the invitation to become part of the recently created Industrial Social Service, SESI, the Regional Department of Pernambuco, set up by the National Industrial Confederation and given legal status by presidential decree.[5]

The invitation was transmitted through a great friend of mine and fellow alumnus of Colégio Oswaldo Cruz, a person to whom I am bound by close ties of friendship, which our political disagreements have never disturbed, to this very day. Our disagreements had to be. They expressed our diverging views of the world, and our understanding of life itself. We have got through some of the most difficult moments of our lives tempering our disagreements, thereby defending our right and our duty to preserve mutual love by ensuring that it will rise above our political options and ideological positions. Without our knowing it, at the time, we were already—each in his or her own way—postmodern! In fact, in our mutual respect, we were actually experiencing the rock-bottom foundation of politics.

His name is Paulo Rangel Moreira. Today he is an attorney of renown, and professor of law at the Federal University of Pernambuco.[6] One bright afternoon in Recife, he came to our house in the Casa Forte district, 224 Rita de Souza Street, and told us—Elza, my first wife, and me—of SESI's existence and what it could mean for us. He had already accepted the invitation extended to him by the young president of the organization, engineer and industrialist Cid Sampaio, to coordinate its social service projects. Every indication was that he would soon move to the legal department of the organization—his dream—to work in the field of his own expertise.

I listened, we listened—silent, curious, reticent, challenged—to Paulo Rangel's optimistic discourse. We were a little afraid, too, Elza and I. Afraid of the new, perhaps. But there was also within us a willingness and a taste for risk, for adventure.

Night was "falling." Night had "fallen." In Recife, night "arrives" suddenly. The sun is "surprised" to find itself still shining, and makes a run for it, as if there were no time to lose.

Elza flicked on the light. "And what will Paul do in this organization?" she asked. "What will it be able to offer Paul besides the salary he needs? How will he be able to exercise his curiosity, what creative work will he be able to devote himself to so that he won't die of sadness and longing for the teaching job he likes so much?"

We were in our last year of law school, in the middle of the school year. Something had already happened, right about the time of the invitation, that was to become very important in my life. I have already referred to it in interviews, and it has been mentioned in biographical notes in books and periodicals. It had made Elza laugh with satisfaction at seeing something happen that she had almost guessed would happen—something she had counted on happening since the beginning of our life together. At the same time, her laugh was a pleasant one, without anything like "I told you so" about it, but just full-to-the-brim of gladness.

I had come home at the end of the day with the tasty sensation of someone correcting a mistake he or she has been making. Opening the door, Elza asked me a question that, on so many people's lips, is not much more than a kind of bureaucratic formality, but which when asked by Elza was always a genuine question, never a rote formula. It expressed lively curiosity, and betokened true investigation. She asked, "Everything all right at the office today?"

And I told her about the experience that had put an end to my brand-new career as a lawyer. I really needed to talk. I needed to recite, word for word, what I had just told the young dentist I had sitting in front of me in my very new office. Shy, frightened, nervous, his hands moving as if suddenly unhooked from his mind, detached from his conscious body, and become autonomous, and yet unable to do anything "on their own," do anything with themselves, or connect with the words that tumbled out of his mouth (God knows how)—the young dentist had said something to me that I needed to speak with Elza about at once. I needed to talk with Elza at that special moment, just as in other, equally special moments in the course of our life. I needed to speak of the spoken, of the *said* and the *not said*, of the heard, of the listened to. To speak of the said is not only to resay the said, but to relive the living experience that has generated the saying that now, at the time of the resaying, is said once more. Thus, to resay, to speak of the said, implies hearing once again what has been said by someone else about or because of the saying that we ourselves have done.

"Something very exciting happened to me this afternoon—just a few minutes ago," I said to Elza. "You know what? I'm not going to be a lawyer. It's not that I see nothing special, nothing captivating, about law. Law is a a basic need. It's a job that has to be done, and just as much as anything else, it has to be based on ethics, and competence, and seriousness, and respect for people. But law isn't what I want." Then I spoke of what had been, of things experienced, of words, of meaningful silences, of the said, of the heard. Of the young dentist before me whom I had invited to come talk with me as his creditor's attorney. The young man had set up his dental office, at least partially, and had not paid his debts.

"I made a mistake," he said. "I guess I was overoptimistic. I took out a loan I can't pay back. But I'm legally required to have certain instruments in order to practice dentistry. So, well, sir, . . . you can take our furniture, in the dining room, the living room . . ." And then, laughing a shy laugh, without the trace of a sneer—with as much humor as irony—he finished up: " . . . Only you can't have my eighteen-month-old baby girl."

I had listened in silence. I was thinking. Then I said to him, "I think you and your wife and your little girl and your dining room and your living room are going to sit in a kind of suspended animation for a while, as far as your debt-troubles are concerned. I'm going to have to wait till next week to see my client and tell him I'm dropping the case. It'll take him another week or so to get another down-and-outer like me to be his attorney. This will give you a little breathing space, even if it is just suspended animation. I'd also like to tell you that, like you, I'm closing down my career before it's even gotten started. Thanks."

The young man, of my own generation, may for all I know have left my office without much of a grasp of what had been said and heard. I squeezed his cold hand warmly with mine. Once he was home again and had thought over what had been said, who knows, he might have begun to understand some of the reasons that had led me to say what I had said.

That evening, relaying to Elza what had been said, I could never have imagined that, one day, so many years later, I would write *Pedagogy of the Oppressed*, whose discourse, whose proposal, has something to do with the experience of that afternoon, in terms of what it, too, meant, and especially in terms of the decision to accept Cid Sampaio's invitation, conveyed to me by Paulo Rangel. I abandoned the practice of law for good that afternoon, once I had heard Elza say, "I was hoping for that. You're an educator." Not many months after, as the night that had arrived in such haste began, I said yes to SESI's summons to its Division of Education and Culture, whose field of experience, study, reflection, and practice was to become an indispensable moment in the gestation of *Pedagogy of the Oppressed*.

Never does an event, a fact, a deed, a gesture of rage or love, a poem, a painting, a song, a book, have only one reason behind it. In fact, a deed, a gesture, a poem, a painting, a song, a book are always wrapped in thick wrappers. They have been touched by manifold *whys*. Only some of these are close enough to the event or the creation to be visible as *whys*. And so I have always been more interested in understanding the process in and by which things come about than in the product in itself.

Pedagogy of the Oppressed could not have gestated within me solely by reason of my stint with SESI. But my stint with SESI was fundamental to its development. Even before *Pedagogy of the Oppressed*, my time with SESI wove a tapestry of which *Pedagogy* was a kind of inevitable extension. I refer to the dissertation I defended in what was then the University of Recife, and later the Federal University of Pernambuco: "Educação e atualidade brasileira." I later reworked my dissertation and published it as *Educação como prática da liberdade,* and that book basically became the forerunner of *Pedagogy of the Oppressed.*

Again, in interviews, in dialogues with intellectuals, including non-Brazilians, I have made references to more remote tapestries that enveloped me, by bits and pieces, from my childhood and adolescence onward, antedating my time with SESI, which was without any doubt a "founding time," a foundational time.

These bits and pieces of time actually lived in me—for I had lived them—awaiting another time, which might not even have come as it came, but into which, if it did come, earlier bits and pieces of time were destined to extend, in the composition of the larger fabric.

At times, it happens to us not to perceive the "kinship" among the times we have experienced, and thus to let slip the opportunity to "solder together" disconnected cognitions, and in so doing to allow the second to shed light on the doubtful brilliance of the first.

There was my experience of infancy and adolescence with youngsters who were the children of rural and urban workers, my life as a child with children whose opportunities for life were so utterly minimal, the way in which most of their parents treated us—Temístocles, my immediately elder brother, and me—their "fear of freedom," which I never understood, nor called it this at the time, their subservient attitude toward their employers, the boss, the owner, which later, much later, I read in Sartre was one of the expressions of the "connivance" of the oppressed with the oppressors.* There were their oppressed bodies, the unconsulted hosts of the oppressors' parasitism.

It is interesting, in a context of childhood and adolescence, in the connivance maintained with the wickedness of the powerful—with the weakness that needed to turn into the strength of the dominated—that the time of SESI's foundation, that time of "solderings" and "splicings" of old, pure "guesses," to which my new knowledge

*Jean-Paul Sartre, preface to Franz Fanon, *Os condenados da Terra* (Rio de Janeiro: Civilização Brasileira).

with its critical emergence gave meaning, was the moment at which I read the why, or some of the whys—the tapestries and fabrics that were books already written and not yet read by me, and of books yet to be written that would come to enlighten the vivid memory that was forming me: Marx, Lukács, Fromm, Gramsci, Fanon, Memmi, Sartre, Kosik, Agnes Heller, M. Ponty, Simon Weil, Arendt, Marcuse, and so many others.

Years later, the putting into practice of some of the "solderings" and "splicings" of the inaugural years of SESI sent me into exile[7]— a kind of "golden spike" that enabled me to connect recollections, recognize facts, deeds, and gestures, fuse pieces of knowledge, solder moments, re-cognize in order to cognize, to know, better.

In this effort to recall moments of my experience—which necessarily, regardless of when they were, became sources of my theoretical reflections for the writing of *Pedagogy of the Oppressed,* as they would continue to be today, as I rethink *Pedagogy*—I feel that it will be appropriate to refer to an excellent example of such a moment, which I experienced in the 1950s. The experience resulted in a learning process of real importance for me—for my theoretical understanding of the practice of political education, which, if it is to be progressive, must, as I have always asserted, take careful account of the reading of the world being made by popular groups and expressed in their discourse, their syntax, their semantics, their dreams and desires.

I was now working in SESI, and specifically on relations between schools and families. I had begun to experiment with various avenues to an improvement of the meeting of minds: to an understanding of the educational practice being carried out in the schools, on the part of families; to an understanding of the difficulties that families from popular areas would have in confronting problems in the implementation of their own educational activity. At bottom, I was looking for a dialogue between them from which might result the necessary mutual assistance that, at the same time—as it would imply more involvement of the families in the school—might enhance the political connotation of that involvement in the sense of opening channels of democratic participation to fathers and mothers in the actual educational policy being implemented in the schools.

I had carried out, by that time, a research project covering some one thousand families of students, throughout the urban area of Recife, the Zona da Mata, the countryside, and what might be called the "doorway" to the desert hinterland of Pernambuco,[8] where SESI had nuclei or social centers in which it offered its members and their families medical and dental assistance, scholastic help, sports and recreation projects, cultural projects, and so on.

My research, which had nothing of the sophisticated about it, asked the parents questions about their relationship with their daughters and sons. I asked about punishments, rewards, the most frequent punishments, the most frequent reasons for it, their children's reaction to the punishment, any change in their behavior, or want thereof, in the direction desired by the person doing the punishing, and so on.

I recall that, when I had sifted through the results, I was astonished, even more than I had expected to be, at the emphasis on corporal punishment, really violent punishment, in the Recife inner city, the Zona da Mata, in the rural areas, and hinterland, by contrast with the almost complete absence, not only of violent corporal punishment, but of any punishment of children, along the fishing coast. It seemed that, along the coast, under the maritime sky, the legends of individual freedom with which the culture is drenched, the fishers' confrontation, in their precarious *jangadas* or rafts,[9] with the forces of the sea, the independent jobber's work done by persons free and proud, the imagination that lends such color to the fishers' fantastic stories—it seemed that all of this had some connection with the taste for a liberty diametrically opposed to the use of violent punishment.

I do not know myself to what extent we might consider the fishers' lifestyle too permissive, wanting boundaries, or whether, on the contrary, with their emphasis on freedom, and conditioned by their own cultural context, the fishers are simply relying on nature itself, on the world, on the sea, in and with which their children they win an experience of themselves, to be the source of freedom's necessary limits. It was as if, softening or trimming down their duty as their children's educators, fathers and mothers shared them with the sea, with the world itself, to which it would fall, through their children's practice, to delineate their responsibilities. In this fashion, the children would be expected to learn naturally what they might and might not do.

Indeed, the fishers lived a life of enormous contradiction. On one side, they felt free and bold, confronting the sea, in fellowship with its mysteries, doing what they called "scientific fishing,"[10] of which they had spoken to me in the sunsets when, relaxing with them in their primitive shelters, their *caiçaras*,[11] I learned to understand them better by listening to them. On the other hand, they were viciously plundered, exploited, now by the middlemen who bought for nothing the product of their hard labor, now by the moneylenders who financed their work tools.

Sometimes, as I listened to them—in my conversations with them in which I learned something of their syntax and semantics, without which I could not have worked with them, or at any rate not effectively—I wondered whether they didn't perhaps notice how unfree they really were.

I recall that, in the fishing season, we delved into the reason why various students were missing school so frequently. Students and parents, separately, replied. The students, "Because we're free." The parents, "Because they're free. They'll go back some day."

Punishments in the other areas of the state that I researched ranged from tying a child to a tree, locking them in a room for hours on end, giving them "cakes" with thick, heavy switches,[12] forcing them to kneel on stones used to grind corn, thrashing them with leather straps. This last was the principal punishment in a town of the Zona da Mata that was famous for its shoemaking.

These punishments were applied for trivial reasons, and people watching the fishing were told, "Hard punishment makes hard people, who are up to the cruelty of life." Or, "Getting hit makes a real man out of you."

One of my concerns, at the time, as valid then as it is now, was with the political consequences of that kind of relationship between parents and children, which later becomes that between teachers and pupils, when it came to the learning process of our infant democracy. It was as if family and school were so completely subjected to the greater context of global society that they could do nothing but reproduce the authoritarian ideology.

I acknowledge the risks to which we expose ourselves in confronting such problems. On the one hand, there is the danger of voluntarism, ultimately a kind of "idealism of the strife" that ascribes to the will of the individual with the power to do all things. On the other hand, there is the peril of a mechanistic objectivism that refuses to ascribe any role to subjectivity in the historical process.

Both of these conceptions of history, and of human beings in that history, end by definitively canceling the role of education. The first, because it attributes to education a power that it does not have; the second, because it denies that it has any power at all.

As for the relationship between authority and freedom—the subject of the research project that I have mentioned—we also run the risk either of denying freedom the right to assert itself, thus exacerbating the role of authority; or else of atrophying the latter and thus hypertrophying the former. In other words, we run the risk of succumbing to the seduction or tyranny of liberty, or to the tyranny of authority, thus acting at cross-purposes, in either hypothesis, with our incipient democracy.

This was not my position then and it is not my position now. And today as yesterday, while on perhaps better foundations than yesterday, I am completely persuaded of the importance, the urgency, of the democratization of the public school, and of the ongoing training of its educators, among whom I include security people, cafeteria personnel, and custodians, and so on. Their formation must be ongoing and scientific. Nor should it fail to instill a taste for democratic practices, among which should be an ever more active intervention on the part of educands and their families as to which direction the school is going. This has been one of the tasks to which I have devoted myself recently, so many years after having first observed this need, and spoken of it in my 1959 academic treatise, "Educação e atualidade brasileira," to address it again as secretary of education for the City of São Paulo from January 1989 to May 1991. Here is the challenge of the democratization of the public school, so neglected by the military governments[13] that, in the name of the salvation of the country from the curse of communism and from corruption, all but destroyed that country.

Finally, with the results of my study in hand, I scheduled a kind of systematic visitation of all of the SESI nuclei or social centers in the state of Pernambuco where we maintain primary schools,[14] as they were called at the time, to go there and speak to the parents about the findings of the inquiry. And to do something more: to join to communication of the findings of the investigation a discussion about the problem of the relationship between authority and freedom, which would necessarily involve the question of punishment and reward in education.

The tour for discussion with the families was preceded by another, which I made in order to *debate*, in seminars as rigorous as it was possible to have, the same question with teachers.

I had put together—in collaboration with a colleague, Jorge Monteiro de Melo, recently deceased, whose seriousness, honesty, and devotion I now reverence—an essay on scholastic discipline, which, alongside the results of the study, became the object of our preparatory seminar in our meetings with the families. In this fashion, we prepared ourselves, as a school, to welcome the students' families— the natural educators of those of whom we were the professional educators.

Back then, I was accustomed to give long talks on the subjects that had been selected. I was repeating the traditional route of discourse *about* something that you would give an audience. Then I would shift the format to a debate, discussion, dialogue about the subject *with* the participants. And, while I was concerned about the order and development of ideas, I proceeded almost as if I were speaking to university students. I say, "almost," because actually my sensitivity had already made me aware of the differences in language, the syntactical and semantic differences, between the working persons with whom I was working and my own language. Hence my talks were always punctuated with, "In other words," or, "That is to say . . ." On the other hand, despite some years of experience as an educator, with urban and rural workers, I still nearly always started out with my world, without further explanation, as if it ought to be the "south" to which their compass ought to point in giving them their bearings. It was as if my word, my theme, my reading of the world, in themselves, were to be their compass.[15]

It was a long learning process, which implied a journey, and not always an easy one, nearly always painful, to the point that I persuaded myself that, even when my thesis and proposal were sure, and I had no doubt in their respect, it was nevertheless imperative, first, to know whether this thesis and proposition coincided with the reading of the world of the groups or social class to whom I was speaking; second, it was incumbent upon me to be more or less abreast of, familiar with, their reading of the world, since only on the basis of the knowledge in its content, or implicit in it, would it be possible for me to discuss my reading of the world, which in turn, maintains, and is based on, another type of knowledge.

This learning process, this apprenticeship, whose story is a long one, is rehearsed in my university dissertation, cited above, continues being sketched in *Educação como prática da liberdade*, and becomes explicit once and for all in *Pedagogy of the Oppressed*. One moment—I could even say, a solemn one, among others, of this apprenticeship—occurred during the one-day seminar to which I have referred, which consisted of talks in which I discussed authority, freedom, and punishment and reward in education. It happened precisely in the SESI nucleus or social center named for President Dutra,[16] at Vasco da Gama[17]—Amarela House—in Recife.

Basing my presentation on an excellent study by Piaget* on the child's moral code, his and her mental representation of punishment, the proportion between the probable cause of punishment and the punishment itself, I spoke at length. I quoted Piaget himself on the subject, and argued for a dialogical, loving relationship between parents and children in place of violent punishments.

My mistake was not in citing Piaget. In fact, how much *richer* my presentation could have been if I had talked about him very concretely, using a map, and showing where Recife is, then the Brazilian Northeast, then to move out to the whole of Brazil, show where Brazil is in South America, relate that to the rest of the world, and finally, point to Switzerland, in Europe, the land of the author I was quoting. It would have been not only richer, but more challenging and instructive, to do that. But my actual mistake was, first, in my use of my language, my syntax, without more effort to get close to the language and syntax of my audience; and second, in my all but oblivion of the hard reality of the huge audience seated before me.

---

*Jean Piaget, *The Moral Judgment of the Child*, trans. Marjorie Worden (New York: Brace World, 1932).

When I had concluded, a man of about forty, still rather young but already worn out and exhausted, raised his hand and gave me the clearest and most bruising lesson I have ever received in my life as an educator.

I do not know his name. I do not know whether he is still alive. Possibly not. The wickedness of the country's socioeconomic structures, which take on stronger colors in the Brazilian Northeast—suffering, hunger, the indifference of the mighty—all this must have swallowed him up long since.

He raised his hand and gave a talk that I have never been able to forget. It seared my soul for good and all. It has exerted an enormous influence on me. Nearly always, in academic ceremonies in which I have had an honorary doctorate conferred on me by some university, I acknowledge how much I owe, as well, to persons like the one of whom I am now speaking, and not only to scholars—other thinkers who have taught me, too, and who continue to teach me, teachers without whom it would have been impossible for me to learn, like the laborer who spoke that night. Actually, were it not for the scientific rigor that offers me greater opportunities for precision in my findings, I should not be able critically to perceive the importance of common sense and the good sense therein residing. In almost every academic ceremony in which I am honored, I see him standing in one of the aisles of that big auditorium of so long ago, head erect, eyes blazing, speaking in a loud, clear voice, sure of himself, speaking his lucid speech.

"We have just heard," he began, "some nice words from Dr. Paulo Freire. Fine words, in fact. Well spoken. Some of them were even simple enough for people to understand easily. Others were more complicated. But I think I understood the most important things that all the words together say.

"Now I'd like to ask the doctor a couple of things that I find my fellow workers agree with."

He fixed me with a mild, but penetrating gaze, and asked: "Dr. Paulo, sir—do you know where people live? Have you ever been in any of our houses, sir?" And he began to describe their pitiful houses. He told me of the lack of facilities, of the extremely minimal space in which all their bodies were jammed. He spoke of the lack of resources for the most basic necessities. He spoke of physical exhaustion, and of the impossibility of dreams for a better tomorrow. He told me of the prohibition imposed on them from being happy— or even of having hope.

As I followed his discourse, I began to see where he was going to go with it. I was slouching in my chair, slouching because I was trying to sink down into it. And the chair was swiveling, in the need of my imagination and the desire of my body, which were both in flight, to find some hole to hide in. He paused a few seconds, ranging his eyes over the entire audience, fixed on me once more, and said, "Doctor, I have never been over to your house. But I'd like to describe it for you, sir. How many children do you have? Boys or girls?"

"Five," I said—scrunching further down into my chair. "Three girls and two boys."

"Well, Doctor, your house must be the only house on the lot, what they call an *oitão livre* house," a house with a yard.[18] "There must be a room just for you and your wife, sir. Another big room, that's for the three girls. There's another kind of doctor, who has a room for every son or daughter. But you're not that kind—no, sir. You have another room for the two boys. A bathroom with running water. A kitchen with Arno appliances.[19] A maid's room—much smaller than your kids' rooms—on the outside of the house. A little garden, with an 'ingress' (the English word) lawn," a front lawn. "You must also have a room where you toss your books, sir—a 'study,' a library. I can tell by the way you talk that you've done a lot of reading, sir, and you've got a good memory."

There was nothing to add or subtract. That was my house. Another world, spacious and comfortable.

"Now Doctor, look at the difference. You come home tired, sir, I know that. You may even have a headache from the work you do. Thinking, writing, reading, giving these kind of talks that you're giving now. That tires a person out too. But, sir," he continued, "it's one thing to come home, even tired, and find the kids all bathed, dressed up, clean, well fed, not hungry—and another thing to come home and find your kids dirty, hungry, crying, and making noise. And people have to get up at four in the morning the next day and start all over again—hurting, sad, hopeless. If people hit their kids, and even 'go beyond bounds,' as you say, it's not because people don't love their kids. No, it's because life is so hard thay don't have much choice."

This is class knowledge, I say now.

This talk was given about thirty-two years ago. I have never forgotten it. It said to me, despite the fact that I didn't understand this at the time, much more than it immediately communicated.

In his intonations, his laborer's syntax and rhythm, the movements of his body, his hands of an orator, in the metaphors so common to popular discourse, he called the attention of the educator there in front of him, seated, silent, sinking down into his chair, to the need, when speaking to the people, for the educator to be up to an understanding of the world the people have. An understanding of the world which, conditioned by the concrete reality that in part explains that understanding, can begin to change through a change in that concrete reality. In fact, that understanding of the world can begin to change the moment the unmasking of concrete reality begins to lay bare the "whys" of what the actual understanding had been up until then.

A change in understanding, which is of basic importance, does not of itself, however, mean a change in the concrete.

The fact that I have never forgotten the fabric in which that discourse was delivered is significant. The discourse of that faraway night is still before me, as if it had been a written text, an essay that I constantly had to review. Indeed, it was the culmination of the learning process I had undertaken long ago—that of the progressive educator: even when one must speak *to* the people, one must convert the "to" to a "with" the people. And this implies respect for the "knowledge of living experience" of which I always speak, on the basis of which it is possible to go beyond it.

That night, in the car on the way back home, I complained to Elza rather bitterly. Though she rarely accompanied me to meetings, when she did she made excellent observations that always helped me.

"I thought I'd been so clear," I said. "I don't think they understood me."

"Could it have been you, Paulo, who didn't understand them?" Elza asked, and she went on: "I think they got the main point of your talk. The worker made that clear in what he said. They understood you, but they needed to have you understand them. That's the question."

Years later, *Pedagogy of the Oppressed* spoke of the theory that became steeped in practice that night, a night whose memory went with me into exile along with the rememberance of so many other fabrics lived.

The moments we live either are instants in a process previously inaugurated, or else they inaugurate a new process referring in some way to something in the past. This is why I have spoken of the "kinship" among times lived—something we do not always perceive, thereby failing to unveil the fundamental why of the way in which we experience ourselves at each moment.

I should like to refer, now, to another of these times, another fabric that powerfully scored my existential experience and had a noticeable influence on the development of my pedagogical thought and educational practice.

Stepping back, now, from the moment to which I am about to refer, which I experienced between the ages of twenty-two and twenty-nine—part of it, then, while I was working in SESI—I see it as not just a moment but a process, whose point of departure occurred toward the end of my childhood and the beginning of my teen years, in Jaboatão.[20]

During the period I am talking about, from the ages of twenty-two to twenty-nine, I used to be overcome by a sense of despair and sadness from time to time. I was a terrible sad sack at these moments, and I suffered terribly from it. Nearly always, I would spend two or three days, or even longer, like this. Sometimes this state of mind would attack me without warning—in the street, in my office, at home. Sometimes it would come gradually, and get the best of me piecemeal. Regardless of which way it came, I felt wounded, and bored with the world, as if I were submerged in myself, in the pain whose reason I did not know, and everything around me seemed strange and foreign. Who wouldn't despair?

One time, a schoolmate from high school managed to hurt and offend me by telling me about something in my behavior of the previous two or three days that he couldn't understand. "You wouldn't talk to me! On Empress Street![21] I was heading for Hospice Street, and you were walking on the other side of the street going the other way. I crossed over, and waved a big hello. I thought you'd stop and say hi! And you just kept on walking! Why did you pretend you didn't see me?"

There were other, less striking, cases than this one. My explanation was always the same. "I didn't see you. Look, I'm your friend! I wouldn't do something like that!"

Elza always had deep understanding for me when this happened, and she helped me in every way she could. And the finest help she could give me, and she gave it, was not to so much as suggest to me that my attitude toward her was changing.

After I had had these experiences for some time, especially as they were beginning to happen more and more often, I began to try to see it in the framework, in which it occurred, see it as a part of the bigger picture. What were the elements, or surrounding elements, of the actual moment at which I felt that way?

When I could see the depression coming, I tried to see what it was that was there around me. I tried to see again, tried to remember, what had happened the day before, tried to hear once more what had been said and to whom it had been said, what I had heard and from whom I had heard it. When you come right down to it, I began to take my depression as an object of curiosity and investigation. I "stepped back" from it, to learn its "why." Basically, I needed to shed some light on the framework in which it was being generated.

I began to perceive that it was repeated, almost identically—my depression, this lack of interest in the world, this pessimism: that it occurred more often in the rainy season, and mostly at or around the time of the trips I would make to the Zona da Mata to speak in SESI schools to teachers and pupils' families on educational problems. This observation called my attention to the trips I made with the same objective to the farming zone of the state. But it didn't happen in connection with these trips. So it wasn't trips that were the cause of my depression.

I find it interesting that I can condense into just a few pages the three or four years of search out of the seven during which that moment was repeated.

My first visit to the city of São Paulo occurred when my search happened to be in full swing.

The day after I arrived, I was in my hotel, that afternoon, and the rain began to pour. I went over to the window to peer out at the world outside. The sky was black, and it was really coming down. But one thing was lacking, in the world that I was observing, by comparison with the pouring rain that would be accompanied with such deep depression. What was missing was green, and mud—the black earth soaking up the water, or the yellow clay turning into the slippery, or else slurpy-sticky, mass that "grabs you like a great, big constrictor," as Gilberto Freyre said of *massapê*, the black clay of the Northeast.[22]

The dark sky of São Paulo that day, and the falling rain, had no effect on me whatsoever.

On my return to Recife, I brought with me a mental portrait that the visit to São Paulo had helped me to put together. My depressions were doubtless connected to rain, and mud—*massapê* clay—and the green of the cane brakes and the dark sky. Not connected to any of these elements in isolation, but to the relationship among them. What I needed now, in order to gain a clear understanding of the experience of my suffering, was to discover the remote framework in which these elements had won or had been winning the power to spark my depression. At bottom, in seeking for the deepest "why" of my pain, I was educating my hope. I never expected things just to "be that way." I worked on things, on facts, on my will. I *invented* the concrete hope in which, one day, I would see myself delivered from my depression.

And so it was that, one rainy afternoon in Recife, under a leaden sky, I went to Jaboatão in quest of my childhood. If it was raining in Recife, in Jaboatão, which was known as the "spout of heaven," there was no describing it.[23] And it was under a heavy rain that I paid my visit to Morro da Saúde, where I had lived as a child. I stopped in front of the house in which I had lived—the house in which my father died in the late afternoon of October 21, 1934. I saw again the long lawn that stretched before the house at the time, the lawn we played soccer on. I saw again the mango trees, their green fronds. I saw my feet again, my muddy feet going up the hill, and me soaked to the skin. I had before me, as on a canvas, my father dying, my mother in stupefaction, my family lost in sorrow.

Then I walked down the hill and went to see once more certain areas where, more out of need than for sport, I had hunted innocent little birds, with the slingshot I had made myself and with which I became an excellent shot.[24]

That rainy afternoon, with the sky dark as lead over the bright green land, the ground soaked, I discovered the fabric of my depression. I became conscious of various relationships between the signs and the central core, the deeper core, hidden within me. I unveiled the problem by clearly and lucidly grasping its "why." I dug up the archeology of my pain.[25]

Since then, never again has the relationship between rain, green, and mud or sticky clay sparked in me the depression that had afflicted me for years. I buried it, that rainy afternoon I revisited Jaboatão. At the same time as I was struggling with my personal problem, I devoted myself to SESI groups of rural and urban workers, worked on the problem of moving from my discourse about my reading of the world to them, and moving them, challenging them, to speak of their own reading.

Many of them had possibly experienced the same process I had lived through—that of unraveling the fabric in which the facts are given, discovering their "why."

Many, perhaps, had suffered, and not just a little, in redoing their reading of the world under the impulse of a new perception—in which it was not actually destiny or fate or an inescapable lot that explained their helplessness as workers, their impotence in the face of the defeated, squalid body of their companion, and their death for want of resources.

Let me make it clear, then, that, in the domain of socioeconomic structures, the most critical knowledge of reality, which we acquire through the unveiling of that reality, does not of itself alone effect a change in reality.

In my case, as I have just recounted, the unmasking of the "why" of my experience of suffering was all that was needed to overcome it. True, I was freed from a limitation that actually threatened both my professional activity and my life in the community of my fellow human beings. It had come to the point that I was politically limited, as well.

A more critical understanding of the situation of oppression does not yet liberate the oppressed. But the revelation is a step in the right direction. Now the person who has this new understanding can engage in a political struggle for the transformation of the concrete conditions in which the oppression prevails. Here is what I mean. In my case, it was enough to know the fabric in which my suffering had been born in order to bury it. In the area of socioeconomic structures, a critical perception of the fabric, while indispensable, is not sufficient to change the data of the problem, any more than it is enough for the worker to have in mind the idea of the object to be produced: that object has to be made.

But the hope of producing the object is as basic to the worker as the hope of remaking the world is indispensable in the struggle of oppressed men and women. The revelatory, gnosiological practice of education does not of itself effect the transformation of the world: but it implies it.

No one goes anywhere alone, least of all into exile—not even those who arrive physically alone, unaccompanied by family, spouse, children, parents, or siblings. No one leaves his or her world without having been transfixed by its roots, or with a vacuum for a soul. We carry with us the memory of many fabrics, a self soaked in our history, our culture; a memory, sometimes scattered, sometimes sharp and clear, of the streets of our childhood, of our adolescence; the reminiscence of something distant that suddenly stands out before us, in us, a shy gesture, an open hand, a smile lost in a time of misunderstanding, a sentence, a simple sentence possibly now forgotten by the one who said it. A word for so long a time attempted and never spoken, always stifled in inhibition, in the fear of being rejected—which, as it implies a lack of confidence in ourselves, also means refusal of risk.

We experience, of course, in the voyage we make, a tumult in our soul, a synthesis of contrasting feelings—the hope of immediate deliverance from the perils that surround us, relief at the absence of the inquisitor (either the brutal, offensive interrogator, or the tactically polite prosecutor to whose lips this "evil, dangerous subversive" will yield, it is thought, more easily), along with, for the extension of the tumult of and in the soul, a guilt-feeling at leaving one's world, one's soil, the scent of one's soil,[26] one's folks. To the tumult in the soul belongs also the pain of the broken dream, utopia lost. The danger of losing hope. I have known exiles who began to

buy a piece of furniture or two for their homes only after four or
five years in exile. Their half-empty homes seemed to speak, elo-
quently, of their loyalty to a distant land. In fact, their half-empty
rooms not only seemed to wish to speak to them of their longing to
return, but looked as if the movers had just paid a visit and they
were actually moving back. The half-empty house lessened the sentiment of blame at having left the "old sod." In this, perhaps, lies a
certain need that I have so often perceived in persons exiled: the
need to feel persecuted, to be constantly trailed by some secret
agent who dogged their step and whom they alone ever saw. To
know they were so dangerous gave them, on the one hand, the
sensation of still being politically alive; and on the other, the sensation of a right to survive, through cautious measures. It diminished
their guilt feelings.

Indeed, one of the serious problems of the man or woman in exile
is how to wrestle, tooth and nail, with feelings, desire, reason, recall,
accumulated knowledge, worldviews, with the tension between a
today being lived in a reality on loan and a yesterday, in their context
of origin, whose fundamental marks they come here charged with.
At bottom, the problem is how to preserve one's identity in the
relationship between an indispensable *occupation* in the new context, and a *preoccupation* in which the original context has to be
reconstituted. How to wrestle with the yearning without allowing it
to turn into nostalgia. How to invent new ways of living, and living
with others, thereby overcoming or redirecting an understandable
tendency on the part of the exiled woman or man always to regard
the context of origin (as it cannot be got rid of as a reference, at least
not over the long haul) as better than the one on loan. Sometimes it
is actually better; not always, however.

Basically, it is very difficult to experience exile, to live with all
the different longings—for one's town or city, one's country, family,
relatives, a certain corner, certain meals—to *live* with longing, and
educate it too. The education of longing has to do with the transcendence of a naively excessive optimism, of the kind, for example, with
which certain companions received me in October 1964 in La Paz:
"You're just in time to turn around. We'll be home for Christmas."

I had arrived there after a month or a little more than a month
in the Bolivian embassy in Brazil, waiting for the Brazilian govern-

ment to deign to send me the safe-conduct pass without which I should not be allowed to leave. Shortly before, I had been arrested, and subjected to long interrogations by military personnel who seemed to think that, in asking these questions of theirs, they were saving not only Brazil but the whole world.

"We'll be home for Christmas."

"Which Christmas?" I asked, with curiosity, and even more surprise.

"This Christmas!" they answered, with unshakable certitude.

My first night in La Paz, not yet under the onslaughts of of the altitude sickness that were to fall upon me the next day, I reflected a bit on the education of longing, which figures in *Pedagogy of Hope*. It would be terrible, I thought, to let the desire to return kill in us the critical view, and make us look at everything that happens back home in a favorable way—create in our head a reality that isn't real.

Exile is a difficult experience. Waiting for the letter that never comes because it has been lost, waiting for notice of a final decision that never arrives. Expecting sometimes that certain people will come, even going to the airport simply to "expect," as if the verb were intransitive.

It is far more difficult to experience exile when we make no effort to adopt its space–time critically—accept it as an opportunity with which we have been presented. It is this critical ability to plunge into a new daily reality, without preconceptions, that brings the man or woman in exile to a more historical understanding of his or her own situation. It is one thing, then, to experience the everyday in the context of one's origin, immersed in the habitual fabrics from which we can easily emerge to make our investigations, and something else again to experience the everyday in the loan context that calls on us not only to become able to grow attached to this new context, but also to take it as an object of our critical reflection, much more than we do our own from a point of departure in our own.

I arrived in La Paz, Bolivia, in October 1964, and another coup d'état took me by surprise. In November of the same year I landed in Arica, in Chile, where I startled my fellow passengers, as we were making our descent toward the airport, by calling out, loud and strong, "Long live oxygen!" I had left an altitude of four thousand meters and was returning to sea level. My body once more became as viable as it had been before. I moved with facility, rapidly, without exhaustion. In La Paz, carrying a package, even a little one, meant an extraordinary effort for me. At forty-three I felt old and decrepit. In Arica, and on the next day in Santiago, I got my strength back, and everything happened almost instantly, as if by sleight of hand. Long live oxygen!

I arrived in Chile with my whole self: passion, longing, sadness, hope, desire, dreams in smithereens but not abandoned, offenses, knowledge stored in the countless fabrics of living experience, availability for life, fears and terrors, doubts, a will to live and love. Hope, especially.

I arrived in Chile, and a few days later started to work as a consultant for renowned economist Jacques Chonchol, president of the Instituto de Desarrollo Agropecuario (Institute for the Development of Animal Husbandry)—the INDAP—subsequently to be minister of agriculture in the Allende government.

Only in mid-January of 1965 were we all back together. Elza, the three girls, and the two boys, with all their terrors, their doubts, their hopes, their fears, their knowledge gotten and being gotten, started a new life with me again in a strange land—a foreign land to which we were giving ourselves in such wise that it was receiving us in a way that the foreignness was turning into comradeship, friendship, siblingship. Homesick as we were for Brazil, we had a sudden special place in our hearts for Chile, which taught us Latin America in a way we had never imagined it.

I reached Chile a few days after the inauguration of Eduardo Frey's Christian Democratic government. There was a climate of euphoria in the streets of Santiago. It was as if a profound, radical, substantial transformation of society had occurred. Only the forces of the Right, at one extreme, and those of the Marxist-Leninist Left at the other, for different reasons, obviously, did not share the euphoria. How vast it was! What a certitude there was, rooted in the minds of Christian Democracy activists, that their *revolution* was fixed on solid ground, that no threat could even get near it! One of their favorite arguments, more metaphysical than historical, was what they called the "democratic and constitutionalist tradition of the Chilean armed forces."

"Never will there be an uprising against the established order," they said, sure as sure can be, in conversations with us.

I remember a meeting that did not go very well at the home of one of these militants, with some thirty of them, in which Plínio Sampaio, Paulo de Tarso Santos,[27] Almino Affonso, and I, participated.

We argued that the so-called tradition of loyalty on the part of the armed forces to the established, democratic order was not an immutable quality, an intrinsic property of the military, but a mere "historical given," and therefore that this "tradition" might become historically shattered and a new process take its place. They answered that Brazilians in exile gave them "the impression of being crybabies who've had their toys taken away," or "frustrated, helpless children." There was no conversing with them.

A few years later the Chilean armed forces decided to change positions. I hope it was without the contribution of any of those with whom we were conversing that night, as I hope as well that none of them had to pay as dearly as thousands of other Chileans did—along with other Latin Americans—under the weight of the perversity and cruelty that came crashing down on Chile in September 1973. It was not by chance, then, that the most backward of the elite, in whom even timid liberal positions stirred threat and fear, frightened at the reformist policy of Christian Democracy, which was then regarded as a kind of middle road, dreamed of the need to put an end to all this bold, too-risky business. Just imagine what Allende's victory meant, then, not only for the Chilean elite, but for the outsiders of the North!

I visited Chile twice during the time of the Popular Unity government, and used to say, in Europe and in the United States, that anyone who wanted to get a concrete idea of the class struggle, as expressed in the most divergent ways, really ought to pay a visit to Chile. Especially, if you wanted to see—practically touch with your hands—the tactics the dominant classes employed in the struggle, and the richness of their imagination when it came to waging a more effective struggle for the resolution of the contradiction between power and government, I would tell my audiences, you really must go to Chile. What had happened is that power, as a fabric of relations, decisions, and force, continued to be the main thing with them, while the government, which was in charge of policy, found itself being propelled by progressive forces, forces in discord with the others. This opposition, this contradiction, had to be overcome, so that both power and government would be in their hands again. The coup was the solution. And so, even within the Christian Democratic party, the Right tended to place obstacles in the way of the democratic policy of the more advanced echelons, especially of the youth. As the process developed, a clearer and clearer tendency to radicalization, and breach between the discordant options, appeared, precluding a peaceful coexistence between them, either in the party or in society itself.

On the outside, the Marxist-Leninist Left, the Communist party and the Socialist party, had their ideological, political, historical, and cultural reasons for not joining in the euphoria. They regarded it as naive at best.

In step with the waxing and deepening of the class struggle or conflicts, the rift between the forces of Right and Left, among Christian Democrats as in civil society, likewise deepened. Thus arose various tendencies on the Left calculated to regiment militants who, in direct contact with the popular bases, or seeking to understand these grassroots elements through a reading of the classic Marxists, began to call on the carpet the reformism that had finally gained the upper hand in the strategic plans of Christian Democratic policy.

The Movimiento Independente Revolucionário, the MIR, was born in Concepción, and was constituted of revolutionary youth who disagreed with what seemed to them to be a deviation on the part of the Communist party—that of a "coexistence" with elements of "bourgeois democracy."

It is interesting, however, that the MIR, which was constantly to the Left of the Communist party, and afterwards, of the Popular Unity government itself, always manifested a sympathy for popular education, something the parties of the traditional Left generally lacked.

When the Communist party and the Socialist party refused, dogmatically, to work with certain *poblaciónes* who, they said, were without a "class consciousness," so that they mobilized only for ad hoc protests and automatically demobilized whenever their demands were met, the MIR thought it necessary, first, to prove the correctness of this attitude toward the *Lumpenproletariat*, the "great unwashed," and second, to observe whether, admitting the hypothesis that their proposition had been verified in certain situations, it would be verified again in a different historical moment. In other words, while there was some truth in the proposition, it could not be taken as a metaphysical postulate.

And so it came about that, now under the Popular Unity government, the MIR launched an intensive campaign of mobilization and organization—itself a piece of political pedagogy—in which it included a series of educational projects in the popular areas. In 1973, I had the opportunity to spend an evening with the leaders of the *población*—settlement or "new city"—of Nueba Habana, which, contrary to the dour forecast, after obtaining what it had been demanding, its own villa, continued active and creative, maintaining countless projects in the area of education, health, justice, social security, and sports. I paid a visit to a lineup of old buses, donated by the government, whose bodies, converted and adapted, had become neat, nicely set up little schoolrooms, which the children of the *población* attended. In the evenings, the bus-schoolrooms would fill with literacy-program clients, who were learning to read the word through a reading of the world. Nueba Habana had a future, then, if an uncertain one, and the climate surrounding it and the experimental pedagogy being plied within it was one of hope.

Alongside the MIR arose the Movimiento de Acción Popular Unitaria, and the Christian Left, further splintering the Christian Democrats. A sizable contingent of more advanced youth among the Christian Democrats joined the MAPU, or else the Christian Left, and even migrated to the MIR as well, or the Communist and Socialist parties.

Today, nearly thirty years later, one readily perceives what, at the time, only a few grasped, and already urged. They were sometimes regarded as dreamers, utopians, idealists, or even as "selling out to the gringos." At this distance, it is easy to see that only a radical politics—not a sectarian one, however, but one that seeks a unity in diversity among progressive forces—could ever have won the battle for a democracy that could stand up to the power and virulence of the Right. Instead, there was only sectarianism and intolerance—the rejection of differences. Tolerance was not what it ought to be: the revolutionary virtue that consists in a peaceful coexistence with those who are different, in order to wage a better fight against the adversaries.

The correct road for the progressive forces standing to the Left of the Christian Democrats would have been to move—within ethical limits of concession on policy—closer and closer to them, not in order to take over the party, nor again in such a manner as to drive it to the Right, nor, indeed, so as to be absorbed into it. And for its own part, Christian Democracy, in all intolerance, rejected dialogue. There was no credibility on either side.

It was precisely by virtue of the inability of all forces to tolerate one another that Popular Unity came to power . . . without power.

From November 1964 to April 1969, I followed the ideological struggle closely. I witnessed, sometimes with surprise, retreats in the area of political ideology by persons who had proclaimed their option for the transformation of society, then became frightened and repentant, and made a fearful about-face in midcourse and turned into hidebound reactionaries. But I also saw the advances made by those who confirmed their progressive discourse by walking consistently, refusing to run from history. I likewise witnessed the progress of persons whose initial position had been timid, to say the least, but who became stronger, ultimately to assert themselves in a radicalness that never extended to sectarianism.

It would really have been impossible to experience a process this rich, this problem-fraught, to have been touched so profoundly by the climate of accelerated change, to have shared in such animated, lively discussion in the "culture circles" in which educators often had to beg the peasants to stop, since they had already gone on practically the whole night, without all of this later winning explication in this or that theoretical position of mine in the book that, at the time, was not even a project.

I was impressed, when I heard about it in evaluation meetings, or when I was actually present, by the intensity of the peasants' involvement when they were analyzing their local and national reality. It took them what seemed like forever to spill everything that was on their minds. It was as if the "culture of silence" was suddenly shattered, and they had discovered not only that they could speak, but that their critical discourse upon the world, their world, was a way of remaking that world. It was if they had begun to perceive that the development of their language, which occurred in the course of their analysis of their reality, finally showed them that the lovlier world to which they aspired was being announced, somehow anticipated, in their imagination. It was not a matter of idealism. Imagination and conjecture about a different world than the one of oppression, are as necessary to the praxis of historical "subjects" (agents) in the process of transforming reality as it necessarily belongs to human toil that the worker or artisan first have in his or her head a design, a "conjecture," of what he or she is about to make. Here is one of the tasks of democratic popular education, of a pedagogy of hope: that of enabling the popular classes to develop their language: not the authoritarian, sectarian gobbledygook of "educators," but their own language—which, emerging from and returning upon their reality, sketches out the conjectures, the designs, the anticipations of their new world. Here is one of the central questions of popular education—that of language as a route to the invention of citizenship.

As Jacques Chonchol's consultant in the Institute for the Development of Animal Husbandry, in the area of what was then called in Chile human promotion, I was able to extend my collaboration to the Ministry of Education, in cooperation with people working in adult literacy, as well as to the Corporation for Agrarian Reform.

Quite a bit later, almost two years before we left Chile, I began to work as a consultant for these same organizations on the basis of my position in another, the Instituto de Capacitación e Investigación en Reforma Agraria (Institute for Ways and Means and Research in Agrarian Reform, or ICIRA), a joint organization of the United Nations and the Chilean government. I worked there for UNESCO, against the will and under the consistent niggardly protest of the Brazilian military government of the period.

And it was as consultant for the Institute for the Development of Animal Husbandry, for the Ministry of Education, and for the Corporation for Agrarian Reform, that, as I traveled practically all over the country, always in the company of young Chileans, who were mostly progressives, I listened to peasants and discussed with them various aspects of their concrete reality. I urged upon agronomists and agricultural technologists a political, pedagogical, democratic understanding of their practice. I debated general problems of educational policy with the educators of the cities and towns I visited.

I still have in my memory today, as fresh as ever, snatches of discourses by peasants and expressions of their legitimate desires for the betterment of their world, for a finer, less-ugly world, a world whose "edges" would be less "rough," in which it would be possible to love—Guevara's dream, too.

I shall never forget what a UN sociologist, an excellent intellectual and no less excellent a person, a Dutchman who wore a red beard, told me after we had assisted, all enthusiastic and full of confidence in the working class, at a two hour discussion on their eagerness for the establishment of agrarian reform by the government (still the Christian Democrats) in a remote corner of Chile. The peasants had been discussing their right to the land, their right to the freedom to produce, to raise crops and livestock, to live decently, to be. They had defended their right to be respected as persons and as workers who were creators of wealth, and they had demanded their right of access to culture and knowledge. It is in this direction that those historico-social conditions intersected in which the pedagogy of the oppressed could take root—and this time I am not referring to the book I wrote—which, in turn, is here being matched by, or prolonged into, a needed pedagogy of hope.

With the meeting over, as we were leaving the wagon shed where it had been held, my Dutch friend with the red beard put his hand on my shoulder and said—choosing his phrases carefully, and speaking with conviction: "It's been worth four days of wandering through these corners of Chile, to hear what we heard tonight." And he added, good-humoredly, "These peasants know more than we do."

I think it is important, at this point, to call attention to something I have emphasized in *Pedagogy of the Oppressed*: the relationship prevailing between political lucidity in a reading of the world, and the various levels of engagement in the process of mobilization and organization for the struggle—for the defense of rights, for laying claim to justice.

Progressive educators have to be on the alert where this datum is concerned, in their work of popular education, since not only the content, but the various manners in which one approaches the content, stand in direct relation with the levels of struggle referred to above.

It is one thing to work with popular groups, and experience the way in which those peasants operated that night, and something else again to work with popular groups who have not yet managed to "see" the oppressor "outside."

This datum continues valid today. The neoliberal discourses, chock-full of "modernity," do not have sufficient force to do away with social classes and decree the nonexistence of differing interests among them, any more than they have the strength to make away with the conflicts and struggle between them.

It happens that struggle is a historical and social category. Therefore it has historicity. It changes from one space–time to another space–time. The fact of the struggle does not militate against the possibility of pacts, agreements between the antagonistic parties. In other words, agreements and accords are part of the struggle, as a historical, and not metaphysical, category.

There are historical moments in which the survival of the social whole, which is in the interest of all the social classes, imposes upon those classes the necessity of understanding one another—which does not mean that we are experiencing a new age devoid of social classes and of conflicts.

The four-and-one-half years that I lived in Chile, then, were years of a profound learning process. It was the first time, with the exception of a brief visit to Bolivia, that I had had the experience of distancing myself geographically, with its epistemological consequences, from Brazil. Hence the importance of those four-and-one-half years.

Sometimes, on long automobile trips, with stops in cities along the way—Santiago to Puerto Mont, Santiago to Arica—I gave myself over to the quest for myself, refreshing my memory when it came to Brazil, about what I had done here, with other persons, mistakes made, the verbal incontinence that few intellectuals of the Left had escaped and to which many today still devote themselves, and through which they reveal a terrible ignorance of the role of language in history.

"Agrarian reform, like it or lump it!" "Either this congress votes laws in the people's interests or we'll close it."

Actually, all of this verbal incontinence, this explosion of verbiage has no connection, none whatever, with a correct, authentic progressive position. It has no connection with a correct understanding of struggle as political, historical practice. It is quite true, as well, that all of this volubility, precisely because it is not done in a vacuum, ends by generating consequences that retard needed changes even more. At times, however, the irresponsible chatter also generates a discovery of the fact that verbal restraint is an indispensable virtue for those who devote themselves to the dream of a better world—a world in which women and men meet in a process of ongoing liberation.

Basically, I sought to reunderstand the fabrics, the facts, the deeds in which I had been wrapped and enveloped. Chilean reality, in its difference from our own, helped me to a better understanding of my experiences, and the latter, reseen, helped me to understand what was happening and could be happening in Chile.

I traversed a great part of that country on trips on which I really learned a great deal. Side by side with Chilean educators, I learned by helping administer training courses for persons proposing to work at the grass roots in agrarian reform projects, those who would work with the peasants on the fundamental problem of the reading of the word, always preceded by a reading of the world. The reading and writing of the word would always imply a more critical rereading of the world as a "route" to the "rewriting"—the transformation—of that world. Hence the hope that necessarily steeps *Pedagogy of the Oppressed*. Hence also the need, in literacy projects conducted in a progressive perspective, for a comprehension of language, and of its role, to which we have referred, in the achievement of citizenship.

It was by attempting to inculcate a maximal respect for the cultural differences with which I had to struggle, one of them being language—in which I made an effort to express myself, as best I could, with clarity—that I learned so much of reality, and learned it with Chileans.

Respect for cultural differences, respect for the context to which one has come, a criticism of "cultural invasion," of sectarianism, and a defense of radicalness, of which I speak in *Pedagogy of the Oppressed*—all of this was something that, having begun to be part of my experience years before in Brazil, whose knowledge I had brought with me into exile, in the memory contained within my own self, was intensely, rigorously experienced by me in my years in Chile.

These elements of knowledge, which had been critically constituted in me since the inauguration of SESI, were consolidated in Chilean practice, and in the theoretical reflection I made upon that practice—in enlightening readings that made me laugh for joy, almost like a teenager, at finding in them a theoretical explanation of my practice, or the confirmation of the theoretical understanding that I had had of my practice. Santiago, to mention just the team of Brazilians living there, sometimes de jure—in exile—sometimes just de facto, unquestionably provided us with a rich opportunity. Christian Democracy, which spoke of itself as a "revolution in freedom," attracted countless intellectuals, student and union leaders, and groups of leftist political leaders from all over Latin America. Santiago, especially, had become a place, or grand context of theory-of-practice, in which those who arrived from other corners of Latin America would discuss, with Chileans and foreigners living there, both what was going on in Chile and what was going on in their own countries.

Latin America was effervescent in Santiago. Cubans were there, threatened as much as ever by the reactionary forces that, all filled with themselves, spoke of the death of socialism. The Cubans showed that changes could be made. There were the guerrilla theories, the "focus theory," the extraordinary charismatic personality of Camilo Torres—in whom no dichotomy existed between transcendentality and worldliness, history and metahistory—liberation theology was there (so soon to provoke fear, trembling, and rage), Guevara's capacity for love was there, as in the line he wrote to Carlos Guijano, as sincere as it was arresting: "Let me tell you, at the risk of appearing ridiculous, that the genuine revolutionary is animated by feelings of love. It is impossible to imagine an authentic revolutionary without this quality."*

In May 1968 came the student movements in the outside world,

---

*Ernesto Guevara, *Obra revolucionária* (Mexico City: Era, 1967).

rebellious, libertarian. There was Marcuse, with his influence on youth. In China, Mao Tse-tung and the cultural revolution.

Santiago had become almost a kind of "bedroom community"[28] for intellectuals, for politicians of the most varied persuasions. In this sense, perhaps Santiago was, in itself, at that time, the best center of "learning" and knowledge in Latin America. We learned of analyses, reactions, and criticisms by Colombians, Venezuelans, Cubans, Mexicans, Bolivians, Argentinians, Paraguayans, Brazilians, Chileans, and Europeans—analyses ranging from an almost unrestricted acceptance of Christian Democracy to its total rejection. There were sectarian, intolerant criticisms, but also open, radical criticisms in the sense that I advocate.

Some of my companions in exile and I learned not only from encounters with many of the Latin Americans I have mentioned who passed through Santiago, but from the excitement of a "knowledge of living experience," from the dreams, from the clarity, from the doubts, from the ingenuousness, from the "cunning"[29] of the Chilean workers—more rural than urban, in my case.

I remember now a visit I made, with a Chilean companion, to an agrarian reform project some hours' distance from Santiago. A number of evening "culture circles" were in operation there, and we had come to follow the process of the reading of the word and rereading of the world. In the second or third circle we visited, I felt a strong desire to try a dialogue with a group of peasants. Generally I avoided this because of the language difficulty. I was afraid my language gaffes might prejudice the smooth functioning of the work. That evening I decided to lay this concern aside, and, asking permission from the educator coordinating the discussion, I asked the group whether they were willing to have a conversation with me.

They accepted, and we began a lively dialogue, with questions and replies on both sides—promptly followed, however, by a disconcerting silence.

I too remained silent. In the silence, I remembered earlier experiences, in the Brazilian Northeast, and I guessed what was going to happen. I knew and expected that, suddenly, one of them, breaking the silence, would speak in his or her name and that of his or her companions. I even knew the tenor of that discourse. And so my own waiting, in the silence, must have been less painful than it was for them to listen to the silence.

"Excuse us, sir," said one of them, " . . . excuse us for talking. You're the one who should have been talking, sir. You know things, sir. We don't."

How many times I have heard this statement in Pernambuco, and not only in the rural zones, but even in Recife. And it was at the price of having to hear statements like that that I learned that, for the progressive educator, there is no other route than to seize the educands' "moment" and begin with their "here" and "now"—but as a stepping-stone to getting beyond, critically, their naïveté. It will do no harm to repeat that a respect for the peasants' ingenuousness, without ironical smiles or malicious questions, does not mean that the educator must accommodate to their level of reading of the world.

What would have been meaningless would have been for me to "fill" the silence of the group of peasants with my words, thus reinforcing the ideology that they had just enunciated. What I had to do was to begin with the acceptance of something said in the discourse of the peasant and make a problem of it for them, and thereby bring them once more to dialogue.

On the other hand, it would have been likewise meaningless—after having heard what the peasant said, begging pardon on behalf of the group for having spoken, when I was the one who knew how to do that, because I "knew"—if I had given them a lecture, with doctoral airs, on the "ideology of power and the power of ideology."

Purely parenthetically, I cannot resist—at a moment like this, as I relive *Pedagogy of the Oppressed,* and speak of cases like this one that I have experienced, the experience of which has given me theoretical foundations for not only advocating, but experiencing respect for the popular groups in my work as an educator—I cannot resist expressing my regret over a certain type of criticism in which I am pointed to as an "elitist." Or, at the opposite pole, where I am sketched as a "populist."

The far-off years of my experiences in SESI, the years of my intense learning process with fishers, with peasants and urban laborers, among the hillocks and ravines of Recife, had vaccinated me, as it were, against an elitist arrogance. My experience has taught me that educands need to be addressed as such; but to address them as educands implies a recognition of oneself, the educator, as one of two agents here, each capable of knowing and each wishing to know, and each working with the other for an understanding of the object of cognition. Thus, teaching and learning are moments in a larger process—that of knowing, of cognizing, which implies re-cognizing. At bottom, what I mean is that the educand really becomes an educand when and to the extent that he or she *knows,* or comes to know, content, cognoscible objects, and not in the measure that the educator is *depositing* in the educand a description of the objects or content.

Educands recognize themselves as such by cognizing objects—discovering that they are capable of knowing, as they assist at the immersion of significates, in which process they also become critical "significators." Rather than being educands because of some reason or other, educands need to become educands by assuming them-selves, taking themselves as cognizing subjects, and not as an object upon which the discourse of the educator impinges. Herein lies, in the last analysis, the great political importance of the teaching act. It is this, among other elements, that distinguishes a progressive educator from his or her reactionary colleague.

"All right," I said, in response to the peasant's intervention. "Let's say I know and you don't. Still, I'd like to try a game with you that, to work right, will require our full effort and attention. I'm going to draw a line down the middle of this chalkboard, and I'm going to write down on this side the goals I score against you, and on this other side the ones you score against me. The game will consist in asking each other questions. If the person asked doesn't know the answer, the person who asked the question scores a goal. I'll start the game by asking you a question."

At this point, precisely because I had seized the group's "mo-ment," the climate was more lively than when we had begun, before the silence.

First question:

"What is the Socratic maieutic?"

General guffawing. Score one for me.

"Now it's your turn to ask me a question," I said.

There was some whispering, and one of them tossed out the question:

"What's a contour curve?"

I couldn't answer. I marked down one to one.

"What importance does Hegel have in Marx's thought?"

Two to one.

"What's soil liming?"

Two to two.

"What's an intransitive verb?"

Three to two.

"What's a contour curve got to do with erosion?"

Three to three.

"What's epistemology?"

Four to three.

"What's green fertilizer?"

Four to four.

And so on, until we got to ten to ten.

As I said good-bye, I made a suggestion. "Let's think about this evening. You had begun to have a fine discussion with me. Then you were silent, and said that only I could talk because I was the only one who knew anything. Then we played a knowledge game and we tied ten to ten. I knew ten things you didn't, and you knew ten things I didn't. Let's think about this."

On the way back home I recalled the first experience I had had, long before, in the Zona da Mata of Pernambuco, like the one I had just had here.

After a few moments of good discussion with a group of peasants, silence fell on us and enveloped us all. What one of them had said then, in Portuguese, was the same thing as I had heard tonight in Spanish—a literal translation of what the Chilean peasant had said this evening.

"Fine," I had told them. "I know. You don't. But *why* do I know and you don't?"

Accepting his statement, I prepared the ground for my intervention. A vivacious sparkle in them all. Suddenly curiosity was kindled. The answer was not long in coming.

"You know because you're a doctor, sir, and we're not."

"Right, I'm a doctor and you're not. But *why* am I a doctor and you're not?"

"Because you've gone to school, you've read things, studied things, and we haven't."

"And why have I been to school?"

"Because your dad could send you to school. Ours couldn't."

"And why couldn't your parents send you to school?"

"Because they were peasants like us."

"And what is 'being a peasant'?"

"It's not having an education . . . not owning anything . . . working from sun to sun . . . having no rights . . . having no hope."

"And why doesn't a peasant have any of this?"

"The will of God."

"And who is God?"

"The Father of us all."

"And who is a father here this evening?"

Almost all raised their hands, and said they were.

I looked around the group without saying anything. Then I picked out one of them and asked him, "How many children do you have?"

"Three."

"Would you be willing to sacrifice two of them, and make them suffer so that the other one could go to school, and have a good life, in Recife? Could you love your children that way?"

"No!"

"Well, if you," I said, "a person of flesh and bones, could not commit an injustice like that—how could God commit it? Could God really be the cause of these things?"

A different kind of silence. Completely different from the first. A silence in which something began to be shared. Then:

"No. God isn't the cause of all this. It's the boss!"

Perhaps for the first time, those peasants were making an effort to get beyond the relationship that I called, in *Pedagogy of the Oppressed*, that of the "adherence" of the oppressed to the oppressor, in order to "step back" from the oppressor, and localize the oppressor "outside" themselves, as Fanon would say.

From that point of departure, we could have gotten to an understanding of the role of the "boss," in the context of a certain socioeconomic, political system—gotten to an understanding of the social relations of production, gotten to an understanding of class interests, and so on and so on.

What would have been completely senseless would have been if, after the silence that had so brusquely interrupted our dialogue, I had given a traditional speech, crammed with empty, intolerant slogans.

CHAPTER
2

Today, at more than twenty-five years' distance from those mornings, those evenings, those nights of seeing, hearing, all but touching with my hands sectarian certitudes that precluded other certitudes, that denied doubts, that asserted a truth possessed by certain groups calling themselves revolutionary, I reassert, as is incumbent upon a pedagogy of hope, the position taken up and argued in *Pedagogy of the Oppressed* against sectarianisms, which always eviscerate, as well as the position I maintain there in defense of a critical radicalism.

The preponderant climate with the factions of the Left was actually one of sectarianism, which, along with rejecting history as opportunity, generates and proclaims a kind of "liberation fatalism." Socialism is on its way . . . necessarily. Carried to its ultimate consequences, then, an understanding of history as "liberation fatalism" prescinds from the struggle, from an engagement in the creation of democratic socialism as a job to do in history. Thus, it conjures away the ethic of struggle and the fineness of the striving. I believe, or rather I am convinced, that we have never needed radical positions, in the sense of the radicalness I advocate in *Pedagogy of the Oppressed*, as we need them today. We need them if we are to get beyond, on the one hand, sectarianisms founding themselves on universal, exclusive truths; and on the other, "pragmatic" accommodations to the facts, as if the facts had turned immutable. Each faction would have its immutability to work with—the former, or modern positions, just as the latter, or modernistic ones. Instead, let us be postmodern: radical and utopian. Progressive.

The last period of my time in Chile—to be precise, the period during which I worked in the Institute for Ways and Means and Research in Agrarian Reform (ICIRA), from the beginning of my third year in the country onward—was one of the most productive moments of my experience in exile. In the first place, I came to this organization only after having already acquired a certain visceral familiarity with the culture of the country, the habits of its peoples, and with the rifts in political ideology within Christian Democracy already clear. Then too, my activity in ICIRA was contemporaneous with the first denunciations lodged against me in and by the more radically rightist sectors of that party. These elements accused me of things I had never done nor ever would do. I always find that one of the ethical and political duties of someone in exile resides in respect for the host country.

Although the condition of exile surely did not transform me into a neutral intellectual, neither did it ever afford me the right to interfere in the party politics of the country. I am not even inclined to go into the facts surrounding the accusations against me, as the latter could easily be demolished by their utter inconsistency. However, upon being informed of the existence of the first rumor, I took the decision to write out in advance the texts of the talks I would give on the subjects on which I was to speak in the training groups. Along with becoming accustomed to writing them out, I got into the habit of discussing them, every time I could, with two great friends I worked with in the ICIRA, Marcela Gajardo, a Chilean, today researcher and professor at the Faculdade Latino-Americana de Ciências Sociais, and sociologist José Luiz Fiori, a Brazilian, today a professor at Rio de Janeiro University.

The hours we spent together, discussing discoveries, and not just my talks, talking over our doubts, wondering together, challenging ourselves, recommending readings, being surprised, being fearful, exerted such a spell on us that, nearly always, the time of day came when our conversation was the only one to be heard in the building. Everyone else had left the office, and there we were, trying to get a better understanding of what was behind a peasant's reply to a challenge with which he had been presented in a culture circle.

With them I discussed various things I wanted to say in *Pedagogy of the Oppressed,* which I was still composing. There is no denying the good that both of their friendships did me, and the contributions that their shrewd intellects added to my mind and my work.

At bottom, in the last analysis, my time at the Instituto de Desarrollo Agropecuaria, the Ministry of Education, and the Corporation for Agrarian Reform; my serious work with their technological teams, through which I found it possible to have a rich experience almost throughout the country, with countless peasant communities, interviewing their leaders; even simply the opportunity to have experienced a life in the historical atmosphere of the time—all of this explained to me the doubts I had had that had led to my exile, deepened my hypotheses, assured me of my positions.

It was in the intense experience I was having in Chilean society— my own experience of their experience, which always sent me back in my mind to my Brazilian experience, whose vivid memory I had brought with me into exile—that I wrote *Pedagogy of the Oppressed,* in 1967 and 1968. Now that that composition has "come of age," I take it once more in hand. To look at it again, rethink it, restate it. And to do some "new" saying, as well: the text in which it is now being said again has its own word to say, as well, and one that, in the same manner, speaks for itself, by speaking of hope.

In more or less a conversational tone—in "conversation" not only with the reader now seeking a living contact with *Pedagogy of the Oppressed* for the first time, but with those who have read it fifteen, twenty years ago, and who, at this moment, as they read this reflection on it, are preparing to read it again—I should like to focus in on a few points through which I might be able to make a better restatement of what I have already said.

I think that an interesting point to begin with might be the actual creation, or procreation, of the book. *Pedagogy of the Oppressed* enwraps the procreation of ideas of course, but thereby it enfolds as well the moment or the moments of activity in which those ideas were generated, together with the moments at which they were put down on paper. Indeed, ideas that need to be argued to—which imply other ideas, ideas that have come to be restated in various "corners" of texts to which authors feel obliged to return from time to time—become generated throughout these authors' practice, within the greater social practice of which the ideas are a part. It is in this sense that I have spoken of the memories that I brought into exile, of which some had been formed in childhood long ago, but are still of genuine importance today for an understanding of my understanding or of my reading of the world. This is also the reason why I have spoken of the exercise to which I always devoted myself in exile—wherever the "loan context" was, the context in which, as I gained experience in it, I thought and rethought my relations with and in the original context. But as ideas, positions, to be made explicit and explained, to be argued in the text, have first seen the light of day in the action-reflection-action in which we are enwrapped (as we are touched by memories of happenings in old fabrics), thus the moment of writing becomes as a time of creation and re-creation, as well, of the ideas with which we come to our desk. The time of writing, let me say again, is always preceded by one of speaking of the ideas that will be set down on paper. At least this was the way it was with me. Speaking of ideas before writing about them, in conversations with friends, in seminars, in talks, was also a way not only of testing them, but of re-creating them, of giving them second birth. Their edges could be better honed down when the thinking managed to reach written form through another discipline, another set of systematics. In this sense, to write is also to redo what has been thought out in various moments of our practice, of our relations-with; to write is as much to re-create, as much to restate what has been said previously, during the time of our activity—just as much as serious reading requires of the one doing it a rethinking of the already-thought, a rewriting of the written, and a rereading, as well, of what before being turned into the writing of the author was some reading of his or her own.

I spent a year or more talking about aspects of *Pedagogy of the Oppressed.* I spoke with friends that visited me, I discussed it in seminars and courses. One day my daughter Madalena came to me to delicately call my attention to something. She suggested greater restraint on my eagerness to talk about the as-yet-unwritten *Pedagogy of the Oppressed.* I did not have the strength to abide by her suggestion. I continued, passionately, to speak of the book as if— and as a matter of fact this was true—I were learning to write it.

I shall never be able to forget something about this oral period of *Pedagogy of the Oppressed*—an entire address in New York, my first, in 1967.

It was my first visit to the United States, where I had been invited by Father Joseph Fitzpatrick and Monsignor Robert Fox, who is now deceased.

It was an exceedingly important visit for me, especially because of what I was able to observe in places where blacks and Puerto Ricans were discriminated against. I visited these places by invitation of educators working with Fox. There was a great deal of similarity between what they were doing in New York and what I was doing in Brazil. The first one to notice the resemblances had been Ivan Illich, who then proposed to Fitzpatrick and Fox that they bring me to New York.

In my trips and visits to the various centers the two priests maintained in areas of New York, I was able to verify, seeing them all over again, behaviors expressive of the "wiliness" or "cunning" demanded of the oppressed if they are to survive. I saw and heard things in New York that were "translations"—not just linguistic ones, of course, but emotional ones, as well—of much of what I had heard in Brazil, and was hearing more recently in Chile. The "why" of the behavior was the same. Only the form—what I might call "trappings"—and the content, were different.

There is a case, among these, which I report in *Pedagogy of the Oppressed,* that it will do no harm to take another look at here, somewhat more extensively.

In one home, with blacks and Puerto Ricans participating in the group, the educator had a large blowup of a photograph carried in and placed on the arms of a chair. It was a picture of a street—as it happened, of the very street that ran in front of the building in which we sat. In the photo, a near mountain of garbage could be seen, piled on a corner of the street.

"What do you see in this picture?" asked the educator.

A silence ensued, as it always did, no matter where we were or to whom we addressed the question. Those present were somehow failing to recognize their own street. Then, emphatically, with false assurance, one of them came out with: "A street in Latin America."

"But the street signs are in English," the educator now pointed out.

Another silence, broken by another attempt to hide the painful, wounding, sorrowful truth. "Maybe a street in Latin America and we're teachin' English down there. Or maybe a street in Africa."

"Why not New York?"

"Because we're in the United States and we don't have nothin' like that here!" And the person speaking pointed to the photograph.

After another, longer silence, a third participant spoke up, and said, with difficulty, and painfully, as if he were relieving himself of some terrible burden: "Might as well admit it's our street. Where we live."

As I recall that session now, so much like so many others I shared in, as I remember how the educands defended themselves in the analysis or "reading" of the codification (the photo), trying to hide the truth, I hear again in my mind something I once heard from Erich Fromm, in Cuernavaca, Mexico: "This kind of educational practice," he told me, in our first meeting, arranged by Ivan Illich, at which I had told him how I thought of and practiced education, "This kind of educational practice is a kind of historico-cultural, political psychoanalysis."

He was dead right, and his words were confirmed by the statements of the educands, one by one, to the approving nods of the others: "It's a street in Latin America . . . we're there and we're teaching English," or "It's a street in Africa," or "We're the US, we can't have anything like that." Two nights before, I had assisted at another meeting, with another group, likewise of Puerto Ricans and blacks, where the discussion was about another fine photo. It was a montage, representing "slices" of New York—more than half-a-dozen shots, one atop the other, representing socioeconomic conditions in various areas of the city, in ascending order of "decency" starting with the bottom "slice."

Once the group had understood what the photo was supposed to represent, the educator asked the group what part of New York in the montage was where they lived. Realistically, the group might have actually lived in the conditions in the second shot from the bottom in the picture, at best.

There was silence, whispering, and opinion swapping. Finally came the group's decision. Their place third from the top!

On the way back to the hotel, sitting next to the educator, who was driving, I continued silently to think about the meetings, of the basic need individuals exposed to such situations have—until they accept themselves as individuals and as a class, until they commit themselves, until they struggle—their need to deny the humiliating truth, a truth that humiliates them precisely because they introject the dominant ideology that sketches them as incompetent and guilty, the authors of their own failures. And yet the actual "why" of those failures is to be found in the perversity of the system.

I thought as well of the moment, several evenings before, when (with Carmen Hunter as simultaneous translator—one of the most competent North American educators, even in those early days) I spoke for the first time at length about *Pedagogy of the Oppressed,* which I was to finalize only in the following year. And I compared the reactions of the educands on those two nights with those of some of the audience of my talk—educators and community organizers.

"Fear of freedom" had marked the reactions in all three meetings. Flight from the real, an attempt to "tame" the real through concealment of the truth.

At this very moment, as I recall these happenings and reactions of times so long ago, something else, something very much like them, comes to mind: an event at which I likewise assisted. It was another case of an expression of the assimilation and interiorization of the dominant ideology by the dominated themselves—I might even say, as I put it in *Pedagogy of the Oppressed,* an expression of the oppressor "inhabiting" and dominating the half-defeated body and soul of the oppressed one.

We were in the midst of the campaign for the governorship of the State of São Paulo, in 1982. Luiz Inácio Lula da Silva, or Lula, was the Workers Party candidate, and, as a party activist, I attended some of the meetings in outlying districts of the city. I did not attend party assemblies, as I do not regard myself as sufficiently competent. These were meetings at recreational clubs or neighborhood associations. At one of these meetings, a workman, some forty years of age, stood up and criticized Lula and his candidacy. His main argument was that he could never vote for somebody just like himself. "Lula's the same as me," said the workman, with conviction. "He don't know how to talk. He don't talk the right kind o' Portuguese to be in government. Lula ain't had no education. He ain't, like they say, 'well-read.' Look," he went on "—if Lula won, what would we do? Think how embarrassed people'd be, if the queen o' England was t' come here again. Lula's wife ain't got no rose garden to receive the queen! She can't be no First Lady!"

In New York, the concealing discourse, which looks for some other geography in which to deposit the garbage, which was making it too plain how discriminated against the audience was, was a discourse of self-rejection. In the same way, it was a discourse of self-rejection, rejection of his class, that the workman had pronounced who refused to look at himself or to see in Lula, because he was a worker himself, a protest against the world that rejected him.

In the most recent presidential campaign, the Northeasterner who worked with us in our house voted, in the first two rounds, for Collor. She told us, with absolute assurance, that she "didn't have anybody to vote for" who would have been a candidate favorable to her own interests.

Basically, she must have agreed with many of the elitists of this country: persons who refer to themselves as *menas gente* cannot imagine any of their own number being president. To say *menas gente,* "lesser people," means, when all is said and done, that you are *menos gente,* "less people" in the adverbial sense of "less": less completely people.

I went back to Chile. Presently I found myself in a new phase of the gestation process of *Pedagogy of the Oppressed.*

I began to use index cards, titling and numbering each one according to what was written on it. I always carried some paper in my pockets, or even a little notepad. Whenever an idea occurred to me—regardless of where I was, in a bus, on the street, in a restaurant, alone, with someone—I jotted down the idea. Sometimes it was just a phrase.

Then in the evening, back home, after dinner, I worked on the idea or ideas I had jotted down, expanding them on two, three, or more file cards. Then I put a title on each card, and a number, in ascending order.

I started working on ideas I culled from reading I had done, as well. There were times when a statement by an author would make a light go on in my head. It would spark a series of reflections in me that might never have been a concern of the author of the book I was reading.

Other times, what one or another author would say would lead me to reflections in the same area as that with which he or she was dealing, but reinforcing some position of mine and making it more clear to me.

In many cases, the sort of thing that challenged me, and about which I wrote on file cards, were statements, or questions, either of peasants whom I was interviewing and whom I had heard discussing codifications in culture circles, or of agricultural technologists, agronomists, or other educators, whom I made sure I kept meeting in training seminars. What kept me from ever looking down on or simply belittling "common sense" may have been the always-respectful contact I had with it, ever since the faraway days of my experience in the Brazilian Northeast, coupled with the never-failing certitude within me that, in order to get beyond "common sense," you had to use it. Just as it is unacceptable to advocate an educational practice that is satisfied with rotating on the axis of "common sense," so neither is an educational practice acceptable that sets at naught the "knowledge of living experience" and simply starts out with the educator's systematic cognition.

The educator needs to know that his or her "here" and "now" are nearly always the educands' "there" and "then." Even though the educator's dream is not only to render his or her "here-and-now" accessible to educands, but to get beyond their own "here-and-now" with them, or to understand and rejoice that educands have gotten beyond their "here" so that this dream is realized, she or he must begin with the educands' "here," and not with her or his own. At the very least, the educator must keep account of the existence of his or her educands' "here" and respect it. Let me put it this way: you never get *there* by starting from *there*, you get *there* by starting from some *here*. This means, ultimately, that the educator must not be ignorant of, underestimate, or reject any of the "knowledge of living experience" with which educands come to school.

I shall return to this subject again, as it appears to me to be central to a discussion of *Pedagogy of the Oppressed*, and not only of the book by that name, but of the actual pedagogy of the oppressed itself.

Then came the time when I began, occasionally, to practically "play" with the file cards. I would calmly read a series of them, say, ten of them, and I would try to discover, first, whether there were any holes to fill in their thematic sequence; and second, whether a careful reading of them called forth in me or gave rise to the emergence of new topics. Basically, my "idea cards" turned into seed cards for other ideas, other topics.

Sometimes—suppose, between card number eight and card number nine—I would sense a vacuum, and begin to work on it. Then I would renumber the cards accordingly, so that they would still be in numerical sequence.

As I recall, now, all of this mechanical work—and it has its nostalgia for me—I admit that it would have saved time and effort, and been more efficient, if I had used a computer from time to time, even a little one like the one that my wife and I have today.

But thanks to that mechanical effort, once I began to write the text—in July 1967, taking the opportunity of a vacation period—in two weeks of work, sometimes working all night long, I wrote the first three chapters of *Pedagogy*. When that much had been typed up—which I thought would be the whole book, just those first three chapters—I turned it over to my great friend, whom I shall never forget, and with whom I always learned so much—Ernani Maria Fiori, to write the preface. When Fiori gave me back his excellent essay in December 1967, I took a few hours at home that night to read through the entire manuscript, from his preface to the last word of chapter 3, which I then thought of as the last.

The year before, in 1966, Josué de Castro,[30] owner of a vanity as lush as that of Gilberto Freyre, but, like the latter, a vanity that disturbed no one, had spent some days in Santiago. One evening when he had no official tasks to perform, we sat together, conversing freely, in one of Santiago's lovely parks, Josué, Almino Affonso, and I. Talking about what he was writing, Josué suddenly told us: "I'll suggest a good habit for a writer to get into. At the end of a book, or article, let it 'marinate' for three months, four months, in a drawer. Then one night, take it out again and read it. People always change 'something,'" concluded Josué, with his hand on the shoulder of one of us.

I took the risk of following his suggestion. The very night of the day Fiori gave me his text, after reading it and the three chapters of *Pedagogy*, I locked everything away in my "box" in my study, and left it there for two months.

I cannot deny the curiosity, and even more, a certain yearning, that the text provoked in me as it lay there, locked away, "all, all alone." Sometimes I had a powerful urge to take it out and read it again; but I thought it would be interesting, too, to take a certain distance from it. So I restrained myself.

There in my study, one night a little more than two months later, I sat down with it a few hours to get reacquainted. It was almost as if I had found an old friend again. In fact, I read it with great emotion—slowly, without even wanting to finish it very soon—the whole text, page by page. (It would have been hard to imagine, just then, that twenty-four years later I would be doing much the same thing, several times, not with the manuscript, but with the book itself—to rethink it, to restate it.)

I did not make many important changes in it. But I did make the basic discovery that the text was unfinished. It needed one more chapter. And so it came about that I wrote the fourth and last chapter, taking advantage, now of lunch period in training seminars in the vicinity of Santiago, now in hotels in cities or towns further away, where I also went to give seminars. After dinner, I would fairly race to my room, and seclude myself there the whole night through, writing chapter 4, till early the next day, when I would begin the work of my seminar once again. I remember now that the only text that could take me away from my writing work was Antonio Callado's excellent *Quarup*.

In those days I was still able to read while the car was lapping up the miles. Thus it was that, on one of my trips to the South of Chile, after taking the opportunity of highway time to spend some hours with my book, I finished reading *Quarup* in the hotel, filled with emotion, as the first light dawned. Then I wrote a letter to Callado, which I was too shy ever to mail. I am sorry to say that the letter was lost, along with letters written to me, when we moved to the United States in 1969.

The gusto with which I gave myself to that exercise, the task of fairly spending myself in writing and thinking (mutually inseparable in the creation or the production of the text), compensated for the lack of sleep with which I returned from trips. I no longer remember the names of the hotels where I wrote parts of the fourth chapter of *Pedagogy,* but I still retain the sensation of pleasure with which I read, before going to sleep, the last pages I had written.

At home, in Santiago, not rare were the times when, so involved in my work, and gratified by it, I was surprised by the morning sun stealing into the little room which I had converted into a library at 500 Alcides de Gasperi Street, Apoquindo, Santiago, and lighting it up—sun and birds, morning, new day. Then I would look out the window, at the little garden Elza had made, the rosebushes she had planted.

I do not know whether the house would still be there, and still be painted blue, as it was at the time.

I should not be able to rethink *Pedagogy of the Oppressed* without thinking upon, without remembering, some of the places where I wrote it, but especially one of them, the house where I lived and was happy, and from where I left Chile, carrying longings, suffering at having to leave but hopeful of being able to respond to the challenges that were waiting for me.

With the fourth chapter finally ready, I looked at the first three again and touched them up, then I handed over the whole text to a typist. Next I made several copies, which I distributed among Chilean friends, and some Brazilian companions in exile and other friends.

In the acknowledgments, when the first Brazilian edition appeared—which only became possible after the book had already been translated into English, Spanish, Italian, French, and German, due to the climate of repression in which we lived—I left out the names of some friends, as well as those of some of my companions in exile.

No one failed to come running, with his or her encouragement, plus concrete suggestions—for the clarification of a point here, for a stylistic improvement there, and so on.

Now, so many years later, and even more convinced how doggedly we must struggle lest ever again, in the name of freedom, democracy, ethics, and respect for the common welfare, we should again have to experience the denial of freedom, outrage to democracy, deception, and contempt for the common weal, such as the coup d'état imposed on us on April 1, 1964 (which picturesquely dubbed itself a revolution), I should like to list the names of all who inspired me with their word, and express to them my sincere thanks: Marcela Gajardo, Jacques Chonchol, Jorge Mellado, Juan Carlos Poblete, Raúl Velozo, and Pelli, Chileans. Paulo de Tarso and Plínio Sampaio, Almino Affonso, Maria Edy, Flávio Toledo, Wilson Cantoni, Ernani Fiori, João Zacariotti, José Luiz Fiori, and Antonio Romanelli, Brazilians.

There is another connection between *Pedagogy of the Oppressed* and the perverse, antidemocratic climate of the military regime that came crashing down on us with such remarkable, hateful fury, that I should like to bring out.

Even though I knew that the book could not be published here— have its first edition in Portuguese, the language in which it was originally written—I did want to get the typescript into the hands of Fernando Gasparian, director of Paz e Terra, which was going to publish it. The question that arose was how to see to the safety not only of the material, but also, and above all, of the courier. At this point, in the early 1970s, we were already staying in Geneva.

I had mentioned the problem to Swiss scholars, professors at the University of Geneva. One of them, who, besides being a professor, was a national councilor, Jean Ziegler, as he was about to leave for Rio de Janeiro on an academic assignment, offered to carry the typescript to Brazil personally. I accepted his offer, since, with his diplomatic passport plus his Swiss nationality, nothing untoward would befall him. He would get through the passport check and customs without questions or searches.

A few days later, Gasparian discreetly acknowledged receipt of the material, asking me to await more favorable times for its publica- tion. I sent the text toward the end of 1970, when the book was already in its first edition in English, or early in 1971. Its publication in Brazil, its first printing, was possible only in 1975. Meanwhile a countless number of Brazilians had read it, in foreign-language edi- tions arriving here by strokes of shrewdness and courage. I came to know, at this time, a young North American sister who worked in the Northeast, who said that, on her return trips from the United States, she had gotten into Brazil several times with a number of copies of *Pedagogy*, covered in book jackets with religious titles on them. In this fashion, her friends, who worked in the outlying districts of Northeastern cities, were able to read the book and discuss it even before its publication in Portuguese.

At about the same time, I received in Geneva, hand-delivered, an excellent letter from a group of workers in São Paulo, of whom I have unfortunately since lost track. They had studied, together, a copy of the original that someone had typed out. It is a pity that so little is left of my Geneva archives. Among many a good thing that was lost, was that letter. But I remember how they ended it. "Paul," they said, or words to this effect, "keep on writing—but next time lay it on a little thicker when you come to those scholarly types that come to visit as if they had revolutionary truth by the tail. You know, the ones that come looking for us to teach us that we're oppressed and exploited and to tell us what to do."

Some time after Ziegler, that excellent intellectual, had gotten the typescript into Gasparian's hands, he, Ziegler, published a book that immediately became a best-seller—*La Suisse au-dessus de tout soupçon* (Switzerland: above all suspicion), in which he disclosed Swiss secrets that were altogether too touchy, especially in the area of the hidden bank accounts of a certain type of Third World folk. Ziegler wounded innumerable interests with his book, and has suffered reprisals that have been by no means easy to deal with. Recently, Jean Ziegler is being put under pressure, and major restrictions, due to the publication of another best-seller of his, in which he discusses the "laundering" of drug-traffic money. As a national councilor, or deputy, from the canton of Geneva, Ziegler recently had his parliamentary immunity restricted by his colleagues, on the allegation that he writes as a professor, a scholar, an academician, while that his parliamentary immunity pertains only to his activity in the Parliament. And so he can be put on trial for what he has written as a scholar.

In view of all of this, and mindful of the unselfish favor he performed in serving as the courier of the forbidden book's typescript, I should like to make public here my solidarity with the great intellectual in whom I see no separation between the professor—the serious, competent scholar—and the watchful representative of the Swiss people, the national councilor.

Finally, I owe one last word of acknowledgment, and posthumous gratitude: to Elza, for all she did in making *Pedagogy* a reality.

— I find that one of the best things that any of us, man or woman, can experience in life, is a loving tenderness in our relationships, however bespattered, from time to time, those relationships may be with a lack of compassion, which simply prove that we are, after all, "ordinary people."

This is the experience I had with Elza, on account of which, when you get right down to it, I became predisposed for a re-creation of myself under the equally unselfish care of another woman who, speaking to me and of us, writes in her excellent book of having to come to me to "reinvent things lost—" hers, with the death of Raúl, her first spouse, and mine, with that of Elza—"life, with love."*

All during the time I spoke about *Pedagogy of the Oppressed* with other persons and with Elza, Elza was always an attentive and critical listener, and became my first, likewise critical, reader when I began the phase of actual writing of the text.

Very early in the morning, she would read the pages I had been writing until daybreak, and had left arranged on the table.

Sometimes she was unable to contain herself. She would wake me up and say, with humor, "I hope this book won't send us into exile!"

I am happy to be able to record this sense of gratitude with the freedom with which I do so, without fear of being accused of being sentimental.

My concern, in this hopeful work, as I have demonstrated to this point, is to stir my memory and challenge it, like an excavation in time, so that I can show you the actual process of my reflection, my pedagogical thought and its development, of which the book is a step—just as my pedagogical thinking is actually developing right in this *Pedagogy of Hope*, as I discuss the hope with which I wrote *Pedagogy of the Oppressed*.

Hence my attempt to discover—in old weavings, facts, and deeds of childhood, youth, and maturity, in my experience with others,

---

*Ana Maria Araújo Freire, *Analfabetismo no Brasil: Da ideologia da interdição do corpo à ideologia nacionalista ou de como deixar sem ler e escrever desde as Catarinas (paraguaçu), Filipas, Anas, Genebras, Apolônias e Gracias até os Severinos* (São Paulo: Cortez, 1989).

within the events, within the instants in the general, dynamic process—not only *Pedagogy of the Oppressed* as it was being gestated, but my life itself. Indeed, it is in the interplay of the fabrics of which life forms a part that life itself wins meaning. And *Pedagogy of the Oppressed* is an important moment of my life—my life of which the book expresses a certain "instant"—demanding of me at the same time that I demonstrate the necessary consistency with what I have said in it.

Among the responsibilities that, for me, writing sets before me, not to say imposes on me, there is one that I always take on. Already experiencing, as I write, the consistency obtaining between my written word and my speech and my deeds, past and present, I likewise come to experience the importance of intensifying this consistency, all through the course of my existence. Consistency, however, is not paralysis. In the process of acting-and-thinking, speaking-and-writing, I can change position. Thus my consistency, still as necessary as ever, comes about within new parameters. What is impossible for me is inconsistency, even recognizing the impossibility of an absolute consistency. At bottom, this quality or this virtue, consistency, requires of us an insertion into a permanent process of search, demands of us patience and humility, which are also virtues, in our dealings with others. And at times, for any number of reasons, we find ourselves lacking these latter virtues, which are fundamental for the exercise of another: consistency.

In this phase of the resumption of *Pedagogy*, I shall be seizing on certain particular aspects of the book, whether or not they have provoked criticism down through the years, with a view to explaining myself better, clarifying angles, asserting and reasserting positions.

Let me say a little something about language: about my taste for metaphor, and about the sexist mark I left on *Pedagogy of the Oppressed*—just as, before that, on *Educação como prática da liberdade*. It seems to me not only important, but necessary, that I now do this.

I shall begin precisely with the sexist langauge that marks the whole book, and of my debt to countless North American women, from various parts of the United States, who wrote to me, from late in 1970 into early 1971, a few months after the first edition of my book had come out in New York. It was if they had gotten together to send me their critical letters, which came into my hands in Geneva over the course of three months, almost uninterruptedly.

Invariably, in their comments on the book, which seemed to them to contain a great deal of good, and to constitute a contribution to their struggle, they also spoke of what they regarded as a large contradiction. In discussing oppression and liberation, in criticizing, with just indignation, oppressive structures, they said, I used sexist, and therefore discriminatory, language, in which women had no place. Almost all of those who wrote to me cited one or other passage in the book, like the one, for example, that I myself now excerpt from the Brazilian edition: "In this fashion, as their consciousness of the situation grows in acuity, men 'appropriate' that situation to themselves as a historical reality that is thereby subject to transformation by *them* [masc.]."* Why not by women too?

I remember reading the first two or three letters I received as if it were yesterday, and how, under the impact of my conditioning by an authoritarian, sexist, ideology, I reacted. And it is important to bring out that, here at the end of 1970 and the beginning of 1971, I had already intensely experienced the political struggle, had spent five or six years of exile, had read a world of serious works, but in reading the first criticisms that I received, still said to myself, or repeated, what I had been taught in my boyhood: "Now, when I say 'men,' that of course includes 'women.'" And why are men not included when we say, "Women are determined to change the world"? No man would feel included in any discourse by any speaker, or in the text of any author, who would write, "Women are determined to change the world." After all, men certainly dislike it when I say to a nearly all-female audience, but with two or three men in it, "Tod*as* vocês deveriam ..." ("You should all [fem.] . . ."). For the men present, either I do not know Portuguese syntax, or else I am trying to "have some fun" at their expense. The one thing they cannot think is that they are included in my discourse. How can one explain, except on an ideological basis, the rule according to which, in a room filled with dozens of women and only one man, I have to say, "El*es* tod*os* são trabalhadores e dedicad*os*" ("You are all workers,

*Paulo Freire, *Pedagogia do oprimido*, 17th ed. (Rio de Janeiro: Paz e Terra, 1987), p. 74.

and dedicated ones"), with all the variable terminations in the masculine gender? Indeed it is not a grammatical problem, but an ideological one.

It is in this sense that I have explicitly stated at the beginning of these comments my debt to those women, whose letters I have unfortunately lost as well, for having made me see how much ideology resides in language.

I then wrote to all of them, one by one, acknowledging their letters and thanking them for the fine help they had given me.

From that date forward, I have always referred to "woman and man," or "human beings." I had rather write an unattractive line sometimes than omit to express my rejection of sexist language.

Now, in writing this *Pedagogy of Hope*, in which I rethink the soul and body of *Pedagogy of the Oppressed*, I shall beg the publishing houses to get over their own sexist language. And let it not be said that this is a minor problem. It is a major problem. Let it not be said that, since the basic thing is to change a wicked world, re-creating it in terms of making it less perverse, the debate over sexist language is therefore of minor importance, especially since women do not constitute a social class.

Discrimination against women, expressed and committed by sexist discourse, and enfleshed in concrete practices, is a colonial way of treating them, and therefore incompatible with any progressive position, regardless of whether the person taking the position be a woman or a man.

The rejection of a sexist ideology, which necessarily involves the re-creation of language, is part of the possible dream of a change of the world. By that very fact, in writing or speaking a language no longer colonial, I do so not in order to please women or displease men, but in order to be consistent with my option for that less-wicked world of which I have spoken before—just as I did not write the book to which I now return in order to seem like a nice person to the oppressed as individuals and as a class, nor simply to beat over the head the oppressors as individuals or as a class. I wrote the book as a political task I understood I had to perform.

It is not pure idealism, let it be further observed, to refuse to await a radical change in the world in order to begin to insist on a change in language. Changing language is part of the process of changing the world. The relationship, language–thought–world, is a dialectical, processual, contradictory relationship. Obviously the defeat of a sexist discourse, like the defeat of any authoritarian discourse, requires of us, or imposes upon us the necessity, that, concomitantly with the new, democratic, antidiscriminatory discourse, we engage ourselves in democratic practices, as well.

What would be intolerable would be simply pronouncing the democratic, antidiscriminatory discourse and maintaining a colonial practice.

An important aspect, under the heading of language, which I should like to emphasize is how much I have always been impressed, in my experiences with urban and rural workers, with their metaphorical language: the wealth of symbolism in their speech. Almost in parentheses, I should call attention to the abundant bibliography, at the moment, of works by linguists and philosophers of language on metaphor and its use in literature and science. Here, however, my concern is to stress how much popular speech, and the absence of *rough edges* therein (there's a metaphor), has always gripped and excited me. From my adolescence, in Jaboatão, my ears began to open to the sonority of popular speech, to which would later accrue, when I was with SESI, a growing understanding of popular semantics and, necessarily, syntax.

My long conversations with the fishers in their hemp shelters on the Pontas de Pedra coast, in Pernambuco, like my dialogues with peasants and urban laborers, in the gullies and hillocks of Recife, not only familiarized me with their language, but sharpened my sensitivity to the lovely way they spoke of themselves—no matter that it be of their sorrows—and the world. Lovely and sure.

One of the best examples of this loveliness and this sureness is to be found in the discourse of a peasant of Minas Gerais[31] in dialogue with professor and anthropologist Carlos Brandão, in one of his many field-research expeditions. Brandão recorded a long conversation with Antônio Cícero de Soza, or Ciço, part of which he used as the preface of the book he was editing.*

---

*Carlos Brandão et al., *A questão política da educação popular* (São Paulo: Brasiliense, 1980).

Now this gen'l'man comes up and asks me, "Ciço, what is edjica-tion?" Yup. Good. What do I think? I say. Well, see, you say "edjication"; an' I say "edjication." Same word, right? Pronuncia-tion, I mean. It's jist one word: "edjication." But then I ask to the gen'l'man: Is it the same thing? Is it the same thing that folks talk about when they say that word? There I say: No. I say to the gen'l'man like this: Nope, it's not. I don't think so.

Edjication—when the gen'l'man comes up and says "edjica-tion," he's comin' from his world. The same . . . 'nother. When it's me talkin' I come from 'nother place, 'nother world. I come from down in the holler where poor folks lives, like people say. What're you comparin' it with, what's this word comin' up with? With school, ain't it? With that fine perfesser, good clothes, smart, new book, spiffy, notebook, fountain pen, all real special, everything just like it should be—from his world, with schoolin', what changes folks into a doctor. Fact? I think so, but I think a ways off, since I never seen that roun' here.

I once proposed to a group of students of a graduate course at PUC-SP[32] that they read Ciço's text and analyze it. Make a critical analysis.

We spent four three-hour sessions reading Cico's four pages.

His thematics, which we gathered as we got into the text, as we unwrapped it, was rich and manifold, and the time just flew by. We never took breaks when we were discussing Ciço—we found the work that exciting.

Something I should like very much to have been able to do, and that, though it was not done, I still have hope of doing some day, is to have discussed or come to discuss this text of Ciço with rural and/ or urban workers. The experience would consist in starting with a reading of Ciço's discourse, and joining my own to it. First, we would take Ciço's text and talk about it. Then it would be my turn to teach any of a number of elements of content about which, like Ciço, if possibly with lesser power of analysis than his, the workers would have a "knowledge of living experience." But the basic thing would be for me to challenge them to go more deeply into the meaning of the themes or content and thereby learn them.

I cannot resist repeating: teaching is not the pure mechanical transfer of the contour of a content from the teacher to passive, docile students. Nor can I resist repeating that starting out with the educands' knowledge does not mean circling around this knowledge ad infinitum. *Starting out* means setting off down the road, getting going, shifting from one point to another, not *sticking*, or *staying*. I have never said, as it is sometimes suggested or said that I have said, that we ought to flutter spellbound around the knowledge of the educands like moths around a lamp bulb.

Starting with the "knowledge of experience had" in order to get beyond it is not *staying* in that knowledge.

Some years ago I visited a capital of the Northeast at the invitation of educators working in rural areas of the state. They wanted to have me with them for the three days they were going to devote to an appraisal of their work with various groups of peasants. At one moment in one of the sessions, the question of language came up—the matter of the sonorous lilt of the peasants' speech, the wealth of their symbolism, and so on. One of those present then recounted the following.

For almost two months, he said, he had wanted to be in on the Sunday meetings a group of peasants regularly held after the nine o'clock Sunday Mass. He had mentioned his wish to the leader, but the green light never seemed to come.

One day he was finally invited. But as the meeting opened, and as he was being introduced to the group, he had to listen to the following speech by the leader.

"Today we have a new member, and he's not a peasant. He's a well-read person. I talked about this with you at our last meeting, whether he could come or not."

Then the leader gave the group a bit of personal data about the new member. Finally, he turned to the candidate himself, and, fixing him intently, said: "We have something very important to tell you, new friend. If you're here to teach us that we're exploited, don't bother. We know that already. What we don't know . . . and need to know from you . . . is, if you're going to be with us when the chips are down."

That is, they might have said, in more sophisticated terms, whether his solidarity went any further than his intellectual curiosity. Whether it went beyond the notes that he would be taking in meetings with them. Whether he would be with them, at their side, in the hour of their repression.

Another educator, perhaps encouraged by the story he had just heard, offered his own testimonial, recounting the following.

He was taking part, with other educators, in a one-day workshop with peasant leaders. Suddenly one of the peasants spoke up: "The way this conversations's goin' nobody's gonna git it. Nope. 'Cause as far as you here're concerned"—and he pointed to the group of educators—"you're talkin' *salt*, and these people here," meaning the others, the peasants, "they wanna know 'bout *seasonin'*, and *salt* ain't but *part* of the seasonin'."

As far as the peasants were concerned, the educators were getting lost in the view of reality that I am wont to call "focalistic," while what they wanted and needed was an understanding of the relationships among the component "partialities" of the totality. They were not denying the salt, it was just that they wanted to understand it in its relationship with the other ingredients that constituted the *seasoning* as a totality.

Speaking of this popular wealth, from which we have so much to learn, I recall suggestions I used to make to various educators who had frequent contact with urban and rural laborers, and who would go and record stories, snatches of conversations, phrases, expressions, in order to supply material for semantic, syntactical, prosodic (and so on) analyses of popular discourse. At a certain moment in a like undertaking, it would be possible to offer various groups of laborers, as if they were codifications, the stories or the phrases, or the scraps of discourse, already studied, with the collaboration of sociolinguists, especially, and test the understanding the educators had had of the phrases, the stories, by submitting them to the laborers. It would be an exercise in a comparison and contrast, between the two syntaxes, the dominant and the popular.

When it comes to language there is something else I should like to bring up here. It is something that I have never accepted—on the contrary, something that I have always rejected. It is the assertion, or even insinuation, that fine, elegant writing, is not scholarly. A scholar does difficult writing, not fine writing. Language's esthetic moment, it has always seemed to me, ought to be pursued by all of us, including rigorous scholars. There is not the least incompatibility between rigor in the quest for an understanding and knowledge of the world, and beauty of form in the expression of what is found in that world.

It would be an absurdity for there to be, or seem to have to be, some necessary association between ugliness and scientific rigor.

It is not by chance that my first readings in Gilberto Freyre, in the 1940s, impressed me so much, just as rereading him today becomes a moment of esthetic pleasure as well.

Personally, ever since I was young, I have liked a discourse without sharp edges, regardless of whether it be pronounced by a peasant, in all naiveté about the world, or by a sociologist of the stature of Gilberto Freyre. Few people in this country, I think, have dealt with language with the good taste that Gilberto has applied.

I have never forgotten the impact, on the adolescents whose teacher of Portuguese I was in the 1940s, of the reading I used to do with them of passages from Gilberto's works. I invariably took him as an example when speaking to them of the problem of where to put objective pronouns in sentences, and emphasizing what a fine style he had. It would have been hard, regardless of whether he was being grammatical or not, for Gilberto Freyre to write something unlovely.

It was he who led me, without a moment's hesitation, in a first esthetic experience, to make my option between "Ela vinha-se aproximando," and "Ela vinha se aproximando"—both meaning, "She gradually drew near." I chose the latter? Why? On account of the sonority resulting from uncoupling the *se* from the auxiliary verb *vinha* and "releasing" it to be attracted by the *a* of the main verb, *aproximando*. It becomes *s'a* when it is released from the first verb, and, as it were, nestles up to the *a* of *aproximando*.

A writer commits no sin against scholarship if, while rejecting the narrow, insipid doctrine we find in grammars, he or she never says or writes, however, a "Tinha acabado-se" ("She had passed on") instead of "releasing" the *se* from the *acabado* and sandwiching it between the other words, or a "Se você *ver* Pedro" ("If you see Peter") using the infinitive instead of the indicative, or a "*Houveram* muitas pessoas na audiência" ("There were many persons in the audience" instead of "Many persons were in the audience"), or a "*Fazem* muitos anos que voltei" ("It's been many years since I returned" instead of "I returned many years ago").

A writer commits no sin against scholarship by refusing to wound the ear and good taste of the person reading or hearing his or her discourse, and may not, in so refusing, simplistically be accused of being "rhetorical," or of succumbing to the "fascination of a linguistic elegance as an end in itself." (On the contrary, otherwise a scholarly writer ought to be accused of having succumbed to the tastelessness of a vacuous flow of words.) Or pointed to as "pretentious," or "snobbish," and seen as ridiculously pompous in his or her way of writing or speaking.

If sociologist Gilberto Freyre—not to mention anyone else, for our purposes just now—had placed any credence in this (about an alleged connection between scholarly rigor and contempt for the esthetic treatment of language), we should not have, today, pages like this one:

> The word *Northeast* is a word, today, disfigured by the expression "Northeast projects"—that is, "antidrought projects." The hinterland of dry sand creaking under your feet. The hinterland of hard landscapes, which hurt your eyes. The cacti known as Peru cereus. The angular oxen and horses. The light shadows, like some souls from another world who fear the sunshine.
>
> But that Northeast of humans and animals stretching almost into El Greco figures is only one side of the Northeast. The other Northeast? Older than the first. This time, the Northeast of fat trees, deep shadows, sluggish oxen, vigorous folk all but puffed up into Sancho Panzas by mill honey, fish cooked with manioc mush, wearisome, monotonous work, rotgut rum, half-fermented sugarcane juice, cocoa beans, worms, erysipelas or "St. Anthony's fire," idleness, sicknesses that make a person bloat up, the special disease you get from eating dirt.

And further on: "An oily Northeast, where at night the moon seems to drip a fat grease of things and people."*

As for *Pedagogy of the Oppressed*, there were criticisms like those reported above—pompousness—as well as of what was regarded as the unintelligibility of my text—criticisms of a language considered all but impossible to understand, a recherché, elitist language that betrayed my "want of respect for the people."

---

*Freyre, *Nordeste*.

In remembering some, and rereading others, of these criticisms, today, I remember a meeting I had in Washington, DC, in 1972 with a group of young persons interested in discussing certain topics in the book.

Among them was a black man, of about fifty, who was involved in problems of community organization. During the discussions, from time to time, after some visible difficulty of understanding on the part of one of the young persons, he would speak up in an attempt to clarify the point, and always did so very well.

At the end of the meeting he came up to me with a friendly smile, and said: "If some of these youngsters tell you they don't understand you because of your English, don't believe them. It's a question of the *thinking* that's expressed in your language. Their problem is, they don't think dialectically. And they don't yet have any actual experience of the hard life led by the sectors of society that suffer discrimination."

It is also interesting to observe that some of the criticisms, of the "hard, snobbish" language of *Pedagogy* in the English-language edition of my book, attributed a certain amount of responsibility to Myra Ramas, my friend, and the book's competent, serious translator. Myra worked with a maximum of professional precision, and absolute dedication. During the process of translation of the text, she would regularly consult with a group of friends. She would call them on the phone and say, "Does this sentence make sense to you?" And she would read the passage she had just translated and was having doubts about. Then again, when she had finished part of a chapter, she would send a copy of the translation, along with the original, to other friends, North Americans who knew Portuguese very well, like theologian Richard Shaull, who wrote the preface to the North American edition, and ask them for their opinion and suggestions.

I was consulted by her myself, a number of times, during my stint in Cambridge as visiting professor at Harvard. I remember her patient inquiry into various hypotheses she had for translating "inédito viavel," one of my metaphors. Finally she selected, "untested feasibility."

Within the limits of my lack of authority in the English language, I have to say that I have a very good feeling about Myra's translation.

And so, whenever I deal with English-language readers, in seminars, in discussions, I have always taken responsibility for the "why" of any criticisms they might make of the language of the book.

I also remember the opinion of the sixteen-year-old son of a black woman who was an excellent student of mine at Harvard. I had asked him to read Myra's translation of the first chapter of *Pedagogy*, which had just arrived in New York. The following week, I was speaking with her and her son, whom I had asked to read the text. "This book," he said, "was written about me. It's all about me." Let us even admit that he might have run into one or another word that was foreign to his young intellectual experience. Even so, it did not deprive him of an understanding of the whole. His existential experience, in a context of discrimination, rendered him *sympathetic* to the text from the moment he began to read it.

Today, after so many words, with *Pedagogy* translated into countless languages, in which it has practically covered the globe, this kind of criticism has significantly diminished. But there is something else.

And that is why I have stayed a bit with this question.

I do not see the legitimacy of a student or teacher closing any book, not just *Pedagogy of the Oppressed*, and simply declaring it to be "unreadable" because he or she has not clearly understood the meaning of a sentence. And especially, doing so without having expended any effort—without having behaved with the necessary seriousness of someone who does studies. There are many people for whom to pause in the reading of a text as soon as difficulties arise in an understanding of it, so that the reader should have to have recourse to the ordinary work tools—dictionaries, including those of philosophy, social sciences, etymology, or synonyms, or encyclopedias—is a waste of time. No, on the contrary, the time devoted to consulting dictionaries or encyclopedias for an elucidation of what we are reading is study time, not wasted time. People will occasionally just "keep on reading," hoping that, magically, on the next page, the word in question might "come up again" in a context in which they will see what it means without having had to "look it up."

Reading a text is a more serious, more exacting, enterprise than this. Reading a text is not a careless, sluggish "stroll through the words." Reading a text is learning the relationships among the words in the composition of the discourse. It is the task of a critical, humble, determined "subject" or agent of learning, the reader.

Reading, as study, is a difficult, even painful, process at times, but always a pleasant one as well. It implies that the reader delve deep into the text, in order to learn its most profound meaning. The more we do this exercise, in a disciplined way, conquering any desire to flee the reading, the more we prepare ourselves for making future reading less difficult.

Most of all, the reading of a text requires that the one who does it be convinced that ideologies will not die. The practical application of this principle here means that the ideology with which the text is drenched—or the ideology it conceals—is not necessarily that of the one who is about to read it. Hence the need for an open, critical, radical, and not sectarian, position on the part of the reader, without which he or she will be closed to the text, and prevented from learning anything through it because it may argue positions that are at odds with those of that reader. At times, ironically, the positions are merely different, and not positively antagonistic.

In many cases, we have not even read the author. We have read *about* the author, and without going to him or her, we accept criticisms of him or her. We adopt them as our own.

Professor Celso Beisiegel, pro-rector for degree candidacy at the University of São Paulo, and one of this country's leading intellectuals, once told me that, on a certain occasion, as he was taking part in a group discussion on Brazilian education, he heard from one of those present, referring to me, that my works were no longer important for the national debate on education. Curious, Beisiegel decided to investigate. "What books of Paulo Freire have you studied?" he asked.

Without a moment's hesitation, the young critic replied, "None. But I've read about him."

It is absolutely fundamental, however, that an author be criticized not on the basis of what is said about him or her, but only after an earnest, devoted, competent reading of the actual author. Of course, this does not mean that we need not read what has been or is being said about him or her, as well.

Finally, the practice of an earnest reading of serious texts ultimately helps one to learn that reading as study is a broad process, requiring time, patience, sensitivity, method, rigor, determination, and passion for knowledge.

Without necessarily identifying the authors of particular criticisms, nor even to the particular chapters of *Pedagogy* to which the objections that I shall now report will refer, I shall extend the present reflection by offering examples of judgments to which I ought to respond, or repeat responses I have already made.

One of these judgments, which is from the 1970s, is one that takes me precisely for what I criticize and combat. It takes me for arrogant and elitist. It regards me as a "cultural invader," and therefore as someone disrespectful of the cultural and class identity of the popular classes—the rural and urban workers. At bottom, this type of criticism, when made of me, and therefore based on a distorted understanding of *conscientização* and a profoundly naive view of educational practice—as it seeks to regard that practice as a "neutral" one, "at the service of the well-being of humanity"—is incapable of perceiving that one of the finest things about this practice is precisely that it is impossible to live it without running risks. For example, there is the risk of not being consistent—of saying one thing and doing something else. And it is precisely the political nature of educational practice, its helplessness to be "neutral," that requires of the educator his or her ethicalness. The task of educator would be all too easy were it to be reducible to the imparting of content that would not even need to be treated aseptically, and aseptically "transmitted," since, as the content of a neutral science, it would already be aseptic. In this case, the educator would have no reason, to say the least, to be concerned with being decent, or to make an effort to be decent, to be ethical, except with regard to his or her training and preparation. The subject or agent of a neutral practice would have nothing to do but "transfer knowledge," a knowledge that would be itself neutral.

Actually, there is no such thing. There neither is, nor has ever been, an educational practice in zero space–time—neutral in the sense of being committed only to preponderantly abstract, intangible ideas. To try to get people to believe that there is such a thing as this, and to convince or try to convince the incautious that this is the truth, is indisputably a political practice, whereby an effort is made to soften any possible rebelliousness on the part of those to whom injustice is being done. It is as political as the other practice, which does not conceal—in fact, which proclaims—its own political character.

What especially moves me to be ethical is to know that, inasmuch as education of its very nature is directive and political, I must, without ever denying my dream or my utopia before the educands, respect them. To defend a thesis, a position, a preference, with earnestness, defend it rigorously, but passionately, as well, and at the same time to stimulate the contrary discourse, and respect the right to utter that discourse, is the best way to teach, first, the right to have our own ideas, even our duty to "quarrel" for them, for our dreams—and not only to learn the syntax of the verb, *haver;* and second, mutual respect.

Respecting the educands, however, does not mean lying to them about my dreams, telling them in words or deeds or practices that a school occupies a "sacred" space where one only studies, and studying has nothing to do with what goes on in the world outside; to hide my options from them, as if it were a "sin" to have a preference, to make an option, to draw the line, to decide, to dream. Respecting them means, on the one hand, testifying to them of my choice, and defending it; and on the other, it means showing them other options, whenever I teach—no matter what it is that I teach!

And let it not be said that, if I am a biology teacher, I must not "go off into other considerations"—that I must *only* teach biology, as if the phenomenon of life could be understood apart from its historico-social, cultural, and political framework. As if life, just life, could be lived in the same way, in all of its dimensions, in a *favela* (slum)[33] or *cortiço* ("beehive"—slum tenement building)[34] as in a prosperous area of São Paulo's "Gardens"![35] If I am a biology teacher, obviously I must teach biology. But in doing so, I must not cut it off from the framework of the whole.

The same reflection will be in order where literacy is concerned. Anyone taking a literacy course for adults wants to learn to read and write sentences, phrases, words. However, the reading and writing of words comes by way of the reading of the world. Reading the world is an antecedent act vis-à-vis the reading of the word. The teaching of the reading and writing of the word to a person missing the critical exercise of reading and rereading the world is, scientifically, politically, and pedagogically crippled.

Is there risk of influencing the students? It is impossible to live, let alone exist, without risks. The important thing is to prepare ourselves to be able to run them well.

Educational practice, whether it be authoritarian or democratic, is always directive.

However, the moment the educator's "directivity" interferes with the creative, formulative, investigative capacity of the educand, then the necessary directivity is transformed into manipulation, into authoritarianism. Manipulation and authoritarianism are practiced by many educators who, as they style themselves progressives, are actually taken for such.

My concern is not to deny the political and directive nature of education—a denial that, for that matter, it would be impossible to reduce to act—but to accept that this is its nature, and to live a life of full consistency between my democratic option and my educational practice, which is likewise democratic.

My ethical duty, as one of the subjects, one of the agents, of a practice that can never be neutral—the educational—is to express my respect for differences in ideas and positions. I must respect even positions opposed to my own, positions that I combat earnestly and with passion.

To quibble that such positions do not exist, is neither scientific nor ethical.

To criticize the arrogance, the authoritarianism of intellectuals of Left or Right, who are both basically reactionary in an identical way—who judge themselves the proprietors of knowledge, the former, of revolutionary knowledge, the latter, of conservative knowledge—to criticize the behavior of university people who claim to be able to "conscientize" rural and urban workers without having to be "conscientized" by them as well; to criticize an undisguisable air of messianism, at bottom naive, on the part of intellectuals who, in the name of the liberation of the working classes, impose or seek to impose the "superiority" of their academic knowledge on the "rude masses"—this I have always done. Of this I speak, and of almost nothing else, in *Pedagogy of the Oppressed*. And of this I speak now, with the same insistence, in *Pedagogy of Hope*.

One of the substantial differences, however, between myself and the authors of these criticisms of me is that, for me, the route to the defeat of these practices is in the defeat of an authoritarian, elitist ideology. The route to the defeat of these practices is in the difficult exercise of the virtues of humility, of consistency, of tolerance, on the part of the progressive intellectual—in the exercise of a consistency that ever decreases the distance between what we say and what we do.

For them, the critics, the route to the defeat of these practices is in the fantasy of a denial of the political nature of education, of science, of technology.

Freire's theory of learning, it was said, in effect, in the 1970s, is subordinate to social and political purposes: and that kind of theory is open to the risks of manipulation. As if an educational practice were possible in which professors and students could be absolutely exempt from the risk of manipulation and its consequences! As if the existence of a distant, cold, indifferent educational practice when it comes to "social and political purposes" were, or ever had been, possible in any space–time!

What is ethically required of progressive educators is that, consistent with their democratic dream, they respect the educands, and therefore never manipulate them.

Hence the watchfulness with which progressive educators ought to act, the vigilance with which they ought to live their intense educational practice. Hence the need for them to keep their eyes always open, along with their ears, and their whole soul—open to the pitfalls of the so-called hidden curriculum. Hence the exigency they must impose on themselves of growing ever more tolerant, of waxing ever more open and forthright, of turning ever more critical, of becoming ever more curious.

The more tolerant, the more open and forthright, the more critical, the more curious and humble they become, the more authentically they will take up the practice of teaching. In a like perspective—indisputably progressive, much more postmodern, as I understand postmodernity, than modern, let alone "modernizing"— to teach is not the simple transmission of knowledge concerning the object or concerning content. Teaching is not a simple transmission, wrought by and large through a pure description of the concept of the object, to be memorized by students mechanically. Teaching—again, from the postmodern progressive viewpoint of which I speak here—is not reducible merely to teaching students to learn through an operation in which the object of knowledge is the very act of learning. Teaching someone to learn is only valid—from this viewpoint, let me repeat—when educands *learn to learn* in learning the reason-for, the "why," of the object or the content. It is by teaching biology, or any other discipline, that the professor teaches the students to learn.

In a progressive line, then, teaching implies that educands, by "penetrating," as it were, the teacher's discourse, appropriate the deeper meaning of the content being taught. The act of teaching, experienced by the professor, is paralleled, on the part of the educands, by their act of knowing that which is taught.

For their part, teachers teach, in authentic terms, only to the extent that they know the content they are teaching—that is, only in the measure that they appropriate it, that they learn it, themselves. Here, in teaching, the teacher re-cognizes the object already cognized, already known. In other words, she or he remakes her or his cognizance in the cognizance of the educands. Thus, teaching is the form taken by the act of cognition that the teacher necessarily performs in the quest to know what he or she is teaching in order to call forth in the students their act of cognition as well. Therefore, teaching is a creative act, a critical act, and not a mechanical one. The curiosity of the teacher and the students, in action, meet on the basis of teaching-learning.

The teaching of a content by appropriating it, or the apprehension of this content on the part of the educands, requires the creation and exercise of a serious intellectual discipline, to be forged from preschool onward. To attempt or claim a critical insertion of educands in an educational situation—which is a situation of cognition—without that discipline, is a vain hope. But just as it is impossible to teach learning without teaching a certain content through whose knowledge one learns to learn, neither is the discipline of which I am speaking taught but in and by the cognitive practice of which the educands become the ever more critical subjects.

CHAPTER

3

There is no room, in the constitution of this needed discipline, for an identification of the act of studying, of learning, of knowing, of teaching, with pure entertainment—learning as a kind of toy or game, without rules or with lax ones. Nor again must it be identified with insipid, uninteresting, boring busywork. The act of studying, teaching, learning, knowing, is difficult, and especially, it is demanding, but it is pleasant, as Georges Snyders never omits to remind us.* It is crucial, then, that educands discover and sense the joy that steeps it, that is part of it, and that is ever ready to fill the hearts of all who surrender to it.

The testimonial role of teachers in the birthing of this discipline is enormous. But once it is at hand, their authority, of which their competence is a part, discharges an important function. Teachers who fail to take their teaching practice seriously, who therefore do not study, so that they teach poorly, or who teach something they know poorly, who do not fight to have the material conditions absolutely necessary for their teaching practice, deprive themselves of the wherewithal to cooperate in the formation of the indispensable intellectual discipline of the students. Thus, they disqualify themselves as teachers.

On the other hand, this discipline cannot emerge from a labor accomplished in the students by the teacher. While requiring the

---

*Georges Snyders, *La joie à l'école* (Paris: PUF, 1986).

effective presence of the teacher—his or her orientation, stimulus, authority—that discipline must be *built* and *adopted* by the students.

I feel led to repeat, by way of emphasizing my position, that a democratic practice consistent with my democratic discourse, which speaks of my democratic option, does not impose on me a silence as to my dreams, nor does the necessary criticism of what Amílcar Cabral* styles "the negativities of culture" make me an "elitist invader" of the popular culture. Criticism, and the effort to overcome these "negativities," are not only to be recommended, they are indispensable. Basically, this has to do with the passage of knowledge from the level of the "knowledge of living experience," of common sense, to the knowledge emerging from more rigorous procedures of approach to knowable objects. And to make this shift belongs to the popular classes by right. Hence, in the name of respect for the culture of the peasants, for example, not to enable them to go beyond their beliefs regarding self-in-the-world and self-with-the-world betrays a profoundly elitist ideology. It is as if revealing the raison d'être, the why, of things, and to have a complete knowledge of things, were or ought to be the privilege of the elite. Suffice it for the popular classes to be able to say, "I think it's . . ." about the world.

What is impermissible—I repeat myself, now—is disrespect for the knowledge of common sense. What is impermissible is the attempt to transcend it without starting with it and proceeding by way of it.

To challenge educands with regard to their certitudes is a duty of the progressive educator. What kind of educator would I be if I did not feel moved by a powerful impulse to seek, without lying, convincing arguments in defense of the dreams for which I struggle, in defense of the "why" of the hope with which I act as an educator?

What is not permissible to be doing is to conceal truths, deny information, impose principles, eviscerate the educands of their freedom, or punish them, no matter by what method, if, for various reasons, they fail to accept my discourse—reject my utopia. This

---

*Amílcar Cabral, *Obras escolhidas*, vol. 1, A *arma da teoria—unidade e luta* (Lisbon: Seara Nova, 1976), p. 141.

would indeed mean I am falling into inconsistency, into the destructive sectarianism that I once upon a time severely criticized in *Pedagogy of the Oppressed* and that I criticize today, in revisiting it, in *Pedagogy of Hope*.

These considerations bring me to another point, one directly connected with them, in regard to which I have likewise had to listen to "corrections" that, it seems to me, themselves stand in need of correction. I refer to the insistence with which, for such a long time now, I have argued the need we progressive educators have never to underestimate or reject knowledge had from living experience, with which educands come to school or to informal centers of education. Obviously there are differences in the way one must deal with this kind of knowledge, if it is a question of one or other of the cases cited above. In each of them, however, to underestimate the wisdom that necessarily results from sociocultural experience, is at one and the same time a scientific error, and the unequivocal expression of the presence of an elitist ideology. It may even be the hidden, concealed, ideological foundation that, on the one hand, blinds a person to objective reality, and on the other, encourages the nearsightedness of those who reject popular knowledge as having led them into scientific error. In the last analysis, it is this "myopia" that, once it becomes an ideological obstacle, occasions epistemological error.

There have been various kinds of negative understanding, and therefore criticism, of this defense of popular knowledge, with which I have been engaged for so long. The mythification of popular knowledge, its superexaltation, is as open to challenge as is its rejection. As the latter is elitist, so the former is "basist."

Still, both basism and elitism, so sectarian in themselves, when taken *at* and *in* their truth become capable of transcending themselves.

One of these ways of criticizing the defense that I have been mounting of the knowledge acquired from living experience, criticisms not infrequently repeated today, to my legitimate astonishment and dismay, is that which suggests or asserts, basically, that I propose that the educator ought to stay spinning in an orbit, along with the educands, around their commonsense knowledge, without any attempt to get beyond that knowledge. And the criticism of this tenor concludes triumphantly by emphasizing the obvious failure of this naive understanding. And it is attributed to me—this defense of a tireless circling around commonsense knowledge.

But I have never actually asserted, or so much as insinuated, "innocence" of such proportions.

What I have said and resaid, untiringly, is that we must not by-pass—spurning it as "good for nothing"—that which educands, be they children coming to school for the first time, or young people and adults at centers of popular education, bring with them in the way of an understanding of the world, in the most varied dimensions of their own practice in the social practice of which they are a part. Their speech, their way of counting and calculating, their ideas about the so-called other world, their religiousness, their knowledge about health, the body, sexuality, life, death, the power of the saints, magic spells, must all be respected.

Indeed, this is a basic theme of ethnoscience[36] today: how to avoid a dichotomy between the knowledges, the popular and the erudite, or how to understand and experience the dialectic between what Snyders* calls "primary culture" and "developed culture."

A respect for both knowledges—a respect of which I speak so much—with a view to getting beyond them, must never mean, in a serious, radical, and therefore critical, never sectarian, rigorous, careful, competent reading of my texts, that the educator must stick with the knowledge of living experience.

With progressive education, respect for the knowledge of living experience is inserted into the larger horizon against which it is generated—the horizon of cultural context, which cannot be understood apart from its class particularities, and this indeed in societies so complex that the characterization of those particularities is less easy to come by.

Respect for popular knowledge, then, necessarily implies respect for cultural context. Educands' concrete localization is the point of departure for the knowledge they create of the world. "Their" world, in the last analysis, is the primary and inescapable face of the world itself.

My concerns with the respect due the local world of the educands continue, from time to time—to my dismay, again—to generate

---

*Snyders, *La joie à l'école*.

criticisms that see me adrift, caught with no means of escape in the blind alley of the narrow horizons of localization. Once more, these criticisms are the upshot of a poor reading of me—or of the reading of texts written about my work by someone who likewise has read me poorly, incompetently, or who has not read me.

I should deserve not only these criticisms, but far more telling ones, as well, if, instead of defending educands' local context as the point of departure for a prolongation of their understanding of the world, I were to defend a "focalistic" position: a position in which, oblivious of the dialectical nature of reality, I should fail to perceive the contradictory relations between partialities and the totality. I would thus have fallen into the error we have seen criticized at a certain moment of this text by peasants in the figure of the relationship they cited between *salt*, as a part, as one of the ingredients, of *seasoning*, and the latter as a *totality*.

This has never been what I have done or proposed, at any time during my practice as an educator—the practice that has furnished me the further undertaking of thinking upon my educational practice, from which latter habit of reflection, in turn, has emerged all that I have ever written, down to this very day.

For me, it becomes difficult, indeed impossible, to understand the interpretation of my respect for the *local*—the local or the regional—as a rejection of the *universal*. For example, I do not understand how, in so rightly criticizing positions that "stifle" or "suppress" the totality implicit in locality—which suppression I call "focalism"—some give as an example of that suppression the category of "universal minimal vocabulary" that I use in my general concept of literacy training.

The "universal minimal vocabulary," of course, emerges from an investigation that has to be conducted, and it is on the basis of this vocabulary that we set up our literacy programs. Never, however, have I said that these programs to be developed on the basis of this universal vocabulary ought to remain absolutely bound up with local reality. If I had said that, I should not have the understanding of language that I have, which is manifest not only in earlier works, but in the present essay as well. In fact, I should be incapable of a dialectical manner of thinking.

Without a great deal of commentary, I refer the reader to any edition of *Educação como prática da liberdade*. I am thinking of the last part of the book, in which I execute an analysis of seventeen selected words among those that have created the "universal vocabulary" on the basis of research conducted in the State of Rio de Janeiro, and applied as well in Guanabara, as Rio was then called.[37] A mere reading of these pages, it seems to me, explains the error of such a criticism.

I believe that it is fundamental to have made clear to educands, or to keep making clear, this obvious fact: the regional emerges from the local just as the national arises from the regional, and the continental from the national as the worldwide emerges from the continental.

Just as it is a mistake to get stuck in the local, losing our vision of the whole, so also it is a mistake to waft above the whole, renouncing any reference to the local whence the whole has emerged.

Back in Brazil on a visit in 1979, I declared in an interview that my Recifeness explained my Pernambucanity, that the latter clarified my Northeastness, which in turn shed light on my Brazilianity, my Brazilianity elucidated my Latin Americanness, and the latter made me a person of the world.

Ariano Suassuna became a universal writer from a point of departure not in the universe, but in Taperuá.[38]

"A critical analysis on the part of popular groups of their way of being in the world of the most immediate everyday, that of their particular customary world," I myself say in *Pedagogy in Process: The Letters to Guinea-Bissau* (1977/1978), page 59, "and the perception of the why of the facts given in it, lead us to *transcend the narrow horizons of the neighborhood* or *even the immediate geographical area*, to gain that *global* view of reality indispensable for an understanding of the task of national reconstruction itself."

But let us go back a way, to my first book, *Educação como prática da liberdade*, completed in 1965 and published in 1967. On page 114, in a comment on the process of the creation of codifications, I say:

> These situations function as challenges to groups. They are codified problem situations, secreting elements that will be decoded by groups with the cooperation of the coordinator. A discussion

of them, like that of those we have from the anthropological concept of culture, will lead groups to *conscientização*, and, concomitantly, literacy.

It is *local situations* [emphasis in the original], however, that open perspectives for an analysis of *national* (and regional) *problems*.

"The written word," Plato said, "cannot be defended when misunderstood."*

I cannot accept responsibility, I must say, for what is said or done in my name contrary to what I do and say. It is of no avail, to make the furious assertion, as someone once did: "You may not have said this, but people who say they're your disciples did." Without claiming, by a long shot, to compare myself to Marx (not because now, from time to time, it is said that he is a "has-been," but on the contrary, precisely because, to me, he continues to be, needing only to be reseen), I find myself inclined to quote one of his letters—the one in which, irritated by inconsistent French "Marxists," he said: "Well, then, all I know is that I'm no Marxist."†

And as long as I have mentioned Marx, let me take the opportunity to comment on certain self-styled "Marxist" criticisms of me in the 1970s. Some of them—as, unfortunately, not infrequently occurs—failed to take into consideration two fundamental points: (1) that I had not died; (2) that I had not yet written *Pedagogy of the Oppressed*—which had years to wait—but only *Educação como prática da liberdade*. Hence the illegitimacy of their extension to a whole body of thought a criticism of one moment of that thought. Certain criticisms may be valid for one or another text, but without foundation if extended to the totality of my work.

One of these criticisms—apparently, at least, more formal, mechanistic, than dialectical—expressed amazement that I had made no reference to social classes—especially, that I had not asserted that "it is the class struggle that moves history." My critics were sur-

*Paul Shorey, *What Plato Said: A Résume and Analysis of Plato's Writings with Synopses and Critical Comment*, limited ed. (Chicago: Phoenix Books/University of Chicago Press, 1965), p. 158.

†"Carta de Engels a Schmidt—Londres, 5.8.188," in Karl Marx, *Obras Escogidas* (Moscow: Progresso), 2:491.

prised that, instead of social classes, I had worked with the "vague concept of the oppressed."

In the first place, it is inconceivable to me that employers and workers, rural or urban, could read *Pedagogy of the Oppressed*, and then conclude, the former, that they were laborers, and the latter, that they were employers. And this because the vagueness of the concept of the oppressed had left them so confused and indecisive that employers hesitated as to whether they should or should not continue to enjoy the usufruct of their "surplus value" and the workers as to their right to strike as a fundamental tool in the defense of their interests!

I now recall something I read in 1981, shortly after my return from exile, written by a young worker of São Paulo in which she asked—answering her own question: "Who are the people? Those who don't ask who the people are."

However, the first time I read one of these criticisms, I sat down for several hours and reread my book, counting the times when, throughout, I had spoken of social classes. Not infrequently, on the same page, I had spoken of social classes two or three times. Only, I had spoken of social classes not as a cliché, or in fear of a possible inspector or ideological censor who might be spying on me and would possibly even call me to account. The authors of such criticisms, generally speaking, although they do not always make this explicit, are in the main uncomfortable with certain particular points, such as: the vagueness of the concept of the oppressed, which I have already mentioned, or of the people; the assertion I make in the book that the oppressed, in gaining liberation, liberate the oppressor; not to have declared, as I have already indicated, that the class struggle is the impulse of history; the treatment I accorded the individual, refusing to reduce him or her to a pure reflex of socioeconomic structures; the treatment I accorded awareness and consciousness, the importance of subjectivity; the role of "conscientization" or consciousness-raising that, in *Pedagogy of the Oppressed*, transcends, in terms of criticalness, that attributed to it in *Educação como prática da liberdade*; the assertion that the "adhesion" to reality in which the great peasant masses of Latin America find themselves dictates that the *consciousness of oppressed class* must pass, if not antecedently, then at least concomitantly, by way of the awareness of *oppressed person.*

Never were all of these points raised at the same time. Rather, one or other of them was brought up in criticisms either written, or verbal (in seminars and discussions), in Europe, the United States, Australia, Latin America.

Yesterday as today, I spoke of social classes with the same independence and consciousness of being right. It may even be, however, that many of those who demanded of me in the 1970s that I constantly explicate the concept, today require the very opposite: that I retract the two dozen times I employed it, because "there are no longer any social classes, nor therefore any class conflict." Hence the fact that these critics now prefer, to the language of the possible, which holds fast to utopia as a possible dream, the neoliberal, "pragmatic" discourse, according to which we must "accommodate" to the facts as given—as if they could be given in no other way, as if we had no duty to fight, precisely because we are persons, to have them given differently.

I have never labored under the misapprehension that social classes and the struggle between them could explain everything, right down to the color of the sky on a Tuesday evening. And so I have never said that the class struggle, in the modern world, has been or is "the mover of history." On the other hand, still today, and possibly for a long time to come, it is impossible to understand history without social classes, without their interests in collision.

The class struggle is not *the* mover of history, but is certainly *one* of them.

As someone dissatisfied with the world of injustice that is here— someone to whom the "pragmatic" discourse recommends I simply adapt—I must, surely, today, just as I did yesterday, be alert to the relationship between tactics and strategy. It is one thing to call on activists who keep on striving for a world less ugly, to attend to the need that, first, their tactics not contradict their strategy, their objectives, their dream; second, that their tactics, *qua* route to the realization of the strategic dream, be, be done, be realized, in concrete history, and therefore that they change; and it is another thing simply to say that all you have to do is dream. Dreaming is not only a necessary political act, it is an integral part of the historico-social manner of being a person. It is part of human nature, which, within history, is in permanent process of becoming.

In our making and remaking of ourselves in the process of making history—as subjects and objects, persons, becoming beings of insertion in the world and not of pure adaptation to the world—we should end by having the *dream,* too, a mover of history. There is no change without dream, as there is no dream without hope.

Thus, I keep insisting, ever since *Pedagogy of the Oppressed:* there is no authentic utopia apart from the tension between the *de*nunciation of a present becoming more and more intolerable, and the "*an*nunciation," announcement, of a future to be created, built— politically, esthetically, and ethically—by us women and men. Utopia implies this denunciation and proclamation, but it does not permit the tension between the two to die away with the production of the future previously announced. Now the erstwhile future is a new present, and a new dream experience is forged. History does not become immobilized, does not *die.* On the contrary, it goes on.

The understanding of history as *opportunity* and not *determinism,* the conception of history operative in this book, would be unintelligible without the *dream,* just as the *deterministic* conception feels uncomfortable, in its incompatibility with this understanding and therefore denies it.

Thus it comes about that, in the former conception the historical role of subjectivity is relevant, while in the latter it is minimized or denied. Hence, in the first, education, while not regarded as able to accomplish all things, is acknowledged as important, since it can do something; while in the second it is belittled.

Indeed, whenever the future is considered as a pregiven— whether this be as the pure, mechanical repetition of the present, or simply because it "is what it has to be"—there is no room for utopia, nor therefore for the dream, the option, the decision, or expectancy in the struggle, which is the only way hope exists. There is no room for education. Only for training.

As project, as design for a different, less-ugly "world," the dream is as necessary to political subjects, transformers of the world and not adapters to it, as—may I be permitted the repetition—it is fundamental for an artisan, who projects in her or his brain what she or he is going to execute even before the execution thereof.

This is why, from the viewpoint of dominant class interests, the less the dominated dream the *dream* of which I speak, in the confident way of which I speak, and the less they practice the political apprenticeship of committing themselves to a utopia, the more open they will become to "pragmatic" discourses, and the sounder the dominant classes will sleep.

The modernity of some of the sectors of the dominant classes, whose position is very far advanced over the posture of the old, retrograde leadership of the "captains of industry" of yesteryear, cannot, however, change its spots. It remains a class position.

And yet this does not mean, to my view, that the working classes ought to close themselves off, in sectarian fashion, from the broadening of democratic spaces that can result from a new kind of relationship between themselves and the dominant classes. The important thing is that the working classes continue to learn, in the very practice of their struggle, to set limits to their concessions—in other words, that they teach the dominant classes the limits within which they themselves may move.

Finally, relationships between classes are a political fact, which generates a class knowledge, and that class knowledge has the most urgent need of lucidity and discernment when choosing the best tactics to be used. Those tactics vary in concrete history, but must be in consonance with strategic objectives.

This is surely not learned in special courses. It is learned and taught precisely at the historical moment at which necessity imposes on social classes the necessary quest for a better relationship between them in dealing with their antagonistic interests. At such historical moments, such as the one in which we are living today, in our country and abroad, it is reality itself that cries out, warning social classes of the urgency of new forms of encounter for the securing of solutions that cannot wait for tomorrow. The practice of setting up these new encounters, or the history of this practice, this attempt, can be studied by labor leaders, not only in courses of the history of workers' struggles, but also in practical theory courses, later, of training for labor leaders. This is what we are experiencing today, in the maelstrom of the fearful crisis we are fighting, in which there have been high moments in discussions between dominant and laboring classes. Hence, however, to say that we are living another history now, a new history in which social classes are disappearing and their conflicts along with them; to say that socialism lies pulverized in the rubble of the Berlin Wall, is something in which I, for my part, do not believe.

The neoliberal discourses, with all their talk of "modernity," do not have the power to do away with social classes and decree the nonexistence of antagonistic interests between them, nor do they have the power to do away with the conflicts and struggle between them. Any appearances to the contrary are to be explained by the fact that struggle is a historical category, and therefore has historicity. It changes from space–time to space–time. Struggle does not rule out the possibility of pacts and understandings, of adjustments between parties in discord. Pacts and understandings are themselves part of the struggle.

There are historical moments at which the survival of the social whole imposes on the classes a need to understand one another— which does not mean, let us repeat, experiencing a new historical time devoid of social classes and their conflicts. A new historical time, yes, but a time in which the social classes continue to exist and to fight for their respective interests.

Instead of simple "pragmatic" accommodation, labor leaders are under the necessity of creating certain qualities or virtues without which, more and more, it is becoming difficult for them to strive for their rights.

The assertion that an "ideological discourse" is a kind of natural clumsiness on the part of the Left, which insists on holding one when there are no ideologies anymore, and when, it is said, no one any longer wishes to hear an ideological discourse, is itself a cunning ideological discourse on the part of the dominant classes. What we have gotten over is not the ideological discourse, but the "fanatical," or inconsistent, discourse, which merely repeats clichés that never should have been pronounced in the first place. What is becoming less and less viable, fortunately, is verbal incontinence—discourse that loses itself in a tiresome rhetoric bereft of so much as sonority and rhythm.

Any progressive, who, all afire, insists on this practice—at times in a tremulous voice—will be contributing little or nothing to the political advance of which we have need. But, then, to up and proclaim the era of the "neutral discourse"? Hardly.

I feel utterly at peace with the interpretation that the wane of "realistic socialism" does not mean, on one side, that socialism has shown itself to be intrinsically inviable; on the other, that capitalism has now stepped forward in its excellence once and for all.

What excellence is this, that manages to "coexist with more than a billion inhabitants of the developing world who live in poverty,"* not to say misery? Not to mention the all but indifference with which it coexists with "pockets of poverty" and misery in its own, developed body. What excellence is this, that sleeps in peace while numberless men and women make their home in the street, and says it is their own fault that they are on the street? What excellence is this, that struggles so little, if it struggles at all, with discrimination for reason of sex, class, or race, as if to reject someone different, humiliate her, offend him, hold her in contempt, exploit her, were the right of individuals, or classes, or races, or one sex, that holds a position of power over another? What excellence is this, that tepidly registers the millions of children who come into the world and do not remain, or not for long, or if they are more resistant, manage to stay a while, then take their leave of the world?

> Some 30 million children under five years of age die every year of causes that would not normally be fatal in developed countries. Some 110 million children throughout the world (almost 20 percent of the age group) fail to complete their primary education. More than 90 percent of these children live in low and medium-low income countries.†

On the other hand, UNICEF states:

> If current tendencies are maintained, more than 100 million children will die of disease and malnutrition in the decade of the 1990s. The causes of these deaths can be counted on one's fingers. Nearly all will die of diseases that were rather fami-

---

*See *Relatório sobre o Desenvolvimento Mundial,* 1990, published for World Bank by Fundação Getúlio Vargas.
†*World Development Report,* 1990, p. 76.

liar in other times in the industrialized nations. They will die parched with dehydration, suffocated by pneumonia, infected with tetanus or measles, or suffocated by whooping cough. These five very common diseases, all relatively easy and inexpensive to prevent or treat, will be responsible for more than two-thirds of infant deaths, and more than half of all infantile malnutrition, in the next decade.

The UNICEF report goes on to say:

> To put the problem in a global perspective: The additional costs, including a program to avoid the great majority of the deaths and infantile undernourishment in the coming years, ought to reach approximately 2.5 billion dollars a year by the end of the 1990s—about the same amount of money as American companies spend annually for cigarette advertising.*

Simply astounding.

What excellence is this, that, in the Brazilian Northeast, coexists with a degree of misery that could only have been thought a piece of fiction: little boys and girls, women and men, vying with starving pups, tragically, like animals, for the garbage of the great trash heaps outlying the cities, to eat? Nor is São Paulo itself exempt from the experience of this wretchedness.

What excellence is this, that seems blind to little children with distended bellies, eaten up by worms, toothless women looking like old crones at thirty, wasted men, skinny, stooped populations? Fifty-two percent of the population of Recife live in slums, in bad weather, an easy prey for diseases that effortlessly crush their enfeebled bodies. What excellence is this, that strikes a pact with the cold-blooded, cowardly murder of landless men and women of the countryside simply because they fight for their right to their word and their labor, while they remain bound to the land and despoiled of their fields by the dominant classes?

What excellence is this, that gazes with serene regard upon the extermination of little girls and boys in the great Brazilian urban

---

*UNICEF (United Nations Children's Fund), *Situação mundial da infância,* 1990, p. 16.

centers—that "forbids" 8 million children of the popular classes to go to school, that "expels" from the schools a great number of those who manage to get in—and that calls all this "capitalistic modernity."

To me, on the contrary, the element of failure in the experience of "realistic socialism," by and large, was not its socialist dream, but its authoritarian mold—which contradicted it, and of which Marx and Lenin are also guilty, and not just Stalin—just as what is positive in the capitalist experience has never been the capitalist system, but its democratic mold.

In this sense, as well, the crumbling away of the authoritarian socialist world—which, in many aspects, is a kind of ode to freedom, and which leaves so many minds, previously calm and contained, stupefied, thunderstruck, disconcerted, lost—offers us the extraordinary, if challenging, opportunity to continue *dreaming* and fighting for the socialist *dream,* purified of its authoritarian distortions, its totalitarian repulsiveness, its sectarian blindness. This is why I personally look forward to a time when it will become even easier to wage the democratic struggle against the wickedness of capitalism. What is becoming needful, among other things, is that Marxists get over their smug certainty that they are *modern,* adopt an attitude of humility in dealing with the popular classes, and become *postmodernly* less smug and less certain—progressively postmodern.

Let us briefly turn to other points already mentioned.

> Inasmuch as the violence of the oppressors makes of the oppressed persons forbidden to be, the response of the latter to the violence of the former is found infused with a yearning to seek the right to be.
>
> Oppressors, wreaking violence upon others, and forbidding them to be, are likewise unable to be. In withdrawing from them the power to oppress and crush, the oppressed, struggling to be, restore to them the humanity lost in the use of oppression.
>
> This is why only the oppressed, by achieving their liberation, can liberate the oppressors. The latter, as oppressing *class* [emphasis in the original], can neither liberate nor be liberated.*

The first observation I might make on the quotation from these

*Paulo Freire, *Pedagogia do oprimido,* p.43.

pages of *Pedagogy of the Oppressed* is that these pages are among those in which I make it very clear of whom I am speaking when I speak of oppressor and oppressed.

Ultimately, or perhaps I might say, in the overall context, not only of the passage cited, but of the whole book (could it have been otherwise?), a particular anthropology is implicit (when not clear and explicit)—a certain understanding or view of human beings as managing their nature in their own history, of which they become necessarily both subject and object. This is precisely one of the connotations of that nature, constituted socially and historically, which not only founds the assertion made in the passage quoted, but in which are rooted, consistently, I feel confident, the positions on political pedagogy that I have argued over the course of the years.

I cannot understand human beings as simply *living*. I can understand them only as historically, culturally, and socially *existing*. I can understand them only as beings who are makers of their "way," in the making of which they lay themselves open to or commit themselves to the "way" that they make and that therefore remakes them as well.

Unlike the other animals, which do not become able to transform *life* into *existence*, we, as *existent*, outfit ourselves to engage in the struggle in quest of and in defense of equality of opportunity, by the very fact that, as living beings, we are radically different from one another.

> We are all different, and the manner in which living beings reproduce is programmed for what we are to be. This is why the human being eventually has need of fashioning the concept of equality. Were we all identical, like a population of bacteria, the notion of equality would be perfectly useless.*

The great leap that we learn to take has been to work not precisely on the *innate*, nor only on the *acquired*, but on the relationship between the two.

"The fashioning of an individual," says François Jacob, in the same passage, "from the physical, intellectual, moral viewpoint, corre-

---

*François Jacob, "Nous sommes programmes, mais pour apprendre," *Le Courrier* (UNESCO, February 1991).

sponds to an ongoing interaction between the innate and the acquired."

We become capable of imaginatively, curiously, "stepping back" from ourselves—from the life we lead—and of disposing ourselves to "know about it." The moment came when we not only *lived*, but began to *know* that we were living—hence it was possible for us to *know* that we know, and therefore to know that we could do more. What we cannot do, as imaginative, curious beings, is to cease to learn and to seek, to investigate the "why" of things. We cannot *exist* without wondering about tomorrow, about what is "going on," and going on in favor of what, against what, for whom, against whom. We cannot *exist* without wondering about how to do the concrete or "untested feasible" that requires us to fight for it.

Why? Because this is the being we are "programmed," but not *determined*, to be. "None of the programs, indeed, is completely rigid. Each defines the structures, which are only potentialities, probabilities, tendencies. Genes determine only the constitution of the individual," so that "hereditary structures and the learning process are found to be strictly interconnected."*

It is because we are this being—a being of ongoing, curious search, which "steps back" from itself and *from the life it leads*—it is because we are this being, given to adventure and the "passion to know," for which that freedom becomes indispensable that, constituted in the very struggle for itself, is possible only because, though we are "programmed," we are nevertheless not determined. It is because this is "the way we are" that we live the life of a vocation, a calling, to *humanization*, and that in *dehumanization*, which is a concrete fact in history, we live the life of a *distortion of the call*—never another calling. Neither one, humanization or dehumanization, is sure destiny, given datum, lot, or fate. This is precisely why the one is calling, and the other, distortion of the calling.

It is important to emphasize that, in speaking of "being more," or of humanization as ontological vocation of the human being, I am not falling into any fundamentalistic position—which, incidentally, is always conservative. Hence my equally heavy emphasis on the fact that this "vocation," this calling, rather than being anything a

---

*Jacob, "Nous sommes programmes."

priori in history, on the contrary is something constituted in history. On the other hand, the striving for it, and the means of accomplishing it—which are also historical, besides varying from space-time to space–time—require, indisputably, the adoption of a utopia. Utopia, however, would not be possible if it lacked the taste for freedom that permeates the vocation to humanization. Or if it lacked hope, without which we do not struggle.

The dream of humanization, whose concretization is always a process, and always a becoming, passes by way of breach with the real, concrete economic, political, social, ideological, and so on, order, moorings that are condemning us to dehumanization. Thus the *dream* is a demand or condition that becomes ongoing in the history that we make and that makes and remakes us.

Not being an a priori of history, *human nature*, which on the contrary is constituted in history, has one of its implications in the *vocation* or calling to which we have referred.

This is why the oppressor is dehumanized in dehumanizing the oppressed. No matter that the oppressor eat well, be well regarded, or sleep well. It would be impossible to dehumanize without being dehumanized—so deep are the social roots of the *calling*. I am not, I do not be, unless you are, unless you be. Above all, I am not if I forbid you to be.

This is why, as an individual and as a class, the oppressor can neither liberate nor be liberated. This is why, through self-liberation, in and through the needed, just struggle, the oppressed, as an individual and as a class, liberates the oppressor, by the simple fact of forbidding him or her to keep on oppressing.

However, liberation and oppression are not inextricably intermeshed in history. Just so, *human nature*, as it generates itself in history, does not contain, as part and parcel of itself, *being more*, does not contain *humanization*, except as the *vocation* whose contrary is *distortion* in history.

The political practice based on a mechanistic and deterministic conception of history will never contribute to the lessening of the risks of men and women's dehumanization.

Throughout history, we men and women become special animals indeed, then. We invent the opportunity of setting ourselves free to the extent that we become able to perceive as unconcluded, limited, conditioned, historical beings. Especially, we invent the opportunity of setting ourselves free by perceiving, as well, that the sheer perception of inconclusion, limitation, opportunity, is not enough. To the perception must be joined the political struggle for the transformation of the world. The liberation of individuals acquires profound meaning only when the transformation of society is achieved.

The dream becomes a need, a necessity.

And, on this subject, another point that has generated criticism has been precisely the role I ascribe, and continue to ascribe, to subjectivity in the process of the transformation of reality, or to the relationship between undichotomizable subjectivity and objectivity, between awareness and the world.

Beginning with the publication of *Pedagogy of the Oppressed*, not infrequent have been the times I have written or spoken of this matter, sometimes in interviews, sometimes in periodicals, sometimes in essays, in seminars. It will do no harm, however, to take up the matter again now and discuss it anew, at least briefly.

In fact, I have no doubt that this subject, which is always present in philosophical reflection, is not only still a current one, but a crucial one, as well, as the century closes. It continues to be an object of philosophical reflection, which reflection is necessarily extended to the fields of epistemology, politics, ideology, language, pedagogy, and modern physics.

We have to recognize, in a first approach to the subject, how difficult it is for us to "walk the streets of history"—regardless of whether we "step back" from practice in order to theorize it, or are engaged in it—succumbing to the temptation either to overestimate our objectivity and reduce consciousness to it, or to discern or understand consciousness as the almighty maker and arbitrary remaker of the world.

Subjectivism or mechanistic objectivism are both antidilectical, and thereby incapable of apprehending the permanent tension between consciousness and the world.

It is only in a dialectical perspective that we can grasp the role of consciousness in history, disentangled from any distortion that either exaggerates its importance or cancels, rejects it.

Thus, the dialectical view indicates to us the importance of rejecting as false, for example, a comprehension of awareness as pure *reflex* of material objectivity, but at the same time the importance of rejecting an understanding of awareness that would confer upon it a determining power over concrete reality.

In like fashion, the dialectical view indicates to us the incompatibility between it and an inevitable tomorrow, an idea that I have criticized before, in *Pedagogy of the Oppressed*, and that I now criticize in this essay. The dialectical view is incompatible with the notion that *tomorrow* is the pure repetition of today, or that *tomorrow* is something "predated," or as I have called it, a *given datum*, a "given given." This "tamed" or domesticated view of the future, shared by reactionaries and "revolutionaries" alike—naturally, each in their own way—posits, in the mind of the former, the *future* as a repetition of the present (which of course must undergo "adverbial" changes), and in the mind of the second, the future as "inexorable progress."* Both of these views or visions imply a fatalistic "intelligence" (in the sense of an interpretative "understanding," an "inner reading") of history in which there is no room for authentic hope.

The idea of the inexorability of a history that will necessarily come in a predetermined manner constitutes what I call "liberation fatalism" or "fatalistic liberation"—a liberation to come as a kind of gift or donation of history: the liberation that will come because it has been said that it will come.

In the dialectical perception, the future of which we dream is not inexorable. We have to make it, produce it, else it will not come in the form that we would more or less wish it to. True, of course, we have to make it not arbitrarialy, but with the materials, with the concrete reality, of which we dispose, and more as a project, a *dream*, for which we struggle.

While for dogmatic, mechanistic positions, the consciousness that I call critical takes shape as a kind of epiphenomenon, a "spin-off"— an automatic, mechanical result of structural changes—for dialectic, the importance of consciousness is in the fact that, not being the maker of reality, neither is it, at the opposite pole, a pure reflex of reality. It is precisely on this point that something of basic importance turns—the basic importance of education as act of cognition

---

*Erica Sherover Marcuse, *Emancipation and Consciousness: Dogmatic and Dialectical Perspectives in the Early Marx* (New York: Basil Blackwell, Ltd., 1986).

not only of the content, but of the "why" of economic, social, political, ideological, and historical facts, which explain the greater or lesser degree of "interdict of the body,"[39] our conscious body, under which we find ourselves placed.

In the 1950s, perhaps more by way of an intuition of the phenomenon than as a critical understanding of the same, at which understanding I was then arriving, I asserted, in the university dissertation to which I have referred in this book, and I repeated later in *Educação como prática da liberdade*, that, while the advance from what I called "semi-intransitive awareness" to "transitive-naive awareness" is automatically at hand, on the strength of infrastructural transformations, the more important passage—that from "naive transitivity" to "critical transitivity"—comes only through serious educational efforts bent to this end.*

To be sure, my experiences with SESI, with which I coupled memories of my childhood and adolescence in Jabotão, helped me to understand, even before my theoretical readings on the subject, the relations prevailing between awareness and world as tending to be dynamic, never mechanistic. I could not avoid, of course, the risks to which I have referred—those of mechanism and of idealistic subjectivism—in discussing those relations, and I acknowledge my slips in the direction of an overemphasis on awareness.

In 1974, in Geneva, Ivan Illich and I presided at a conference under the patronage of the Department of Education of the World Council of Churches, in which we took up once more the concepts of "descholarization" (Illich) and *conscientização* (I). I wrote a little document for the conference, from which I am now going to quote an extended passage instead of simply referring the reader to it. (It originally appeared in the WCC periodical *RISK*, in 1975).†

> . . . Although there can be no consciousness-raising (*conscientização*) without the unveiling, the revelation, of objective reality as the object of the cognition of the subjects involved in process

*Paulo Freire, *Educação como prática da liberdade* (Rio de Janeiro: Paz e Terra, 1969).

†In Brazil, it appears in *Ação cultural para a liberdade e outros escritos* (Rio de Janeiro: Paz e Terra, 1976). In the United States, it appears under the title, *The Politics of Education* (Massachusetts: Bergin and Garvey, 1986).

of consciousness-raising, nevertheless that revelation—even granting that a new perception flow from the fact of a reality laying itself bare—is not yet enough to render the consciousness-raising authentic. Just as the gnoseological circle does not end with the step of the acquisition of existing knowledge, but proceeds to the phase of the creation of new knowledge, so neither may consciousness-raising come to a halt at the stage of the revelation of reality. Its authenticity is at hand only when the practice of the revelation of reality constitutes a dynamic and dialectical unity with the practice of transformation of reality.

I think that certain observations can and should be made on the basis of these reflections. One of them is a criticism I make of myself, and it is that, in *Educação como prática da liberadade,* in considering the process of consciousness-raising, I took the moment of the revelation of social reality as if it were a kind of psychological motivator of the transformation of that reality. My mistake, obviously, was not in recognizing the basic importance of the cognition of reality in the process of its transformation; rather my mistake consisted in not having addressed these poles—knowledge of reality and transformation of reality—in their dialecticity. I had spoken as if the unveiling of reality automatically made for its transformation.*

---

*Paulo Freire, *Ação cultural para a liberdade e outros escritos* (Rio de Janeiro: Paz e Terra, 1987).

CHAPTER

4

If my position at the time had been mechanistic, I would not even have spoken of the raising of consciousness, of *conscientização*. I spoke of *conscientização* because, even with my slips in the direction of idealism, my tendency was to review and revise promptly, and thus, adopting a consistency with the practice I had, to perceive that practice as steeped in the dialectical movement back and forth between consciousness and world.

In an antidialectically mechanistic position, I would have rejected, like all mechanists, the need for *conscientização* and education before a radical change in the material conditions of society can occur.

Neither, as I have asserted above, is an antidialectical perspective compatible with an understanding of critical awareness other than as an epiphenomenon—"as a result of social changes, not as a factor of the same" (Erica Marcuse, 1986).

It is interesting to observe that, for the idealistic, nondialectical comprehension of the relationship between awareness and world, one can still speak of *conscientização* as an instrument for changing the world, provided this change be realized only in the interiority of awareness, with the world itself left untouched. Thus, *conscientização* would produce nothing but verbiage.

From the viewpoint of a mechanistic dogmatism, there is no point in speaking of *conscientização* at all. Hence the dogmatic, authoritarian leaderships have no reason to engage in dialogue with the popular classes. They need only tell them what they should do.

Mechanistically or idealistically, it is impossible to understand

what occurs in the relations prevailing between oppressors and oppressed, whether as individuals or as social classes.

Only in a dialectical understanding, let us repeat, of how awareness and the world are given, is it possible to comprehend the
phenomenon of the introjection of the oppressor by the oppressed,
the latter's "adherence" to the former, the difficulty that the oppressed have in localizing the oppressor outside themselves.*

Once again the moment comes to mind when, twenty-five years
ago, I heard from Erich Fromm, in his house in Cuernavaca, his
blue eyes flashing: "An educational practice like that is a kind of
historico-sociocultural and political psychoanalysis."

This is what dogmatic, authoritarian, sectarian mechanists fail to
perceive, and nearly always reject as "idealism."

If the great popular masses are without a more critical understanding of how society functions, it is not because they are naturally
incapable of it—to my view—but on account of the precarious conditions in which they live and survive, where they are "forbidden to
know." Thus, the way out is not ideological propaganda and political
"sloganizing," as the mechanists say it is, but the critical effort
through which men and women take themselves in hand and become agents of curiosity, become investigators, become subjects in
an ongoing process of quest for the revelation of the "why" of things
and facts. Hence, in the area of adult literacy, for example, I have
long found myself insisting on what I call a "reading of the world
and reading of the word." Not a reading of the word alone, nor a
reading only of the world, but both together, in dialectical solidarity.

It is precisely a "reading of the world" that enables its subject or
agent to decipher, more and more critically, the "limit situation" or
situations beyond which they find only "untested feasibility."

I must make it clear, however, that, consistently with the dialectical position in which I place myself, in terms of which I perceive
the relations among world-consciousness-practice-theory-reading-
of-the-world-reading-of-the-word-context-text, the reading of the
world cannot be the reading made by academicians and imposed on
the popular classes. Nor can such a reading be reduced to a compla-
cent exercise by educators in which, in token of respect for popular

---

*See, among others, Sartre, Fanon, Memmi, and Freire.

culture, they fall silent before the "knowledge of living experience" and adapt themselves to it.

The dialectical, democratic position implies, on the contrary, the *intervention* of the intellectual as an indispensable condition of his or her task. Nor do I see any betrayal of democracy here. Democracy is betrayed when contradicted by authoritarian attitudes and practices, as well as by spontaneous, irresponsibly permissive attitudes and practices.

It is in this sense that I insist once more on the imperative need of the progressive educator to familiarize herself or himself with the syntax and semantics of the popular groups—to understand how those persons do their reading of the world, to perceive that "craftiness" of theirs so indispensable to the culture of a resistance that is in the process of formation, without which they cannot defend themselves from the violence to which they are subjected.

Educators need an understanding of the meaning their festivals have as an integral part of the culture of resistance, a respectful sense of their piety in a dialectical perspective, and not only as if it were a simple expression of their alienation. Their piety, their religiousness, must be respected as their right, regardless of whether we reject it personally (and if so, whether we reject religion as such, or merely do not approve the particular manner of its practice in a given popular group).

In a recent conversation with Brazilian sociologist Professor Otávio Ianni, of UNICAMP, I received a report from him of some of his encounters with young activists of the Left, one of them in prison, in Recife, in 1963. Ianni not only made no effort to hide his emotion at what he had seen and heard, but approved and endorsed the way these militants respected popular culture, and within that culture, the manifestations of their religious beliefs.

"What do you need," Ianni asked the young prisoner.

"A Bible," he answered.

"I thought you'd want Lenin's *Que fazer?* (What is to be done?)," said Ianni.

"I don't need Lenin just now. I need the Bible. I need a better understanding of the peasants' mystical universe. Without that understanding, how can I communicate with them?"

Besides the democratic, ethical duty to proceed in this way, incumbent on the progressive educator, such a procedure is also demanded by requirements in the field of communication, as the young person in Recife had discerned.

Unless educators expose themselves to the popular culture across the board, their discourse will hardly be heard by anyone but themselves. Not only will it be lost, and inoperative, it may actually reinforce popular dependency, by underscoring the much-vaunted "linguistic superiority" of the popular classes.

It is once more against the background of a dialectical comprehension of the relationship between world and awareness, between economic production and cultural production, that it seems valid to me to call progressive educators' attention to the contradictory movement between culture's "negativities" and "positivities." There can be no doubt, for example, that our slavocratic past[40] marks us as a whole still today. It cuts across the social classes, dominant and dominated alike. Both have worldviews and practices significantly indicative of that past, which thereby continues ever to be present. But our slavocratic past is not evinced exclusively in the almighty lord who orders and threatens and the humiliated slave who "obeys" in order to stay alive. It is also revealed in the relationship between the two. It is precisely by obeying in order to stay alive that the slave eventually discovers that "obeying," in this case, is a form of struggle. After all, by adopting such behavior, the slave survives. And it is from learning experience to learning experience that a culture of resistance is gradually founded, full of "wiles," but full of *dreams*, as well. Full of rebellion, amidst apparent accommodation.

The *quilombos*[41]—the hiding places used by runaway slaves—constituted an exemplary moment in that learning process of rebellion—of a reinvention of life on the part of slaves who took their existence and history in hand, and, starting with the necessary "obedience," set out in quest of the invention of freedom.

In a recent public discussion entitled, "Presence of the People in the National Culture," in which I participated, along with the Brazilian sociologist I have already mentioned, Otávio Ianni, the latter, referring to this slavocratic past of ours and the marks it has left on our society, brought out its positive signs as well—the slaves' resistance, their rebellion. He spoke of the corresponding struggles, today, of the "landless," the "homeless," the "schoolless," the "foodless," the "jobless," as current kinds of *quilombos,* or "underground railroads."

It is our task as progressive educators to take advantage of this tradition of struggle, of resistance, and "work it." It is a task that, to be sure, is a perverted one from the purely idealist outlook, as well as from the mechanistic, dogmatic, authoritarian viewpoint that converts education into pure "communication," the sheer transmission of neutral content.

Another consideration that I cannot refrain from entertaining in this book is the question of the programmatic content of education. I seem to be misunderstood on this matter at times.

This calls for a reflection on educational practice itself, which is taking shape before our eyes.

Let us "step back" from educational practice—as I now do in writing, in the silence, not only of my office, but of my neighborhood—in order the better to "close in" on it again, take it by surprise, in its component elements in their reciprocal relationship.

As an object of my curiosity, which curiosity is now operating epistemologically, the educational practice that, by "taking my distance" from it, I "close in" on, begins to reveal itself to me. The first observation I make is that any educational practice always implies the existence of (1) a subject or agent (the person who instructs and teaches); (2) the person who learns, but who by learning also teaches; and (3) the object to be imparted and taught—the object to be re-cognized and cognized—that is, the content; and (4) the methods by which the teaching subject approaches the content he or she is mediating to the educand. Indeed, the content—in its quality as cognoscible object to be re-cognized by the educator while teaching it to the educand, who in turn comprehends it only by apprehending it—cannot simply be transferred from the educator to the educand, simply deposited in the educand by the educator.

Educational practice further involves processes, techniques, expectations, desires, frustrations, and the ongoing tension between practice and theory, between freedom and authority, where any exaggerated emphasis on either is unacceptable from a democratic perspective, which is incompatible with authoritarianism and permissiveness alike.

The critical, exacting, consistent educator, in the exercise of his or her reflection on educational practice, as in the practice itself, always understands it in its totality.

He or she will not center educational practice exclusively on, for example, the educand, or the educator, or the content, or the methods, but will understand educational practice in terms of the relationship obtaining among its various components, and will perform that practice consistently with his or her understanding, in all use of materials, methods, and techniques.

There has never been, nor could there ever be, education without content, unless human beings were to be so transformed that the processes we know today as processes of knowing and formation were to lose their current meaning.

The act of teaching and learning—which are dimensions of the larger process of knowing—are part of the nature of the educational process. There is no education without the teaching, systematic or no, of a certain content. And "teach" is a transitive-relative verb. It has both a direct and an indirect object. One who teaches, teaches something (content) to someone (a pupil).

The question that arises is not whether or not there is such a thing as education without content (which would be at the opposite pole from a "contentistic," purely mechanistic education), since, let us repeat, there has never been an educational practice without content.

The fundamental problem—a problem of a political nature, and colored by ideological hues—is who choses the content, and in behalf of which persons and things the "chooser's" teaching will be performed—in favor of whom, against whom, in favor of what, against what. What is the role of educands in the programmatic organization of content? What is the role, on various levels, of those at the bases—cooks, maintenance workers, security personnel, who find themselves involved in a school's educational practice? What is the role of families, social organizations, and the local community?

Nor let it be said, in a spirit of smoldering, venomous aristocratic elitism, that students, students' fathers, students' mothers, janitors, security people, cooks, have "no business meddling in this"—that the question of programmatic content is of the sole jurisdiction or competency of trained specialists. This discourse is like peas in a pod with another—the one that proclaims that an illiterate does not know how to vote.[42]

In the first place, to argue in favor of the active presence of pupils, pupils' fathers, pupils' mothers, security people, cooks, and custodians in program planning, content planning, for the schools, as the São Paulo Municipal Secretariat of Education does today in the Workers party administration[43] of Luiza Erundina, does not mean denying the indispensable need for specialists. It only means not leaving them as the exclusive "proprietors" of a basic component of educational practice. It means democratizing the power of choosing content, which is a necessary extension of the debate over the most democratic way of dealing with content, of proposing it to the apprehension of the educands instead of merely transferring it from the educator to the educands. This is what we are doing in the São Paulo Municipal Secretariat of Education.[44] It is impossible to democratize the choice of content without democratizing the teaching of content.[45]

Nor let it be said that this is a populist, or "democratistic" position. No, it is not democratistic, it is democratic. It is progressive. But it is the position of progressives and democrats who see the urgency of the presence of the popular classes in the debates on the destiny of the city. Their presence in the school is a chapter in that debate, and is a positive sign, and not something evil, something to be deterred. This is not the position of self-styled "democrats" for whom the presence of the people in facts and events, a people organizing, is a sign that democracy is not doing well.

Besides considering the importance of this kind of intervention in the destiny of the school in terms of a democratic learning process, we can also imagine what a school will be able to learn from, and what it will be able to teach, cooks, janitors, security guards, fathers, and mothers, in its indispensable quest for a transcendence of the "knowledge of living experience" in order to arrive at a more critical, more precise knowledge, to which these persons have a right. This is a right of the popular classes that progressives have to recognize and fight for if they are to be consistent—the right to know better than they already know—alongside another right, that of sharing in some way in the production of the as-yet-nonexistent knowledge.

Something that likewise seems to me to be important to bring out, in any discussion or conceptualization of content, in a critical, democratic outlook on curriculum, is the importance of never allowing ourselves to succumb to the naive temptation to look on content as something magical. And it is interesting to observe that, the more we look on content as something magical, the more we tend to regard it as neutral, or to treat it in a neutral manner. For someone understanding it as magical, content in itself has such power, such importance, that one need only "deposit" it in educands in order for its power to effect the desired change. And it is for this reason that, when content is rendered magical, or is thus understood, when it is regarded as having this force in itself, then the teacher seems to have no other task than to transmit it to the educands. Any discussion about social, political, economic, or cultural reality—any critical, in no way dogmatic, discussion—is regarded as not only unnecessary, but simply irrelevant.

This is not the way I see things. As object of cognition, content must be delivered up to the cognitive curiosity of teachers and pupils. The former teach, and in so doing, learn. The latter learn, and in so doing, teach.

As object of cognition, content cannot be taught, apprehended, learned, known, in such a way as to escape the implications of political ideology—which implications, as well, are to be apprehended by the cognizing subject. Once more a "reading of the world" is imperative that stands in dynamic interrelationship with the cognition of word-and-theme, of content, of cognoscible object.

That every reader, everyone engaged in any teaching or learning practice, explicitly wonder about his or her work as teacher or pupil, in mathematics, history, biology, or grammar classes, is of little importance. That all explicitly interrogate themselves, and see themselves, as participating as teacher or pupil in the experience of critical instruction in content, that all explicitly engage in a "reading of the world" that would be of a political nature, is not of the highest necessity.

What is altogether impermissible, in democratic practice, is for teachers, subreptitiously or otherwise, to impose on their pupils their own "reading of the world," in whose framework, therefore, they will now situate the teaching of content. The battle with the authoritarianism of the Right or the Left does not lead me into that impossible "neutrality" that would be nothing but a cunning way of seeking to conceal my option.

The role of the progressive educator, which neither can nor ought to be omitted, in offering her or his "reading of the world," is to bring out the fact that there are other "readings of the world," different from the one being offered as the educator's own, and at times antagonistic to it.

Let me repeat: there is no educational practice without content. The danger, of course, depending on the educator's particular ideological position, is either that of exaggerating the educator's authority to the point of authoritarianism, or that of a voiding of the teacher's authority that will mean plunging the educand into a permissive climate and an equally permissive practice. Each of the two practices implies its own distinct manner of addressing content.

In the former case, that of the exaggeration of authority to the point of authoritarianism, the educator is ascribed the "possession" of *content*. In this fashion, educators who feel that they "possess" content, hold it as their property—regardless of whether they have had a share in its selection—since they possess the methods by which they manipulate the object, they will necessarily manipulate the educands as well. Even when calling themselves progressive and democratic, authoritarian educators of the Left, inconsistent with at least a part of their discourse, feel so uncomfortable with critical educands, educands who are investigators, that they cannot bring themselves to terminate their discourse, any more than can authoritarian educators of the Right.

In the latter case, we have an annihilation of the teacher's authority that plunges the educands into the above-mentioned permissive climate and equally permissive practice, in which, left to their own devices, they do and undo what they please.

Devoid of limits, spontaneous practice, which shreds to pieces something so fundamental in human beings' formation—spontaneity—not having sufficient strength to deny the necessity of content, nevertheless allows it to trickle away in a never-justifiable pedagogical "Let's pretend."

And so, when all is said and done, there is nothing the progressive educator can do in the face of the question of content but join battle for good and all in favor of the democratization of society, which necessarily implies the democratization of the school in terms, on the one hand, of the democratization of the programming of content, and on the other, of the democratization of the teaching of that content. The democratization of the school, especially when we have some say-so over the "network" or "subsystem" of which it is a part, so that we can make a contribution to governmental change in a democracy, is part of the democratization of society. In other words, the democratization of the school is not a sheer epiphenomenon, the mechanical result of the transformation of society across the board, but is itself a factor for change, as well.

Consistent progressive educators need not await the comprehensive democratization of Brazilian society in order to embrace democratic practices with respect to content. They must not be authoritarian today in order to be democratic tomorrow.

What they simply may not do, in critical terms, is look to municipal, state, and federal governments of a conservative mold, or to "progressive" governments nevertheless tinged with the *dogmatism* I have always criticized, to democratize the organization of curriculum or the teaching of content. Concretely, we need neither authoritarianism nor permissiveness, but democratic substance.

In 1960 I wrote, for the symposium, "Education for Brazil," sponsored by the Recife Regional Center for Educational Investigations, a paper entitled, "A Primary School for Brazil" and published by the *Revista Brasileira de Estudos Pedagógicos*, no. 35 (April–June 1961). I shall cite a brief passage from this text here for the sake of its bearing on the question under discussion in this part of this book.

> The school we need so urgently [I said in 1960] is a school in which persons really study and work. When we criticize, on the part of other educators, the intellectualism of our schools, we are not attempting to defend a position with regard to the school in which the study disciplines, and the discipline of studying, would be watered down. We may never in all of our history have had more need of teaching, studying, learning, than we have today. Of learning to read, write, count. Of studying history, geography. Of understanding the situation or situations of our country. The intellectualism we fight is precisely that hollow, empty, sonorous chatter, bereft of any relationship with the real-

ity surrounding us, in which we are born and reared and on which, in large part, we yet feed today. We must be on our guard against this sort of intellectualism, just as we must be on our guard against a so-called antitraditionalist position that reduces schoolwork to mere *experiences of this or that,* and which excuses itself from performing the hard, heavy work of serious, honest, study, which produces intellectual discipline.[46]

It is precisely the authoritarian, magical comprehension of content that characterizes the "vanguardist" leaderships, for whom men's and women's awareness is an empty "space" waiting for content—a conceptualization I have severely criticized in *Pedagogy of the Oppressed.* And I criticize it again today as incompatible with a *pedagogy of hope.*

But let me make one thing perfectly clear: it is not every conscious mind, not every awareness, that is this empty "space" waiting for content, for the authoritarian vanguardist leaders. Not their own awareness, for example. They feel they belong to a special group in society (Erica Marcuse, 1986), which "owns" critical awareness as a "datum." They feel as if they were already liberated, or invulnerable to domination, so that their sole task is to *teach* and *liberate* others. Hence their almost religious care—their all but mystical devotion— but their intransigence, too, when it comes to dealing with content, their certitude with regard to what ought to be taught, what ought to be transmitted. Their conviction is that the fundamental thing is to teach, to transmit, what *ought* to be taught—not "losing time," in "mindless chatter" with popular groups about their reading of the world.

Any concern with educands' expectations, whether these persons be primary-school children, high-school students, or adults in popular education courses, is pure democratism. Any concern on the part of the democratic educator not to wound the cultural identity of the educands is held for harmful purism. Any manifestation of respect for popular wisdom is considered populism.

This conception is as consistent, on the Left, with a dogmatic thinking, of Marxist origin, in terms of which a critical, historical awareness is given, as I have already mentioned, almost as if it were just "put there" (Erica Marcuse, 1986); as it is consistent, on the Right, with the elitism that would have the dominant classes, by nature, knowing, and the dominated ones, by nature, ignorant. Thus, the dominant teach when and if they feel like it; the dominated learn at the price of much effort.

A dogmatic activist working in a school as a teacher is indistinguishable from her or his colleague working on behalf of a union, or in a slum, except for the material differences in their respective activities. For the former, it is imperative to "fill" the "empty" awareness of educands with content whose learning process he or she as educator already knows to be important and indispensable to the educands. For the latter, it is likewise imperative to "fill" the "empty" consciousness of popular groups with the working-class consciousness that, according to this individual, the workers do not have, but which the middle class judges and asserts themselves to have.

I can never forget what four German educators, of the former East Germany, said one evening, in the early 1970s, as we sat in the home of one of them. One spoke, while the others nodded their assent: "I recently read the German edition of your book, *Pedagogy of the Oppressed*. I was very glad you criticized students' absence from discussions of programmatic content. In bourgeois societies," he went on, dogmatically, "you have to talk about this, and fire the students up about it. Not here. We know what the students should know."

From this point forward, after what I said to them in response, it was hard to keep up the conversation. The visit came to an end, and I retired earlier than I had expected to the home of a friend who was putting me up.

It took me a while to get to sleep. I thought not only about what I had just heard that evening in Berlin, but about what I had heard all day long there, in a group of young scientists, university scholars. The contrast was huge. The young people criticized the authoritarianism of the regime: for them it was retrograde, antidemocratic, and arrogant. And their criticism was lodged from within the socialist option, not from the outside.

The educators with whom I had just been speaking were an example of the very thing the young scientists had spoken to me about and had opposed.

It was hard to sleep, thinking of the supercertitude with which those "modern" educators wove their discourse, their declaration of unshakable faith: "Not here. We know what the students should know."

This is the certitude, always, of the authoritarian, the dogmatist, who knows what the popular classes know, and knows what they need even without talking to them. At the same time, what the popular classes already know, in function of their practice in the interwoven events of their everyday lives, is so "irrelevant," so "disarticulate," that it makes no sense to authoritarian persons. What makes sense to them is what comes from their readings, and what they write in their books and articles. It is what they already know about the knowledge that seems basic and indispensable to them, and which, in the form of content, must be "deposited" in the "empty consciousness" of the popular classes.

If anyone, on the other hand, assuming a democratic, progressive position, therefore argues for the democratization of the programmatic organization of content, the democratization of his or her teaching—in other words, the democratization of curriculum—that person is regarded by the authoritarian as too spontaneous and permissive, or else as lacking in seriousness.

If, as I have declared above, the neoliberal discourse has no power to eliminate from history the existence of social classes, on one hand, and the struggle between them, on the other, then the rug is pulled out from under the authoritarian positions that characterize so-called realistic socialism and underly a vertical discourse and practice of curricular organization.

Neoliberals err when they criticize and reject us for being ideological in an era, according to them, in which "ideologies have died." The discourses and dogmatic practices of the Left are mistaken not because they are ideological, but because theirs is an ideology that connives with the prohibition of men's and women's curiosity, and contributes to its alienation.

"I do not authentically think unless others think. I simply cannot think for others, or for others, or without others." This assertion, owing to its implicit dialogical character, unsettles authoritarian mentalities. This is also why they are so refractory to dialogue, to any idea swapping between teachers and students.

Dialogue between teachers and students does not place them on the same footing professionally; but it does mark the democratic position between them. Teachers and students are not identical, and this for countless reasons. After all, it is a *difference* between them that makes them precisely students or teachers. Were they simply identical, each could be the other. Dialogue is meaningful precisely because the dialogical subjects, the agents in the dialogue, not only retain their identity, but actively defend it, and thus grow together. Precisely on this account, dialogue does not *level* them, does not "even them out," reduce them to each other. Dialogue is not a favor done by one for the other, a kind of grace accorded. On the contrary, it implies a sincere, fundamental respect on the part of the subjects engaged in it, a respect that is violated, or prevented from materializing, by authoritarianism. Permissiveness does the same thing, in a different, but equally deleterious, way.

There is no dialogue in "spontaneism" any more than in the omnipotence of the teacher. But a dialogical relation does not, as is sometimes thought, rule out the possibility of the act of teaching. On the contrary, it founds this act, which is completed and sealed in its correlative, the act of learning,* and both become authentically possible only when the educator's thinking, critical and concerned though it be, nevertheless refuses to "apply the brakes" to the educand's ability to think. On the contrary, both "thinkings" become authentically possible only when the educator's critical thinking is delivered over to the educand's curiosity. If the educator's thinking cancels, crushes, or hinders the development of educands' thinking, then the educator's thinking, being authoritarian, tends to generate in the educands upon whom it impinges a timid, inauthentic, sometimes even merely rebellious, thinking.

Indeed, dialogue cannot be blamed for the warped use sometimes made of it—for its pure imitation, or its caricature. Dialogue must not be transformed into a noncommittal "chewing the fat"[47] to the random rhythm of whatever happens to be transpiring between teacher and educands.

Pedagogical dialogue implies not only content, or cognoscible object around which to revolve, but also a presentation concerning it made by the educator for the educands.

---

*See, in this regard, Eduardo Nicol, *Los principios de la ciencia* (Mexico City: Fondo de Cultura Económica, 1965).

Here I should like to return to reflections I have previously made about the "expository lesson."*

The real evil is not in the expository lesson—in the explanation given by the teacher. This is not what I have criticized as a kind of "banking." I have criticized, and I continue to criticize, that type of educator-educand relationship in which the educator regards himself or herself as the educands' sole educator—in which the educator violates, or refuses to accept, the fundamental condition of the act of knowing, which is its dialogical relation (Nicol, 1965), and therefore establishes a relation in which the educator transfers knowledge about a or b or c objects or elements of content to an educand considered as pure recipient.

This is the criticism I have made, and still make. The question now is: will every "expository classroom," as they are called, be this? I think not. I deny it. There are expository classrooms in which this is indeed attempted: pure transferrals of the teacher's accumulated knowledge to the students. These are vertical classrooms, in which the teacher, in a spirit of authoritarianism, attempts the *impossible,* from the viewpoint of theory of knowledge: to transfer knowledge.

There is another kind of classroom, in which, while appearing not to effect the transfer of content, also cancels or hinders the educand's ability to do critical thinking. That is, there are classrooms that sound much more like children's songs than like genuine challenges. They house the expositions that "tame" educands, or "lull them to sleep"—where, on the one side, the students are lulled to sleep by the teacher's pretentious, high-sounding words, and on the other, the teacher likewise doing a parcel of self-babying. But there is a third position, which I regard as profoundly valid: that in which the teacher makes a little presentation of the subject and then the group of students joins with the teacher in an analysis precisely of that presentation. In this fashion, in the little introductory exposition, the teacher challenges the students, who thereupon question themselves and question the teacher, and thereby share in plumbing the depths of, developing, the initial exposition. This kind of work

---

*Paulo Freire and Sérgio Guimaraes, *Sobre educação—diálogos* (Rio de Janeira: Paz e Terra, 1984).

may in no wise be regarded as negative, as traditional schooling in the pejorative sense.

Finally, I find yet another kind of teacher whom I do not regard as a banker. It is that very serious teacher who, in conducting a course, adopts a relationship with the subject, with the content, of which she or he is treating, that is one of profound, affectionate, almost loving respect, whether that content be constituted of a text composed by the teacher or a text composed by someone else. Ultimately, he or she is bearing witness to the educands as to how he or she studies, "approaches," or draws near a given subject, how she or he thinks critically. Now the educands' must have, or create and develop, the critical ability to accompany the teacher's movement in his or her attempt to approach the topic under consideration.

From a certain point of view, this kind of teacher also commits an error. It consists in ignoring the fact that the knowledge relation does not terminate in the object. In other words, the knowledge relationship is not exclusively between a cognizing subject and a cognoscible object. It "bridges over" to another subject, basically becoming a subject-object-subject relation.

As a democratic relationship, dialogue is the opportunity available to me to open up to the thinking of others, and thereby not wither away in isolation.

Pedagogy of the Oppressed first saw the light of day twenty-four years ago, under the impulse of this sentiment with which, more touched by it and enveloped in it than before, I revisit it in this *Pedagogy of Hope.*

I began this book by saying that a poem, a song, a sculpture, a painting, a book, a piece of music, a fact or deed, an occurrence, never have just one reason to explain them. An event, a fact, a deed of love or hatred, a poem, a book, are always found wrapped in thick webs, tapestries, frameworks, and touched by manifold *whys*, of which some are more proximate to the occurrence or creation— more visible as a *why.*

A great proportion of the first part of this book has centered on a grasp of certain of the tapestries or frameworks in which *Pedagogy of the Oppressed* took its origin.

Now, in the latter part of this volume, I shall speak of facts, occurrences, tapestries, or frameworks in which I have shared and am sharing and which have revolved around *Pedagogy of the Oppressed*.

Published in New York in September 1970, *Pedagogy* immediately began to be translated into various languages, sparking curiosity, and favorable criticism in some cases, unfavorable in others. By 1974 the book had been translated into Spanish, Italian, French, German, Dutch, and Swedish, and its publication in London by Penguin Books carried *Pedagogy* to Africa, Asia, and Oceania, as well.

The book appeared at an intensely troubled moment in history. Social movements appeared, in Europe, the United States, and Latin America, each with its own space–time and particular characteristics. There was the struggle with sexual, racial, cultural, and class discrimination. In Europe, there was the struggle waged by the Greens to protect the environment. Coups d'état with a new face, in Latin America, with new military governments replacing those of the previous decade. Now the coups were ideologically based, and all of them were coupled in one way or another to the locomotive of the North going full steam ahead for what seemed to it the capitalist destiny of the continent. There were the guerrilla wars in Latin America, the base communities, the liberation movements in Africa, independence for former Portuguese colonies, the battle in Namibia. There were Amílcar Cabral, Julius Nyerere, their leadership in Africa and its repercussions outside Africa. China. Mao. The Cultural Revolution. A lively loyalty to the meaning of the May of 1968. There were the political and pedagogical union movements—all of them obviously political, especially in Italy. There was Guevara, murdered the decade before, present as a symbol not only for Latin-American revolutionary movements, but for progressive leaders and activists the world over. There was the Vietnam War, and the reaction in the United States. There was the fight for civil rights, and the climate of the 1960s in the area of political culture overflowed, in that country, into the 1970s.

These, with their numberless implications and developments, were some of the social, cultural, political, and ideological historical fabrics that explain, in part, both the curiosity the book aroused, and with the tenor of the reading and the acceptance with which it met—whether it was accepted or rejected, and what criticisms were made of it.

As I did not systematically keep and duly comment on the letters that came to me from each respective linguistic region of the world after each new translation of *Pedagogy* is something I regret today with an almost physical pain. They were letters from the United States, Canada, Latin America, and after the publication by Penguin Books, Australia, New Zealand, the islands of the South Pacific, India, and Africa, such was the effectiveness of that publisher's distribution network. After the letters, or sometimes with them, came invitations to discuss and debate theoretico-practical points of the book. Not infrequently, in Geneva, for a day or longer, I would host a group of university students, accompanied by their teacher, who would be running a course or seminar on *Pedagogy*, or a group of workers, especially Italian workers, but also immigrant workers in Switzerland, who—from a more political perspective than the one maintained by the university students—wanted to have points explained and aspects illuminated bearing directly on their practice.

I remember now, for example: there was a series of coinciding positions on political pedagogy, my positions in the book and positions in the general view maintained by the Italian union leaders then heading up the battle for what they called the "fifty hours." The movement was finally victorious in obtaining recognition of workers' right to take courses on work time.

On various occasions, in Geneva, or in Italy, I met with some of these leadership teams to discuss points of practical theory in their struggle in terms of dimensions of the book.

It was in those days that we began to form a group and hold discussions just among ourselves: Elza Freire, Miguel Darcy de Oliveira, Rosiska de Oliveira, Claudius Ceccon, myself, and, later, Marcos Arruda and the Institute for Cultural Action. The IDAC team was playing a truly important role just then, in seminars on *Pedagogy of the Oppressed* held throughout Europe, the United States, and Canada. A time or two, as first director of IDAC, I participated in some of those seminars analyzing the book.

It would be difficult to exaggerate how much I was enriched by the discussions I held, for hours on end, with German university youth, whether in Geneva or in their universities in Germany. I could not help being struck with their strong liking for theoretical discussion, and the seriousness with which they challenged me on the basis of their careful, rigorous reading, which they had done either by themselves or along with their professor. Or how much it likewise enriched me to engage in discussions with Italian or Spanish labor leaders—with the former, as I have said, in meetings in Geneva or Italy, while with the latter I could only meet in Geneva, since at that time *Pedagogy of the Oppressed* was contraband in Spain and Portugal alike. Franco Spain, like Salazar's Portugal,[48] had shut us both out. *Pedagogy* and me.

It was at that time, and on account of *Pedagogy,* that I came in contact with the harsh reality of one of the most serious traumas of the "Third World in the First": the reality of the so-called guest workers—Italians, Spaniards, Portuguese, Greeks, Turks, Arabs, in Switzerland, in France, in Germany—and their experience of racial, class, and sexual discrimination.

In one of the seminars in which I took part in Germany, on literacy and postliteracy programs for Portuguese workers, I was told by some of the latter that their German colleagues despised them to the point, and in such a way, that they regarded them as incapable of ever speaking their language, so that when they spoke to them in German they put all the verbs in the infinitive mood. And surely enough, one of the Portuguese workers told me, in German, referring to a fellow worker: "He to like the meeting very much, but not to understand everything."

In Paris, in one of these seminars on *Pedagogy of the Oppressed,* a Spanish worker, enraged and almost in physical pain, protested a lack of class solidarity on the part of his French colleagues. "Lots of 'em come up and kick our butt," he said, with irritation, "if we're not lookin'!"

Behavior like this could reinforce today's neoliberal discourse, according to which the social classes are vanishing. They no longer exist, we hear. They existed, though, at the moment of the above-mentioned unburdening on the part of the Spanish worker, and they exist today as well. But their existence does not necessarily betoken a level of solidarity on the part of their members, especially internationally. At the same time, sectors of the dominated themselves are steeped in the authoritarian, discriminatory, dominant ideology. It becomes installed in them, and causes them to see and feel themselves to be superior to their companions who have left the land of their origin and wear the mark of need.

One of the serious problems that alert, politically engaged guest-worker leaders had to confront in the 1970s, and they discussed it with me in connection with their reading of *Pedagogy*, was a lack of motivation on the part of their companions for any commitment to the political struggles transpiring in the lands of their origin.

I myself took part in meetings in Switzerland, France, and Germany with immigrant workers at which I heard discourses evincing far more concern for an easier life in their experience far from their native lands, than of a desire to return to those lands one day in conditions appreciably better than those in which they had once left them. It was readily perceptible, in those days, whether in the meetings I have mentioned, or in conversations with leaders in which I was told of these difficulties of mobilization and political organization, that a great many of the workers who had emigrated to the new, "loan" context were taken, on the one hand, with a feeling of relief and joy that they had *work* now, and at the same time, with a sense of fear: fear of losing the tiny bit of security that they had found in their "loan" context. Their feelings of insecurity were too great for the minimal courage they would have needed for the adventure and risk of political commitment, however slight a commitment. The time that they had spent living in their countries of origin, the hope of employment, of security, had caused them to stake everything on *employment*, in the loan context, instead of on structural changes in their own context. These persons, a great proportion of the guest workers-to-be, had left their context of origin under the crushing burden of a weariness that I called, in those days, "existential weariness"—not a physical weariness, but a spiritual weariness, which left those caught in it emptied of courage, emptied of hope, and above all, seized with a fear of adventure and risk. And with the weariness came what I dubbed: "historical anesthesia."

On one of my visits to Germany for a discussion with Portuguese guest workers, which was held in a Catholic parish that was sponsoring an excellent program in political pedagogy, I heard from a young priest the following story: "A short while ago I received a complaint from three Portuguese workers that they and many of their companions were being severely exploited by the landlords of their little shacks: super-high rent, flouting of the law governing tenant rights and obligations, and so on.

"So I decided," continued the father, "after talking about it at Mass one Sunday, to call a meeting of anyone willing to discuss the question with me and try to figure out what could be done. Several parishioners came to the meeting. We worked together for two sessions, and we programmed a strategy against the almighty landlords: complaints in the newspapers, fliers, walks through the parish neighborhood, and so on.

"So we began putting the plan in practice—until a committee of tenants, including one of the ones who had made the complaint to me in the first place, came to me personally and requested that I call off the campaign. They had been threatened with eviction unless I stopped the accusations." And I still remember the words with which the priest concluded his story: "I felt a powerful tension, an ethical tension, between continuing to fight the exploiters, who now had gone so far as to take advantage of the emotional dependency of the oppressed and were blackmailing them, and respecting the tenant's pusillanimity and calling off the struggle, thereby restoring to them a sense of relative security—basically a false security, but one they couldn't do without—in which they lived."

In line after line of *Pedagogy of the Oppressed,* I discuss this phenomenon. Fanon and Memmi* did the same, or had done it before me. I mean the fear that fills the oppressed, as individuals and as a class, and prevents them from struggling. But fear is no abstraction, and neither is the "why" of fear an abstraction. Fear is altogether concrete, and is caused by concrete considerations—or considerations that seem concrete, so that, in the absence of any demonstration to the contrary, they might as well be.

And so the leadership, which, for any number of reasons, enjoys a different, higher level of "immunization" to the fear that affects the masses, must adopt a special way of leading where that fear is concerned. Once more, then, it becomes incumbent upon them to maintain a serious, rigorous relationship between tactics and strategy, a relationship of which I have already spoken in this book. In

---

*Franz Fanon, *Os condenados da Terra*; Albert Memmi, *The Colonizer and the Colonized* (Boston: Beacon Press).

the last analysis, the problem facing the leaders is: they must learn, through the critical reading of reality that must always be made, what actions can be tactically implemented, and on what levels they can be so implemented. In other words, what can we do now in order to be able to do tomorrow what we are unable to do today? In the case I have just narrated of the German parish, the solution to the problem from which the workers' *fear* could not be eliminated was found in a tactical freeze on the action initiated. Here was an action that could be resumed further down the line, after a project in political pedagogy from which a victory over the fear, at least in part, would be won. That project would reveal to the workers that their landlords are vulnerable, too. Guevara, as well, spoke about this aspect of the dialectical relationship between oppressors and oppressed—of the need for the latter to be given objectives whereby they can become convinced of the vulnerability of the former, as a decisive moment in the struggle. Indeed, the more the oppressed see the oppressors as "unbeatable," endowed with an invincible power, the less they believe in themselves. Thus has it ever been. One of the tasks of a progressive popular education, yesterday as today, is to seek, by means of a critical understanding of the mechanisms of social conflict, to further the process in which the weakness of the oppressed turns into a strength capable of converting the oppressors' strength into weakness. This is a hope that moves us.

While I lived one-half of the decade of the sixties in the climate of the Brazilian transition that was shattered by the 1964 coup, and the other half in Chile, where I wrote *Pedagogy*—in the seventies, with the book multiplying in various languages, I saw myself exposed, along with it, to challenges that sparked analyses on my part, and these analyses in many cases confirmed and reinforced the book's basic theses.

It is impossible, in my view, to overrate the importance of the innumerable meetings and encounters in which I took part with students and professors of German, Swiss, English, Dutch, Belgian, Swedish, Norwegian, French, Latin-American, African, Asian, United States, and Canadian universities. This is why I speak so much of them here. And sprinkled among these meetings of an academic nature, the no less rich Saturdays to which I was subjected by groups of workers.

The tonic administered by the former—a First World audience—with an occasional exception, came in the form of a theoretical analysis. My interlocutors would assess the degree of rigor with which I had approached this theme or that one, or the precision of my language, or the evident influence on me of this thinker or that one (whose work, at times, I had not read!). Or the inconsistency into which I had slipped between something I had said on, for instance, page 25, and something else on page 122. The German students loved this kind of critique.

When the encounters occurred with Third World students, a different tonic was administered. Here, discussion turned preponderantly on political questions, and these led us to philosophical, ethical, ideological, and epistemological questions.

In my meetings with immigrant workers, Italians, Spaniards, Portuguese, of whom a large proportion had also read *Pedagogy,* in Italian, Spanish, or French, interest always centered on a more critical understanding of practice in order to improve future practice.

While the university people, generally speaking, tried to find and "understand a certain practice imbedded in a theory," the workers sought to sneak up on the theory that was imbedded in their practice. Regardless of the world I found myself in with labor leaders who were immersed in personal experience of politics and policy for changing the world, this is how it always was. It did not matter whether those leaders belonged to the Third World of the Third or to the Third World of the First. This is always the way it was.

Once or twice, in Geneva or away, I had the opportunity of working in long seminars with workers and academicians, obviously progressive. I hope they still take that position today, and have not given in to the ideology of those who decree the death of the ideologies and who proclaim that the *dream* is a way of fleeing the world instead of re-creating it.

I had one of the encounters to which I have just referred, a hugely rich one, with academicians and a Spanish laborer, one weekend some time in the 1970s, in Germany, in Frankfurt, to be precise. Two or three groups of progressive intellectuals, respectively Marxists and Christians, who did not relate well with each other, agreed to come together for a study day provided I took part.

I have always found it worthwhile to serve as the pretext for a good cause. So I accepted the invitation and went, along with two German friends—theologians, both of them, clear-sighted, creative, serious intellectuals: Werner Simpfendoerfer, who was to translate *Pedagogy* into German, and Ernst Lang, now deceased, director of the World Council of Churches, who had invited my collaboration in that body and who was to write the preface to the German edition.

The language of the meeting was German, with a simultaneous translation into English for me, and from English into German for the others, except for the theologians.

One of the groups had invited a laborer, a Spanish guest worker, who spoke German without any difficulty.

The presence of the Spanish worker had the effect of keeping the meeting on a level of equilibrium between the necessary abstraction and a quest for the concrete. In other words, the presence of the laborer lessened the risk that abstraction might renounce its authentic nature and meander about in a vagueness ever more distant from the concrete.

When we took our first coffee break, the worker came over to me and we began to converse in Spanish. We alone understood each other now. No one in hearing, other than ourselves, understood Spanish, as was to be expected.

After a few perfunctory remarks, with which we were actually working up to a little conversation, the Spanish worker said: "I have to admit intellectual qualities in these young people that make me admire them. They're devoted to the cause of the working class. They work tirelessly. But they seem to think that revolutionary truth is pretty much their private property. Well, now, we guest workers . . . ," he added, with a twinkle in his eye, " . . . we're a sort of new game for them."

There was wisdom, there was grace in his discourse, without grief, and without anger. It was as if the truth infusing his words gave him the peace with which he spoke. He spoke of the problem he had mentioned with the tranquility of someone who knew his "why."

We chatted a while longer, commenting on the elitism, the authoritarianism, the dogmatism of the positions he had criticized. At one point he told me: "I have an interesting experience to tell you about—something I was involved in before I read your *Pedagogy of the Oppressed*.

"I'm an activist in a Leftist political movement working both in Spain and outside. One of our jobs is training immigrants politically so that we can then all go out and try to mobilize and organize other guest workers.

"A year ago, or so, five of us got together to try to work out a course in political problems to offer our fellow immigrants. We met for a discussion, just among ourselves, one Saturday afternoon in the home of one of these activists. We figured out what we thought the course ought to be, content and presentation. Finally, the way you academics like to do, we laid it all out on in a nice, orderly package ready to bestow on our future pupils. We were sure we knew not only what our people would like to know, but what they ought to know. So why waste time listening to them? All we had to do was communicate to them what they could expect in the course. All we'd have to do was announce the course and enroll the applicants.

"Once we had the program worked out, with the weekend times, the place, the whole thing—we started looking for students.

"Total failure. No one was interested. We spoke to everybody we could. We laid out the content, we visited a number of people and explained how important the program was, how important the course was, and . . . nothing came of it.

"We got together one Saturday to try to figure out why we'd failed. Suddenly I got an idea.

"Why not take a survey, in the factories? Why not talk with lots of people, one at a time, and find out what each one'd like to do? Why not ask them what they prefer, and what they usually do on weekends? Then, on the basis of that, we ought to be able to figure out how to 'get to them,' instead of just starting out with what we're so sure they ought to know.

"We decided to give it a try. We gave ourselves two weeks to conduct the survey, and scheduled another meeting of the five of us after that, for an evaluation. And out we went to conduct the survey.

"After two weeks we got together again as planned, the five of us, each with a report on the job we'd done. Lots of the Spaniards liked to play cards on weekends. Then there was a bunch that liked to go for hikes. Some others went to parks, or to supper in each other's houses, or would sit around drinking beer, and so on.

"We picked the card games. Maybe this would be an 'in' with them, to get to political problems. So we practiced up at cards," the Spanish worker went on, enthusiastically, "and we started going around stopping in on the groups that would play cards on weekends, in each other's homes. Then during the week we'd get together, the five of us, for an evaluation.

"Sometimes during a game, with my cards in my hand, not looking at anybody, I'd just kind of casually ask, 'Know what happened yesterday in Madrid?'

"'No,' they'd say.

"'Cops raided some of our guys and locked 'em up. For one little protest march.'

"Nobody said a word.

"I didn't either.

"'Well, gotta go,' I'd say, then I'd stop in on another game, and then another. Another question, a political question.

"All five of us kept doing this, in different places.

"After four months, we could finally get a bunch of them together to discuss if we'd like to get up some systematic meetings on politics. There were thirty of us at the first meeting, and we made a joint decision to run a real course on political problems. And we've had the best results we've ever had."

He laughed when I told him, "That proves that if we want to work *with* the people and not just *for* them we have to know their 'game.'"

This is precisely what authoritarian educators are always fighting. They claim to be progressive, and yet they regard themselves as proprietors of knowledge, which they need only *extend* to the ignorant educands. These people always see signs of permissiveness or "spontaneism" in the respect that radical democrats show for educands.

These people will never understand what it means to *start* with the reading of the world, the comprehension of the world, had by the educands. All surprised, as if they had made a great discovery, they say their practice proves that *staying* on the lower level of knowledge that the groups have, without trying to teach them anything beyond that knowledge, does not work. Of course it does not work. It is so obvious that it does not work that there is no point in bothering to prove it. One of the main reasons for the lack of spirit and inspiration in team members who get together to evaluate their practice is that the person running the evaluation process has no more sophisticated knowledge than the team has. No research is needed to establish the inviability of an evaluation seminar in which the coordinator lacks that particular knowledge with which he or she might explain the obstacles encountered by the participants in their practice. The normal tendency will be the failure of the seminar. So will a physics course fail unless the teacher knows physics. One does not teach what one does not know. But neither, in a democratic perspective, ought one to teach what one knows without, first, knowing what those one is about to teach know and on what level they know it; and second, without respecting this knowledge. One begins with that which is implicit in the reading of the world of those about to learn what the one about to teach knows.

This is what my practice, consistent with my democratic option, has taught me. This is also what the Spanish workers I have just spoken of were taught by their practice.

I should like to suggest certain further considerations in connection with the Spanish workers' experience. First let me present a consideration along the lines of political ethics. Educators have the right, even the duty, to teach what seems to them to be fundamental to the space–time in which they find themselves. That right and that duty fall to the educator by virtue of the intrinsic "directivity" of education. Of its very nature, education always "outstrips itself." It always pursues objectives and goals, dreams and projects. I have asked before, in this book: what sort of educator would I be if I had no concern for being maximally convincing in my presentation of my dreams? But that does not mean that I may reduce everything to my truth, my "correctness." On the other hand, even though I may be convinced, like the Spanish worker-activists, for example, that reflection on the political life of a town or city is essential, I may not on that account dictate the themes on which that political analysis and reflection must bear. A rather moralistic viewpoint would brand as disloyal the tactic of the Spanish workers in using card games to make a political approach to their companions and thereby render viable their objective of seriously studying the political question in Spain with them. This is not how I see it. They are as ethical as academicians could be in their own research.

The second reflection I should like to offer is far more positive. It regards the validity, in Latin America today, not only of the principle invoked by the Spanish workers, but of their work method. The popular educator must make a democratic option and act consistently with that option. I fail to see how popular education, regardless of where and when it is practiced, could prescind from the critical effort to involve, on the one side, educators, and on the other, educands, in a quest for the "why" of the facts. In other words, in a popular education focusing on cooperative production, union activity, community mobilization and organization so that the community can take the education of its sons and daughters in hand through community schools—without this having to mean an excuse for the state to neglect one of its duties, that of offering the people education, along with care for their health, literacy, and their education after the attainment of literacy—in any hypothesis, there is no discarding the gnoseological process. The process of knowing belongs to the very nature of education, and so-called popular education is no exception. On the other hand, popular education, in a progressive outlook, is not reducible to the purely *technical* training of which groups of workers have a real need. This will of course be the narrow training that the dominant class so eagerly offers workers—a training that merely *reproduces* the working class as such. Naturally, in a progressive perspective as well, a technical formation is also a priority. But alongside it is another priority, which must not be shoved out of the picture. For example, the worker learning the trade of machinist, mechanic, or stonemason has the right and the need to learn it as well as possible—but also has the right to know the "why" of the technical procedure itself. The worker has the right to know the historical origins of the technology in question, and to take it as an object of curiosity and reflect on the marvelous advance it implies—along with the risks it exposes us to, of which Neil Postman warns us of in an extraordinary recent book.* This is doubtless not only a profoundly current issue of our time, but a vital one, as well. And the working class should not be part of the employer-employee relationship simply in the way the worker in "Mod-

---

*Neil Postman, *Technopoly—the Surrender of Culture to Technology* (New York: Knopf, 1992).

ern Times" saw himself wildly struggling to tighten the screws that came along the assembly line, in the critique we have from the genius of Charlie Chaplin.

It seems to me to be fundamental for us today, whether we be mechanics or physicists, pedagogues or stonemasons, cabinetmakers or biologists, to adopt a critical, vigilant, scrutinizing attitude toward technology, without either demonizing it or "divinizing" it.

Never perhaps, has the almost trite concept of exercising control over technology and placing it at the service of human beings been in such urgent need of concrete implementation as today—in defense of freedom itself, without which the dream of a democracy is evacuated.

The progressive postmodern, democratic outlook in which I take my position acknowledges the right of the working class to be trained in such a way that they will know how their society functions, know their rights and duties, know the history of the working class and the role of the popular movements in remaking society in a more democratic mold. The working class has a right to know its geography, and its language—or rather, a critical understanding of language in its dialectical relationship with thought and world: the dialectical interrelations of language, ideology, social classes, and education.

In a recent brief trip through Europe, I heard from a European sociologist, a friend of mine recently returned from Africa, that political activists of a certain African country were saying that the "Freire era" had come and gone. What is needed now, they were saying, is no longer an education faithfully dedicated to a critical understanding of the world, but an education strictly devoted to the technical training of a labor force. As if, in a progressive view, it were possible to dichotomize technology and politics! The ones who attempt this dichotomy, as I have emphasized above, are the dominant class. Hence the wealth of discourse with which we are besieged today in favor of the pragmatic ideal of adjusting ourselves to the world at hand in the name of the values of capitalism. In this new history of ours, without social classes, and thus without any conflicts other than purely personal ones, we have nothing other to do than to let the calloused hands of the many and the smooth ones of the few remake the world at last into a festival.

Really, I do not believe in this. But I hear and regret the mistake in which the above-mentioned African activists are caught: the long, intensely tragic experience that has so long victimized them, their rejection as John, as Mary, as persons, as sex, as race, as culture, as history, the disregard for their lives, which to a perversely murderous white supremacy are of no value, so that those lives can just "be there," stand there practically like an inanimate object that nevertheless moves and speaks and is under white command, and any black life can simply die or disappear and white supremacy will not care one little bit. This long, tragic experience, so worthily humanized by their people's struggle, by that fine, high struggle, has nevertheless bequeathed them, through and through, that same kind of existential weariness that suddenly came upon the guest workers in Europe, as I have described above. The illusion is that today's historical moment calls on the men and women of their country to wage a completely different struggle from the one before—a struggle in which technology would replace people's political formation altogether. At the same time, the blurring of political parameters reinforces the fatalism that marks "existential weariness," inviting us to resign ourselves to a "hope" in which only an adverbial change is possible in the world.

But the truth is: regardless of what society we are in, in what world we find ourselves, it is impermissible to train engineers or stonemasons, physicians or nurses, dentists or machinists, educators or mechanics, farmers or philosophers, cattle farmers or biologists, without an understanding of our own selves as historical, political, social, and cultural beings—without a comprehension of how society works. And this will never be imparted by a supposedly purely technological *training*.

Another concern on which popular education must never turn its back is epistemological research, antecedent to or concomitant with teaching practices, especially in peasant regions. This is a task that has become dear to the ethnoscience being plied among us today in Brazil: to know how rural popular groups, indigenous or not, know—how they organize their *agronomic* knowledge or science, for example, or their medicine, to which end they have developed a broadly systemized taxonomy of plants, herbs, trees, spices, roots. It is interesting to observe how they integrate their meticulous taxonomy with miraculous promises—for example an herbal tea that heals both cancer and the pangs of unrequited love, or battles male impotence; or special leaves for protection in childbirth, for "fallen breastbone," and so on.

Recent research in Brazilian universities has verified the actual medical usefulness of certain discoveries made by popular wisdom.

For example, to discuss with peasants this ongoing university-level verification of their knowledge is a political task of high pedagogical importance. Such discussion can help the popular classes win confidence in themselves, or augment the degree of confidence they have already attained. Confidence in themselves is so indispensable to their struggle for a better world! I have already made reference to the need for it in this book.

What seems to me to be unconscionable, however, today as yesterday, would be to conceive—or even worse, to practice—a popular education in which a constant, serious approach were not maintained, antecedently and concomitantly, to problems like: what content to teach, in behalf of what this content is to be taught, in behalf of whom, against what, and against whom. Who selects the content, and how is it taught? What is teaching? What is learning? What manner of relationship obtains between teaching and learning? What is popular knowledge, or knowledge gotten from living experience? Can we discard it as imprecise and confused? How may it be gotten beyond, transcended? What is a teacher? What is the role of a teacher? And what is a student? What is a student's role? If being a teacher means being superior to the student in some way, does this mean that the teacher must be authoritarian? Is it possible to be democratic and dialogical without ceasing to be a teacher, which is different from being a student? Does dialogue mean irrelevant chitchat whose ideal atmosphere would be to "leave it as it is to see if it'll work"? Can there be a serious attempt at the reading and writing of the word without a reading of the world? Does the inescapable criticism of a "banking" education mean the educator has nothing to teach and ought not to teach? Is a teacher who does not teach a self-contradiction? What is *codification*, and what is its role in the framework of a theory of knowledge? How is the "relation between practice and theory" to be understood—and especially, experienced—without the expression becoming trite, empty wordage? How is the "basistic," voluntaristic temptation to be resisted—and how is the intellectualistic, verbalistic temptation to engage in sheer empty chatter to be overcome? How is one to "work on" the relationship between language and citizenship?

It is impossible to make education both a political practice and a gnosiological one, fully, without the constant stimulus of these questions, or without our constantly answering them.

Finally, I believe that the way I pose these questions in this book implies my answers to them—answers that express the positions on political pedagogy that I reaffirm in this book.

CHAPTER
5

O
ne day I received a phone call at my home in Geneva. It was a Sunday morning, a very cold, cloudy morning, and the French mountains you can see in the distance were swathed in clouds. A typical Swiss January Sunday.

The call was from a Spanish guest worker, who asked if he and two of his companions might drop in for an interview with me some evening in the coming week. He told me they wanted to talk about a children's education program they had planned and were setting up. He mentioned that they were reading *Pedagogy of the Oppressed*, and that they would like to talk about that too. "Who knows," he said, "—if you were to have time, and were interested, we might meet more than once."

We agreed on a day, and, at the scheduled time, they arrived with certain documents and certain children's exercises.

We chatted a bit about the climate, and the hard winter. They told me about Spain and asked me about Brazil. Then they broached the question that had brought us together. However, to be methodical, they had to introduce that question with an introduction explaining their political option, their activism. They spoke of their experience as guest workers, of the restrictions on their right to have their families with them to which so many of them were subjected, of the obligation imposed on them, simply because they had been in Switzerland for a year, to go back to Spain and renew (or fail to renew) their privilege of spending another one-year term here the following year.

This legal determination, besides relieving the Swiss government of the burden of expenditures for education and health, not to mention other considerations, obliged them to live in a state of constant tension. Their vital insecurity was one more "why" for the "existential weariness" I have talked about. They gave examples. Many of their companions found themselves on an emotional roller coaster, living in a present that, despite their now having the work that they had been without in their own country, was a today with a doubtful, too doubtful, tomorrow. It was a today in which, missing the love and tenderness, as well as physical presence, of their families, they found their activity, their strength, their resistance, all undermined. Many among them, then, awash in "existential weariness" and "historical anesthesia," simply gravitated around their personal problems and concerns of the moment, unable to glimpse the "untested feasibility" that lay beyond the "limited situation" in which they found themselves immersed.* Hence also the difficulty of moving them out of their "historical anesthesia," which spawned a kind of apathy, a kind of paralysis, when it came to a concern for or discussion of political questions. Then, added to the "historical anesthesia" in which so many of them were caught, there was the cultural, political, and ideological climate of Switzerland, which was unfavorable to public political dissent. I remember how, just about the time of the encounter of which I now speak, in reaction to a strike by construction workers on a huge site in Geneva, an official or quasi-official declaration was issued, in the guise of a union document, denouncing the workers' position, and deploring that "for the first time in the history of Switzerland, and therefore in scant consonance with the uses and customs of this country, they have had recourse to force in order to have their demands met: they have had recourse to a strike." Obviously a notice like this was not very encouraging to an effort to enable the guest workers to overcome their apathy and participate in the political projects being conducted by their leaders.

On the contrary, the explicitly open nature of the letter condemning the strike reinforced in the guest workers the "historical anesthesia" of which I am speaking.

---

*For "limit situations" and "untested feasibility," see my *Pedagogia do oprimido*, pp. 90ff.

But from the viewpoint of the immigrant Spanish workers' leadership, the political reaction implied in the note appeared as a challenge, as well as a confirmation of their conviction as to the need for their Spanish companions' political training.

The pedagogical project they had come to me about was a special one, and bore directly on their children—the sons and daughters of those Spanish workers who, under Swiss law, could bring their families with them from Spain. When you come right down to it, it was a counterschool project. Their "school" would be established precisely for the purpose of conducting an ongoing criticism of the Swiss schools attended by the Spanish children. It would be a "school" that would *problematicize* the Swiss school—render it problematic in the eyes of the workers' children.

The decade of the 1970s was just under way, and Althusserian studies had burst upon the scene denouncing the school system as an instrument for the reproduction of the dominant ideology (studies not always invulnerable to distortions and exaggerated interpretations). I do not believe, as far as I can recall, that we made any reference to the Althusserian theory of reproduction, but our conversation did basically turn on a critical understanding of the role of the school, and of the role in the school that progressive or conservative educators might play. In other words, the conversation bore on the power of the dominant ideology, and how that power might be blocked. And indeed, the program of which the Spanish workers were speaking to me with such justifiable enthusiasm focused precisely on the Swiss school their children were attending—Swiss schooling in all its aspects. This is what they were planning to do, and this is what they had come to speak with me about on that evening.

These Spanish workers were planning to set up, alongside the scholastic practice maintained by the Swiss school, in its particular manner, in doing its own teaching, another school that would take the Swiss school as the object of a critical analysis. A child could attend their school only under one condition: he or she would have to decide, after a short trial period, whether to continue to attend. And classes would be held not every day, or for long periods of time, but for only two hours or so at a time, and only three times a week. Nor was the new school intended as a substitute for the Swiss school.

It would complement it, through the experience of critical thinking about the world. The Spanish workers who conversed with me that evening were convinced of their children's need to study seriously, to learn, to create study habits, which, at least in part, they seemed to be doing in the Swiss schools.

The children would spend the regular school day in the Swiss schools, and then, on certain days, go to this other school, as well, where they would "rethink" what they had learned or were learning.

The workers' primary, overriding purpose was, on the one hand, to diminish the risk of having to watch the alienation of their children, cut off as these children were from their own culture—a risk greatly intensified by the Swiss school, which was unquestionably competent from the viewpoint of the dominant interests—and on the other hand, to stimulate in the children a critical way of thinking, as I now have brought out. Hence their project. Hence their sui generis school, which would take the other one as the object of its study, critically examine its practice, and analyze its curriculum—not only in its explicit elements, but in its hidden ones, as well.

The educators in the "challenge school" would not always be the same persons. Teachers would rotate, serving when they had free time. They would be trained in occasional evening or weekend seminars, in which they would rehearse their task.

They would also discuss with the children the ideology imbedded in the books of children's stories, whether or not these were being used in the Swiss schools.

One of the stories they repeated to me, laughing with almost childlike amusement, but critical of the ideology that permeated it, told of the simple, happy family life of a family of pigs—a papa pig, a mama pig, and three little piglets. The youngest piglet was always getting into things, overcome with curiosity. He did not like routine. He tried everything, and was always looking for something new and different.

But nothing ever worked for him. His older siblings followed convention to the letter, and got along fine. One autumn Sunday, under a clear blue sky, the youngest piglet decided to set out for the day and give his curiosity free rein. Nothing worked out. The moment he stepped beyond established bounds, he was attacked by a little dog. Wounded, and escaping by the skin of his teeth, he thought he saw another dog, and "poked the dog with a little stick." The "dog" turned out to be a swarm of bees. The poor little pig was all but stung to death by the horrible, diabolical attack of the enraged bees. From failure to failure he goes, returning home at nightfall dejected and subdued, now without the courage to so much as think of a new adventure. His commonsensical father was waiting for him, and wisely tells him, with the benign air of a gentle pedagogue, "I knew that you would do this some day. For you, there was no other way to learn that we need not leave the beaten path. Try to change something, and we run the risk of being hurt very painfully, as must have happened to you today."

Silent and contrite, the little pig listened to the "sensible" discourse of his well-behaved father.

It was against such a hamstringing suggestion, it was against programs like these, calculated to tame, that the Spanish workers' challenging, questioning school was being created. They dreamed of an open, democratic education, one that would instill in their children a taste for questioning, a passion for knowledge, a healthy curiosity, the joy of creating, and the pleasure of risk without which there can be no creation.

Hence the community of views between *Pedagogy of the Oppressed*, about which we spoke in meetings we held after this one, and the experience of the school in which children were taught to question things.

Their reading of *Pedagogy* had confirmed the Spanish workers in some of the pedagogical intuitions that had moved them to the concretization of their experiment—the book's whole analysis of the dialectical relationship between oppressors and oppressed, of the process of the introjection of the dominator by the dominated; its reflections on a "banking" education and its authoritarianism, on an education that challenges the status quo, on dialogue, on democratic initiatives; on the need, in a progressive educational process, for educands to have their curiosity challenged; on the critical presence of educators and educands who, while teaching and learning respectively, nevertheless all learn and teach, without any implication either that their relationship is one of homogeneous reciprocity, or that the teacher does not learn and the learner does not teach. All of this stimulated them, as I had been stimulated by reading

Fanon and Memmi back in the days when I was putting the final touches on *Pedagogy*.

Perhaps, in the process of their experience with *Pedagogy of the Oppressed*—as they read of the educational practice to which I was holding—perhaps they felt the same emotion with which I was taken when I plunged into *The Wretched of the Earth* and *The Colonizer and the Colonized*—the satisfying sensation with which we are taken when we find a confirmation of the "why" of the certitude we find within ourselves.

The positive results they had achieved had led the parents of the children of the questioning and challenging school—they had told me in our meeting—to come to them and ask them to do something like that for themselves, the parents, as well. They said they would like another school, in which they would be able to discuss, together, their presence in Switzerland, the political situation in Spain, and so on.

It had been by way of the implementation of the idea of a school that would challenge their children's school, that, now, the parents had come for courses or seminars, or political training meetings. In Geneva, the "game" was no card game.

The following year—the year after I became acquainted with that experiment in which these workers, turned educators, were calling their children's school in question and challenging them to think critically, Claudius Ceccon, the remarkable Brazilian cartoonist, then residing in Geneva, recounted to me the following case, that of his son Flávio.

One day, dejected and hurt, Flávio had told him that his teacher had torn up one of his drawings. At home, Flávio had learned freedom of expression, and was gradually encouraged to use it more and more, as he grew up exercising his curiosity in a climate of respect and affection. Curiosity was not forbidden. And so Flávio's creativity enjoyed the necessary conditions of self-expression. He could not understand why in the world his teacher would destroy one of his drawings! That had offended him deeply, nor had he been the only one to take offense. It had been as if his teacher had ripped up a little piece of himself. After all, his drawing was a creation of his, was it not? Had it not deserved as much respect as a story or a poem he might have written?

As any father or mother would have done who had embraced a democratic option and whose behavior was consistent with that option, Claudius went to the teacher to talk about what had happened.

The teacher had a high regard for the child. She spoke of him in terms of high praise, emphasizing his talent and his capacity for freedom.

As Claudius watched the teacher, he noticed by her gestures by her tone of voice that it could never have entered her head that he had come to voice his disapproval of what she had done to Flávio's drawing—for that matter, his disapproval of what she had done to Flávio himself, with his creativity that she had all but torn to shreds.

Delighted at a visit from the parent of one of her students whom she genuinely admired, she paced back and forth, fairly skipping, speaking of her class activities.

Claudius listened, and followed her narratives, awaiting an opportunity to speak with her about what had happened. His rage had abated now. He was calmer.

All of a sudden the teacher showed Claudius a series of nearly identical drawings. The drawings were all of a black cat—a single cat, multiplied, with the alteration of some trait here or there.

"What do you think of *that?*" the teacher asked, and without waiting for an answer, exclaimed, "My students did these. I brought them a little statue of a cat for them to draw."

"Why not bring a live cat into the classroom—one that would walk and run, and jump?" Claudius asked. "Then the children would draw the cat as they understood it, as they perceived it. The children would actually *reinvent* the cat. They would be free to make any cat they felt like. They would be free to create, to invent and reinvent."

"No, no!" the teacher fairly shouted. "Perhaps that might do for your child. Perhaps. I don't know, but perhaps with him that might do, for Flávio, with his lively, intelligent, free spirit. But what about the others? I remember how I was when I was a child," the teacher went on. "I was terrified in situations where I felt obliged to choose, decide, create. That's why a few days ago I took a drawing away from Flávio," she said, euphemistically, referring to its destruction at her hands. He had drawn a cat that couldn't exist. A cat of all different impossible colors. I couldn't accept his drawing. It would have been harmful not only to him but to the others, too—even more harmful to them than to him."

And that, it appeared, was the way the entire school functioned. It was not merely that one educator who shook with fear at the very mention of freedom, creation, adventure, risk. For the whole school, as for her, the world should not change, and just as in the story of the little pig, we ought never to leave the beaten path, or deviate from the established norm, in our passage through this world. Walk in the footsteps others have left for us. Lo, our lot and destiny.

Blaze trails as we go? Re-create the world, transform it? Never!

It was because of incidents like this, along with other, more serious occurrences, that the Spanish guest workers had created their school—the school that called their children's other school, the Swiss school, into question.

Of the memories that I retain of facts and events, over the course of the seventies, which were closely connected with *Pedagogy of the Oppressed,* there are moments that I shall never forget, so vivid and vital do they remain in my recollection.

Just now I am speaking of various encounters I had in Geneva—whether in my office at the World Council of Churches, or in the apartment we had in Grand Lancy—with intellectuals, teachers, students, religious, blacks, whites from South Africa. During the 1970s, rarely did a month go past that someone, a native of South Africa or at least someone who lived there and was passing through Geneva, did not come to speak with me of the tragic, absurd, unthinkable experience of racism.

Rare too was the occasion, in those days, when I did not have a conversation with a woman or man, white or black, of South Africa—on her or his way to the United States—on the same subjects as those of my other meetings in Geneva, as well as on different issues.

Rarely did much time pass between occasions when the phone would ring and I would pick it up to hear, "I landed in Geneva two days ago. I'm flying to South Africa tonight. I knew it'd be too risky for me to take *Pedagogy of the Oppressed* into the country with me, so I spent all last night reading it. Could I talk to you today, before I leave?" Naturally I never said no. I postponed other meetings, canceled interviews, changed agendas, but never said no to any of those requests. Headache, upset stomach, bad mood, weariness, homesickness for Brazil, reading to do, writing to do, no such reason could make me say no to any of these requests whatsoever. In the face of the emotional, and not only political, need with which they were accompanied in the one making the request, all such considerations became secondary ones. They carried no weight with me as an argument for refusing a meeting that, at times, was requested for a Saturday afternoon or Sunday morning.

The very moment someone asked on the phone whether he or she might come and consult with me, I felt the importance and urgency of the meeting so powerfully that I needed it as much as the one asking for it. I would have been frustrated myself, had I refused it.

My rebellion against every kind of discrimination, from the most explicit and crying to the most covert and hypocritical, which is no less offensive and immoral, has been with me from my childhood. Since as far back as I can remember, I have reacted almost instinctively against any word, deed, or sign of racial discrimination, or, for that matter, discrimination against the poor, which, quite a bit later, I came to define as class discrimination.

The evidence I heard from South Africans, white or black, in Geneva or in the United States, shocked me, and continues to shock me today when I recall it, as I am doing now. The brutality of racism is something beyond what a minimum of human sensitivity can encounter without *trembling*, and saying, "Horrible!"

I have heard from South African whites, or whites living in South Africa, who are as revulsed as I, who are as antiracist as I, traumatic accounts of unthinkable *discriminatory* practices. And from blacks as well. "I'm not allowed to say, 'My God,'" a young black church person told me, to my dismay and near incredulity at what I was hearing. "I have to say, 'Your God.'"

Blacks and whites, South Africans or residents of South Africa, with whom I conversed usually spoke of relations between oppressors and oppressed, colonizers and colonized, whiteness and blackness, employing theoretical elements common to Fanon, Memmi, and *Pedagogy of the Oppressed*. They were especially interested in discussing how to attack concrete situations, and how, through an in-depth approach to the "why" or "whys" of the sense of being crushed that the popular classes have of themselves, they might revise their earlier perceptions. In other words, they wanted to learn how to perceive their old perception of reality and adopt a new apprehension of the world, but without this meaning that, by reason of being perceived differently, the world were suddenly transformed. It meant that, on the basis of a new *apprehension* of the world, it would be possible to acquire the *disposition* to change it.

Today, I fear that some men and women, rightly disturbed, some intellectuals in revolt who sought me out in those days, may now be among those who have allowed themselves to be tamed by a certain high-sounding neoliberal discourse. They may have been won to the cause of those who find that, when all is said and done, "This is the way it is," this is how history is, this is how life is. The competent run things and make a profit, and create the wealth that, at the right moment, will "trickle down" to the have-nots more or less equitably. The discourse upon and in favor of social justice no longer has meaning, and if we continue to hold that discourse in this "new history" of ours, we shall be mounting obstacles to the natural process in which it is the capable who make and remake the world. Among these persons are to be found those who declare that we no longer have any need today of a militant education, one that tears the mask from the face of a lying dominant ideology; that what we need today is a *neutral* education, heart and soul devoted to the *technical training* of the labor force—dedicated to the transmission of content in all the emaciation of its technicity and scientism. But that's the old discourse!

These visits from South Africans or residents of South Africa, with their expressions of justifiable anger and necessary indignation, were contemporaneous with my first visit to Africa—to Zambia and Tanzania, once again in connection with *Pedagogy of the Oppressed*. I was to stop over in Zambia, where I would hold a week-long seminar in Kitwe, in a center for theological studies, Mindolo Ecumenical Foundation, then I would go on to Tanzania, for another seminar, at the University of Dar es Salaam. In both encounters, discussion would turn on *Pedagogy*, which was central to the "why" of the invitations I had been extended. While I was changing planes in Lusaka for a local flight to Kitwe, I was summoned to the "meeting area" on the airport public address system. Waiting for me there I found a young North American couple, whom I had met, I believe, in Boston, two or three years before. They were working in Zambia as volunteers, and had very good relations with the leadership of the MLA, the Movement for the Liberation of Angola.

We greeted each other with an embrace, and they asked me whether I could stay in Lusaka that day, and fly to Kitwe the next. The MLA team in Lusaka would like a conversation with me on problems of education and struggle, literacy programs in liberated areas, and so on. If I should accept, my friends told me, they would see to flight arrangements and advise the theological center in Kitwe.

By one o'clock that afternoon I was having lunch in the young couple's home with the MLA leaders, headed by Lúcio Lara, who within a few years would be second in the Angolan government and chief of the party's political bureau.

We spent an afternoon and night of work, using some documentary films to flesh out our conversations.

Lara started us off with a realistic report on the status of the liberation struggle, then we went back and forth about the educational practice to be applied during the struggle itself. We dwelt on an analysis of how to take advantage of the need for sheer survival in the struggle by turning that need to account in the discovery of more effective and more rigorous means or procedures than, for example, *benziduras* (spells) or simple talismans. But in no wise, not even here, where going beyond commonsense knowledge was a matter of life and death, would it be legitimate to belittle that knowledge or look down on it. It must be respected. A transcendence of commonsense knowledge, I was already saying back in those days, must be achieved only by way of that very knowledge.

Indeed, this was a conception dear to the heart of Amílcar Cabral, the great African leader who, alongside others, inspired the liberation movements in what are now the former Portuguese colonies: a more rigorous empowerment of his comrades through seminars in which they would be authentically trained and their methods evaluated, which he would conduct on his visits to the battle front. Cabral's objective was to overcome what he called *culture weaknesses* or *debilities*. He put it this way:

Let no one imagine that the officers of the revolutionary forces approve the notion that, if we carry a talisman in our belt, we shall not die in battle. No, we shall not die in battle if we do not wage war or attack the enemy from a position of weakness. If we make mistakes, if we are in a position of weakness, we shall certainly die. There is no way around that. You can tell me a string of stories that you have in your heads: "Cabral doesn't know. We've seen cases where it was the talisman that snatched our comrades from the jaws of death. The bullets were headed right for them, and they turned around and ricocheted back the other way." You can say that. But I have hope that our children's children, when they hear that, will be glad that PAIGEC [African Party for the Independence of Guinea and Cape Verde] was able to wage the struggle in accordance with the reality of their land—and not have to say, "Our grandparents fought really hard, but they believed in superstitions." This conversation may mean nothing to you now. I'm talking about the future. But I have certitude that the majority understand what I say, and know I am right.*

Interspersing our conversation with documentaries, we also discussed, at length, the question of literacy, and the imperative need that the struggle itself, as a process, enjoined upon its leadership: that they bend serious efforts to this end—in terms of activists' technical training, of course, with a view to the progress of the struggle, and to the use of more modern and more sophisticated weapons, which could require more sophisticated knowledge on the part of the activists. Simultaneously with this kind of preparation, however, should come the activists' political training. These persons, in the framework of Cabral's critical understanding, ought always to be armed *militants*—activists, yes, military never.

Years later, I had the opportunity to continue some of these conversations with Lúcio Lara, in Luanda, when he was working as chief of the party's Political Bureau, and when, at his invitation and that of the minister of education in Angola then, the poet Antônio Jacinto, who had spent seven years in the colonial dungeons, I

*Amílcar Cabral, *Obras escolhidas*, vol. 1, *Arma da teoria*, p. 141.

worked as a consultant to his ministry through the World Council of Churches.

That meeting in Lusaka left a deep mark on me. The same is true of my meeting in Dar es Salaam with the FRELIMO (Mozambique Liberation Front) leaders, at the Formation Campus for leaders and administrators, a short distance outside Dar in a lovely location placed at the disposal of the front by the Tanzanian government. Finally, I was invited to hold a dialogue with experienced activists currently engaged in the struggle and therefore having no time for woolgathering or intellectual tours de force. What they wanted was to dive into a critical, theoretical reflection with me on their practice, their struggle, as a "cultural fact and a factor of culture" (Cabral, 1976). Their confidence in me as a progressive intellectual was genuinely important to me. They did not criticize me for citing a peasant along with Marx. Nor did they regard me as a bourgeois educator because I maintained the importance of the role of consciousness in history.

That was a satisfaction. I, a thinker in the field of educational practice, had been understood by activists currently caught up in their struggle, and had been invited to hold a dialogue with them precisely concerning that struggle, sometimes an armed one and sometimes not. It was a satisfaction that accompanied me all through the seventies, and that has accompanied me to this very day, most recently in my visit to El Salvador, of which I speak at the end of this book. The same was true of my journey through all of the former Portuguese colonies (with the sole exception of Mozambique), my trips to Tanzania, my conversations with President Nyerere, in which we discussed "education as self-reliance" and *Pedagogy of the Oppressed,* my sojourns in Nicaragua, Grenada (that lovely Caribbean island that was the victim of an invasion), my encounter with Cuba. But along with the satisfaction of these encounters came the joy of so many others, at the four corners of the earth, with progressive folk who dreamt the possible dream of changing the world. And almost always, *Pedagogy of the Oppressed* had preceded me in these corners of the earth, in some sense paving the way for my own arrival there.

I remember writing, during my nights in Africa, in Kitwe, in Dar es Salaam, a harsh, strong report of my visit. My report transcribed stories I had heard from Africans from the period preceding the independence of Zambia or Tanzania, and I myself wrote of the cruel marks of colonialism and racism.

"A few years ago," a Tanzanian professor told me as we walked into the bar of the hotel where I was staying in Dar, "I wouldn't have been able to walk into this bar like this. Things were different. The warnings posted along our beaches were unbelievable: 'Blacks and Dogs Prohibited,' 'Blacks and Dogs Prohibited.'" My friend from the University of Dar was murmuring these words, softly, in a kind of singsong, facing me across the table in the bar, as if by repeating the offensive words of the shameful sign, he were somehow expressing the righteous wrath of women and men the world over in the face of the outrage represented by racism.

Afterwards I strolled along the beach with him—the beach that had once been off-limits for him, and accessible only to whites. His "genetic inferiority," according to the "science" of a professor who "coincidentally" was white, counterindicated that his Negro feet tread those white areas, and that his Negro body "pollute" the blue waters of his own sea. "Blacks and Dogs Prohibited," he kept whispering, as we left the beach and headed for his house for dinner.

There are no such signs posted on the beaches of Tanzania. But racism is alive and well, crushing, shredding people's lives, and besmirching the world.

As Patrick Lekota, Popo Molefe's comrade—two extraordinary black South African leaders—put it in a letter to a friend:

> Today we are receiving judgment. Earlier on I had some anxiety for my family. All my years are going to our struggle, and the question must cross their minds as to whether I still remember my obligations toward them. But now, all that has suddenly changed into unbridled rage with this system of South African law. This past week, an Afrikaner bully, Jacobus Vorster, was fined [$1,200] for tying an African laborer to a tree and beating him to death. He was then released to go back to his farm with an order that he pay the widow [$43] per month for five years. The laborer (deceased) had accidentally killed Vorster's one dog

and injured another one. . . . African life remains extremely
cheap in this country.*

So here is an instance of racism. But it is only one out of millions
of such violent, shameful, absurd instances.

Between January 3 and mid-February 1973, at the invitation of
the religious leaders associated with the World Council of Churches,
I visited twelve states of the United States. On that pilgrimage I
found myself together with countless educators. Once more with
Pedagogy of the Oppressed as mediator, I discussed their practice
with them, seeking to understand it critically in its given context.
Not always, let it be said in passing, were the groups in agreement
with the analyses I made of certain components of their historico-
social context. But none of the divergencies—even when they bore
on substantive issues, as we shall see below—rendered inviable a
generally rich, dynamic dialogue.

Working from an ecumenical perspective, the team responsible
for the study days had contacted the various groups of social workers,
scattered throughout the twelve states, who wished to be included
in these seminars, and set up with them a coordinating committee
to arrange the calendar of meetings.

On weekdays I met with groups, or leaders of movements that,
although they declined to join church groups for the process, were
not thereby excluded from the same.

On weekends, in a city of one of the states in which I was working,
a larger seminar would be held, with upwards of seventy participants. The main lines and themes of the discussions had been set
down minutely and in advance. For the last weekend, representatives of the twelve seminars crowded together for an evaluation
meeting in New York, whose framework had been constituted from
the reports of each of the twelve seminars.

As I have said, beginning in 1967 I visted the United States regularly, participating in meetings and giving talks, even apart from the
time I lived in Cambridge, at 371 Broadway (nearly a year). But
never had I been exposed in such systematic, direct contact with

*Rose Moss, "Shouting at the Crocodile," in *Popo Molefe, Patrick Lekota and
the Freeing of South Africa* (Beacon Press, 1990).

the complex and highly technologized reality of North America. Those forty-five days challenged me to the maximum, and taught me a great deal. I relearned things I had learned before, obvious things like the fact that *oneness in difference* will be the only effective response of those forbidden to be, those prevented from living, to the ancient rule of the mighty: *divide and conquer.* Without unity in diversity, the so-called minorities could not even struggle, in the United States, for the most basic (and therefore the "least," if we may so say) rights, let alone overcome the barriers that keep them from "being themselves," from being "minorities *for* themselves," *with* one another and not *against* one another.

The first time I made this statement on *unity in diversity* was in one of the weekend seminars of which I have just spoken. It was at a seminar in Chicago. It had begun in the morning, in the hotel where Elza and I had been put up, and where I had one of the most concrete experiences of discrimination I have ever had. We were sitting in the restaurant having breakfast. The waiters were going back and forth, taking care of customers to our right, to our left, in front of us, and at some tables a little way behind us, but passing us by as if we did not exist, or were under the effect of one of those marvelous science-fiction drugs that make you invisible.

It was an experience of discrimination that I shall never forget. And the reason why I shall never forget it is precisely that, after all the years I had lived without having it happen to me, it was suddenly happening to *me.* Deep down inside, I realized, I had not conceived of myself as a possible object of discrimination. Of course, this betokened a lack of humility on my part, to say the least.

We went without breakfast, even though (after my righteous protests, and the explosion of my no less righteous anger, softened a bit by Elza's more gentle manner) we left the restaurant to the accompaniment of the profuse apologies of the manager on duty, who was as racist as the waiters.

The hour was upon us: the seminar was scheduled to begin in a few moments. So we went to a cafe on the corner for an orange juice and a cup of coffee.

And so I walked into the big auditorium, where the participants had been waiting. I felt burdened—with a kind of sorrow, a great deal of anger, and a sense of helplessness, along with a little hunger, not to mention a hefty dose of frustration at not having my favorite American breakfast: "eggs up and a toasted English."

The coordinator opened the meeting. Then, one by one, the leaders of each of the various groups stood up and said, "We're black, and we'd like to meet just among ourselves." Or, "We're Indians. We'd like to be by ourselves." Or, "We're Mexican Americans, and we'd like a room to talk." Then, his voice ringing with sarcasm, a young black pointed at a group of whites and said: "This is the 'other' group!" The whites had been silent. And silent they remained.

In relations between blacks and whites, if I am not completely mistaken, there seems to be, on the part of many whites who do not regard themselves as racists, something that encumbers them in their dealings with blacks, and prevents them from mounting an authentic battle against racism. Here is what I mean. It seems—at least to me—that whites have strong guilt feelings with regard to blacks. And if there is anything that annoys those who suffer discrimination, it is to have someone dealing with them in a guilty tone. The presence of this feeling of guilt suggests, at the least, the existence of vestiges of the actual "why" of the guilt: in this case, traces of the preconception itself. Here is the reason for the posture of accommodation adopted by so many whites in the way they behave in situations like the one just described. What I mean to say is this. In my relations with blacks, with Chicanos, with gays and lesbians, with homeless persons, with workers white or black, there is no need for me to treat them paternalistically, brimming over with guilt. What I ought to be doing is discussing and debating things with them, disagreeing with them, as new comrades, or at least as possible comrades-to-be, comrades in the battle, companions along the way.

Actually, what the rejected ones need—those forbidden to be, prevented from being—is not our tepidity but our *warmth*, our solidarity—yes, and our love, but an unfeigned love, not a mistrustful one, not a soppy love, but an "armed" love, like the one of which poet Thiago de Melo tells.[49]

It was precisely amidst the silence that ensued among after the various "minority" leaders had claimed the right to isolation, that I spoke up.

"I respect your position," I said,

but I am convinced that the more the so-called minorities accept themselves as such, and close off from one another, the sounder the only real minority—the dominant class—will sleep. All through history, among the many self-proclaimed rights of power, power has always arrogated the right, as an intrinsic condition of its very being, to paint the portrait of those who have no power. And the picture the powerful paint of the powerless, to be incarnated by them, obviously will reinforce the power of those who have power, by reason of which they do their portrait painting. The colonized could never have been seen and portrayed by the colonizers as cultivated, capable, intelligent persons worthy of their liberty, or, for example, as the producers of a language that, because it is a language, advances and changes and grows historico-socially. On the contrary, the colonized will have to be barbarous, uncultured, "nonhistorical" persons—until the arrival of the colonizers, who 'bring' them history. They speak dialects, not languages, fated never to express "scientific truth," or "the mysteries of transcendence," or the "loveliness of the world."

Generally speaking, the powerless, in the early moments of their historical experience, accept the sketch the powerful draw of them. They have no other picture of themselves than the one imposed on them. One of the signs of nonconformism on the part of the powerless is rebellion against the portraits created of them by the powerful.

The so-called minorities, for example, need to realize that, when all is said and done, they are the majority. The path to their self-acceptance as the majority lies in concentrating on the similarities among themselves, and not only the differences, and thus creating *unity in diversity,* apart from which I fail to see how they can improve themselves, or even build themselves a substantial, radical democracy.

My discourse annoyed some of those present. "That's white talk," said the young black leader, lifting his index finger solemnly and looking daggers at me.

"No, this isn't white talk," I said. "It's intelligent, clear-sighted, progressive talk, and it could have been uttered by a black man, a black woman, a blue-eyed Irishman, a Chicano, anybody at all, as long as they're progressive. The only person who can't do this kind of talk is somebody whose self-interest would be served by the maintenance of the status quo. The only person who cannot logically speak in this way is a racist. Of course, it may be that, historically, right now, for any number of reasons, it is impossible to attain this oneness in difference. It may be, for example, that the grass roots of each 'minority' have not matured as yet, or have not sufficiently matured, to accept dialogue, accept 'being with' one another (or, more likely, their leaders have not). That's something else again. But to say that 'unity in diversity' is 'white talk'? No, that's not right."

The groups had divided up and isolated themselves. They held their discussions and arrived at various conclusions on certain problems.

CHAPTER

6

When the seminar was over, I took advantage of the fact that the matter had come up, and talked about it again. I insisted that, on the journey in quest of unity in diversity—a long, difficult, but completely necessary journey—the "minorities" (who, once more, are ultimately the majority) at odds with the majority have a great deal to learn.

After all, no one walks without learning to walk—without learning to walk by walking, without learning to remake, to retouch, the dream for whose cause the walkers have set off down the road. And I have heard tell of this again just recently, so long after that Saturday morning in Chicago. This is what the current leader of the *seringueiros* among the Rain Forest Peoples—Osmarino Amâncio, one of the disciples of Chico Mendes, recently the victim of a cowardly assassination— spoke of recently in ECO-Rio 92, with such candor and energy. His words, and the emphasis with which he uttered them in the presence of Chief Ianomami, reminded me of that seminar in Chicago.

"In the beginning," Amâncio declared, "we believed the story we were told by the mighty—that the Indians were our enemies. The Indians, on their side, manipulated by these same mighty ones, believed them as well—that we were their enemies. As time went by, we discovered that our differences should never be the reason for our killing one another on behalf of the interests of the mighty. We discovered that we were all 'Rain Forest People,' and that we have always desired only one thing around which we could unite: the rain forest. Today," he concluded, "we are a unity in our differences."

There is another learning process, another apprenticeship, of exceeding importance, but exceedingly difficult, especially in highly complex societies like that of North America. I mean the process of learning that a critical comprehension of the so-called minorities of one's culture is not exhausted in questions of race and sex, but requires a comprehension of the class division in that culture, as well. In other words, sex does not explain everything. Nor does race. Nor does class. Racial discrimination is by no manner of means reducible to a problem of class. Neither is sexism. Without a reference to the division between the classes, however, I, for one, fail to understand either phenomenon—racial discrimination or sexual—in its totality, or even that against the "minorities" in themselves. Besides skin color, or sex differentiation, ideology, too, has its "color."

Cultural pluralism is another serious problem that ought to be subjected to this kind of analysis. Cultural pluralism does not consist of a simple juxtaposition of cultures, and still less is it the prepotent might of one culture over another. Cultural pluralism consists in the *realization* of freedom, in the *guaranteed* right of each culture to move in mutual respect, each one freely running the risk of being different, fearless of being different, each culture being "for itself." They need the opportunity to grow together, but preferably not in the experience of an ongoing tension provoked by the almightiness of one culture vis-à-vis all the others, which latter would all be "forbidden to be."

The needed ongoing tension, among cultures in a cultural pluralism, is of a different nature. The tension that is needed is the tension to which the various cultures expose themselves by being different, in a democratic relationship in which they strive for advancement. The tension of which the cultures have need in a multicultural society is the tension of not being able to escape their self-construction, their self-creation, their self-production, with their every step in the direction precisely of a cultural pluralism, which will never be finished and complete. The tension in this case, therefore, is that of the "unfinishedness" that each culture accepts as the raison d'être of its very search and self-concern, the *why* of its nonantagonistic conflicts—conflicts ungenerated by fear, by prideful arrogance, by "existential weariness," by "historical anesthesia," nor, again, by an explosion of vengeance, by desperation in the face of an injustice that seems to go on forever.

We must also realize that the society to whose space other ethnic groups, for economic, social, and historical reasons, have come, to be "absorbed" here in a subordinate relationship, has its dominant class, its class culture, its language, its syntax, its class semantics, its tastes, its dreams, its ends—its projects, values, and historical programs. The society to whose space other ethnic groups have come has its dreams, projects, values, and language that the dominant class not only defends as its own—and since they are its own, calls them "national"—but also therefore "offers" to the others (along any number of paths, among them the school), and will not take no for an answer. There is no genuine bilingualism, therefore, let alone multilingualism, apart from a "multiculturality," and no multiculturality arises spontaneously. A multiculturality must be created, politically produced, worked on, in the sweat of one's brow, in concrete history.

Hence the need, once more, for the invention of unity in diversity. The very quest for this oneness in difference, the struggle for it as a process, in and of itself is the beginning of a creation of multiculturality. Let us emphasize once more: multiculturality as a phenomenon involving the coexistence of different cultures in one and the same space is not something natural and spontaneous. It is a historical creation, involving decision, political determination, mobilization, and organization, on the part of each cultural group, in view of common purposes. Thus, it calls for a certain educational practice, one that will be consistent with these objectives. It calls for a new ethics, founded on respect for differences.

In the early stages, the struggle for unity in diversity, which is obviously a political struggle, means mobilizing and organizing all the various cultural forces—without ignoring the class rift—and bringing these forces to bear on a broadening, a deepening, a transcending of a pure, laissez-faire democracy. We must adopt that democratic radicalness for which it is not enough merrily to proclaim that in this or that society man and woman enjoy "equal freedom," meaning the right to starve, have no schools to send their children to, and be homeless—so, the right to live in the street, the right not to be taken care of in old age, the right simply not to be.

It is imperative that we get beyond societies whose structures beget an ideology that ascribes responsibility for the breakdowns and failures actually created by these same structures to the *failed* themselves, as individuals, instead of to the structures of these societies or to the manner in which these societies function. If black urchins do not learn English well it is their own fault! It is due to their "genetic" incompetency, and not to the racial or class discrimination to which they are subjected, not to the authoritarian elitism that presumes to impose a "cultural standard"—an elitism that ultimately goes perfectly hand in hand with a complete disrespect for popular knowledge and popular speech. It is the same thing as occurs in Brazil. The little boys and girls of the hill and gully country fail to learn because they are *born* incompetent.

These were some of the subjects discussed in the study day of which I speak.

In the case of most of the positions I held in those days, and still hold, the reaction was not long in coming.

The worst thing would have been a well-behaved silence, concealing the discord. It was a good thing that the various groups—most of them, at any rate, expressed themselves, no matter that it have been against my view of the facts and problems.

Things have not changed a great deal between 1973 and 1994, when it comes to an all but systematic refusal on the part of antiracist and antisexist movements, even serious movements, to admit the concept of *social class* into a comprehensive analysis either of racism and sexism themselves, or of the struggle against them. And the same is true for the struggle against the thesis of unity in diversity.

Recently a university professor, black, female, a friend of mine, a serious, competent scholar, in conversation with me, my wife Nita, and Professor Donaldo Macedo, in Boston, vehemently denied any relationship between social classes and racism.

We listened to her, she listened to us, we listened to each other respectfully, as I listened in 1973 to those who who said no to my analyses.

If she had been offended by us, or we by her—because, for us, even though racism is not reduced to social class, we cannot understand the former without the latter, while for my friend this is not the case—had we offended each other, we would have fallen into a sectarian position as reprehensible as the racism we were execrating.

Even more recently, in July of this year, I experienced tough resistance on the part of a group of competent intellectuals, mostly of Mexican or Puerto Rican origin, in California, to the possible dream, the necessary utopia, of transcending this almost invincible taste for shutting oneself up in a ghetto, and moving on to the political invention of unity in diversity. On this occasion, too, my interlocutors extended their reaction to or rejection of the category of class to any analysis of North American reality.

Between sessions in the seminar I delighted in the reading of Manning Marabele.*

Another study day, with its unforgettable moments, marked my first visit to the Caribbean, with a program of meetings and discussions held on various islands, starting in Jamaica.

And on all the islands, with an occasional exception, the seminars were planned and coordinated by organizations working in popular regions in an advisory capacity on behalf of social movements on various levels and in various areas.

Once more, a reading of *Pedagogy of the Oppressed* and the application of some of its suggestions nearly always occasioned a discussion of matters in which I was confronted with identical problems, if "clothed" in different "trappings."

In the interest of brevity, I have selected three of the richer moments of my voyage, and I shall concentrate on them.

The first is connected with my being forbidden to enter Haiti, in whose capital I was to hold one of the seminars to discuss literacy and postliteracy programs.

In Geneva, through the World Council of Churches, I had obtained an entry visa for Haiti. Upon arriving in Kingston, however, I was informed by program organizers that Haitian authorities had informed them that I was prohibited from entering the country. So they had switched the seminar from Haiti to the Dominican Republic.

---

*Manning Marabele, *The Crisis of Color and Democracy: Essays on on Race, Class and Power* (Monroe, Maine: Common Conrage Press, 1992).

It will be worthwhile here more to underscore the attitudes of arbitrary power—of fear of freedom (and anger with freedom), of a horror of culture, of contempt for thought in the authoritarian and unpopular regimes—than for any other reason. It helps to understand just how it came about that I was prevented from entering Haiti in those days. I was told that, upon learning of the seminar coordinators' request that I enter the country, the national authorities, perhaps out of sympathy with the Brazilian military regime, decided to consult our embassy in Port-au-Prince.

The response, according to the same source, was a categorical "No." Obviously I can prove none of this, but none of it is very significant in comparison with the absurd pressure that, during the military regime, which called itself serious, democratic, and pure, was exerted not only against me, but against so many other Brazilians in exile. The first honorary doctorates that I received were bestowed in spite of ridiculous pressures put on the universities not to bestow them. My trip to UNESCO under FAO auspices occasioned incredibly flimsy and disgustingly petty reactions on the part of the military government then in power in Brazil.

After a great deal of pressure by my first wife, Elza, on the Brazilian consulate in Geneva, where she insisted on her own right and that of her minor children to carry the passport whose renewal had been denied them more than three years before, the Brazilian government then in power ordered that they be issued a document valid only for Switzerland, as if they had needed a passport to travel from Geneva to Zurich! I frequently referred, in the outside world, to the "creativity" of the Brazilian Foreign Affairs Ministry in this matter. It all came down to national diplomacy's having invented a "stay-in-port," with which it "took the wind out of the sails" of the life of less dangerous exiles!

The interesting thing is that Elza traveled with me through part of the world with her "stay-in-port." In the airports, the police carefully scrutinized that diplomatic anomaly, smiled, and stamped it, thereby manifesting their acceptance not only of the "stay-in-port" but of the human person who used it.

Let us return to our case.

As I was prevented from entering Haiti, another meeting had been arranged instead, in the Dominican Republic. It was to be with a popular education group, under Catholic auspices. Twenty to twenty-five educators wished to discuss with me, in particular, the question of the Generative Thematic, the actual programming of programmatic content, and my criticism of "banking" education. Heading toward the Dominican Republic, we made a stop in Port-au-Prince. I was traveling with a United Nations technologist and a Jamaican educator. For technical reasons, the flight to the Dominican Republic would not leave for three more hours. And so my friend the United Nations technologist telephoned a friend of his, who quickly came to the airport to drive us around the city.

I entered the country under prohibition from doing so, with my Swiss document inserted beneath my friend's passport. It was a blue passport, which, by "bluing" my own, preserved me from examination.

The little city struck me. Especially all the popular artists, who displayed their paintings in various corners of the squares. Their pictures were full of color, and spoke of the life of their people, the pain of their people, the joy of their people. It was the first time that, in the face of such loveliness, such artistic creativity, such a quantity of colors, I felt as if I were, as indeed I was, faced with a multiplicity of discourses on the part of the people. It was if the Haitian popular classes, forbidden to be, forbidden to read, to write, spoke or made their discourse of protest, of denunciation and proclamation, through art, the sole manner of discourse they were permitted.

By painting, they not only supported themselves and their families, but also supported, maintained, within themselves, possibly without knowing it, the desire to be free.

Some time ago, I conceived a huge desire to return to Haiti, legally, during the tenure of the elected, democratic government that has recently been overthrown by one more adventurer bent on defacing his world and imprisoning his people. Now, with this betrayal of the Haitian people, it is no longer possible. It is a pity that we have come to the end of the century, and the end of the millennium, still running the historical risk of suffering these cowardly coups against freedom, against democracy, against the right to be. Once again the dominant minority, invested with the economic and political power upon which their firepower, their destructive violence, rests, crushes the popular majorities in Haiti. Defenseless, these latter return to silence and immobility. Perhaps they will plunge into the popular arts—their festivals, their music, the very rhythm of their bodies. These things they must never renounce, and now they are an expression of their resistance, as well.

Little did I imagine, as I headed for the Dominican Republic, what awaited me there.

As a Brazilian citizen, I had not applied for an entry visa, since none was required by the Dominican regime then in power. The problem was that I did not even have my Brazilian "do-not-pass-port." I only had a Swiss travel document.

For the police at the airport, I was not Brazilian, I was a Swiss. And the Swiss needed a visa. As I had none, I was prohibited from entering. I was escorted, and none too politely, to "Departures" to reboard my plane, which would now go on to Puerto Rico.

My friend the United Nations technologist left the boarding area for the reception area, found the priest who had come to meet me, and told him what was happening.

Some fifteen minutes later, so soon after having been "recycled" to Puerto Rico, and from there to Geneva, via New York, I was sought out by the same police officer who had so discourteously escorted me to the waiting area from which I was to leave the country. "Kindly come with me, sir," he said, in a much different, more delicate, tone. "You are to enter the country."

At the moment I was far readier to leave than to stay, but the persons who were awaiting me must not be punished, nor must I fail to accomplish the task for which I had come to the Dominican Republic. I accompanied the police officer, to the tune of his profuse apologies, to the passport checkpoint, where the priest stood who would still have quite a time getting me into the country. I was listed as "disapproved," it seemed, in the airport register, now surely replaced by computers. My name—no, there was no mistake—was there, "Paulo Reglus Neves Freire," whole and entire, carefully penned, correct to the letter. This meant that I might not enter the country after all, and this time for far more serious reasons than merely not having a visa. Not this time. This time I found myself on an exceedingly lengthy list of "undesirables"—"dangerous subversives," who posed a "threat," as, for example, traffickers in contraband.

The only solution, said the chief of the Airport Police, who had been summoned for his opinion, was for the priest who had invited me to speak with the national security chief. The latter alone had the authority to make the final decision. The police chief himself made the call, then handed the phone to the priest.

"Yes, General. Yes," said the priest, "if Professor Freire is willing to accept these conditions, I shall be responsible for him."

And with his hand over the mouthpiece, the priest asked me: "Will you stay the five days here without leaving the building where we're having the seminar? And the press must not know you're in the country. No one must know. Do you accept?"

"Of course I accept. I came here to converse, to teach, and to learn, not to make side trips or give interviews. I accept. There is no problem," I replied.

"Very well, General. Professor Freire is grateful for the opportunity of entering our country under the conditions you have established, and I guarantee that they will be fulfilled to the letter."

He handed the phone to the chief of police, who listened to the orders of the national security chief.

I got in. I worked five days. I heard excellent reports on work in progress in rural and urban areas.

This is what I had come for. It would have betokened political immaturity on my part if, out of some personal vanity, and feeling belittled, I had refused the general's proposal.

In the five days I spent in the country, without giving any interviews, without appearing in the streets, without touring the city, I nevertheless did what I had come there to do.

On the last day, on the trip back to the airport, the father made some discreet detours through the city so I could get a general idea of it.

Beyond a doubt, this experience is not to be compared with the one I had some months later, when I was arrested one night in a hotel in Libreville, Gabon, in Africa, where I had arrived at the invitation of the recently installed government of São Tomé and Príncipe.

What an irony, by the way, to be arrested in a city called Libreville, for being "exceedingly dangerous," and having "written a sub-versive book," as I was informed, without any beating around the bush!

"But sir," I said to the officer whose demeanor was certainly that of a chief of police, "I'll only be in your country for twenty-four hours, while I wait for my flight to São Tomé tomorrow afternoon. Besides, I'm passing through here at the invitation of the government of São Tomé and Príncipe. So I only see an abuse of power here in what you have just communicated to me, and I protest that abuse: that I will be held at the hotel until tomorrow's flight."

"You are not under arrest. You are our guest. Only, you may not leave your room."

A few moments later, at the hotel, my room was locked from the outside.

Not under arrest! Strange terminology.

There was one thing about that first visit to the Caribbean that impressed me a great deal: the experiment I visited on the lovely little isle of Dominica.

Peasants living on a large, financially troubled ranch, which had been a key contributor to the country's agricultural production, had persuaded the government to buy the ranch (with the cooperation of the British company that ran it) and hand it over to them, where-upon they undertook to purchase it over the course of so-and-so many years.

The peasants then created a cooperative, with the technological assistance of an agricultural engineer who had been working with them. When I visited the experiment, they had already been manag-ing the property for a little over a year, and were having excellent results.

There is a personal aspect of my visit that I should like to make public in this book—an experience of which I spoke of with my children after my return to Geneva. I was visiting the ranch as the guest of the president of the peasant cooperative that was managing the economic, social, and educational life of the ranch. He lived with his wife—no children—in a very simple house, without elec-tricity, on a little hill, the kind of hillock we call a *morro* in Brazil. In front of the house stood a lush mango tree, some bushes, and a green lawn.

It was raining when I got out of the car to climb the slippery, muddy slope—its clay a "cousin" to the *massapé* of Brazil's Northeast. With a slip here and a slide there, my right hand tight on the arm of the president of the cooperative, my feet groping for a foothold, finally we got to the house, which was lighted by a kerosene lamp.

We spoke a bit, the president and I. His wife, in a corner of the room, was listening, but not venturing to say anything.

I was tired, and I had my mind more on going to bed than on anything else.

Before going to my room—their own room, which they had put at my disposition in a gesture of siblingship—naturally I wanted to use the bathroom. Then it was that I perceived how far removed I was from the concrete daily life of peasants, despite my having written the book they had read in their study circles and therefore invited me to come talk with them.

The more I needed to go to the bathroom, the less casual I felt about asking where it was. This could be complicated. I said to myself, if I ask where the bathroom is, and there is no bathroom, how will I be understood?

Suddenly I said to myself: am I not being a bit like the white liberals who feel guilty when they talk with blacks?—the behavior to which I have referred a few pages earlier. Only, this time the division is a class one. I summoned up my courage, then, and asked my friend: "Where's the bathroom?"

"The bathroom? The bathroom is the world," said Mr. President, courteously conducting me beneath the mango tree, where we both raised the level of the water flowing down through the grass.

Other than the bathroom, my major problem was, the next day, how to take my morning bath. My morning bath, in the fashion that I take it, has to do with my class position—just as does the way I speak, for example with the verb agreeing with the subject, or my dress, or my gait, or my tastes.

It was a fine thing for me to be living and dealing not only with the couple with whom I stayed, but with the other peasants there. It was a fine thing, especially, to be able to observe how they came at the question of education, culture, technical training—they and their companions in the co-op.

To this purpose, I spent two or three days actually out in the fields, besides joining in a conference set up by the leadership and attended by well-nigh seventy peasants at which we discussed questions of curricular organization and problems of teaching and the learning process.

After a little over a year of being their own bosses, under a democratic regime—without, therefore, the abuses of, on the one hand, permissiveness and unlimited freedom, or on the other, unlimited authority—the work of the ranch was genuinely exemplary. The contribution of the agronomist, their educator, with his seriousness and competence, was lauded by all.

The peasants had set up some ten centers throughout the area— ten "nuclei," each managed by a team and headed by an elected officer. They had built ten rustic adobe meeting rooms. They had gotten sawhorses and laid boards on them for tables. The little rooms each had an extension, or a corner, that served as a kitchen, where the members of that particular center met for lunch and social refreshment. All of the members of the area around each center would bring whatever they could—a chicken, a fish, some fruit, or the like. Teams of two persons, a man and a woman, took turns preparing the food.

Every day the workers had two hours for lunch, during which time they discussed problems of daily experience. One of the members of each center, also in rotation, was in charge of noting down the subjects discussed, or even broached, in the daily meeting. These subjects, the material of the daily meetings, would then be brought up at the big meeting held every other Saturday at the co-op office itself, with the agricultural engineer or other experts present. The ranch in its entirety was regarded by the peasants not only as a center of economic production, but as their cultural center, as well. When you got right down to it, the ten "cultural nuclei" were the best way they had found to divide up the ranch as a totality, in the process of improving their knowledge and training, just as the biweekly meeting was the effort to, shall we say, "retotalize" the divided totality.

It was an experiment in popular education directly connected with production, and I saw it functioning in an exemplary manner. This was in the 1970s.

Recently, participating in an international conference in Montego, Jamaica (May 1992), I met an educator from the Dominican Republic. We got on the subject of things that had happened years ago, and I immediately asked her whether she knew how the work on the community ranch was going. "It's all over. Politics," she said.

Toward the end of 1979 and the beginning of 1980, I was twice more in the Caribbean. On these occasions my destination was Grenada, the magnificent little island that, seemingly overnight, almost magically, had mounted a revolution that, all fine and gentle that it was, nevertheless failed to escape the fury of the teeth-gnashing, raging folk who own the world—any more than that of the raging folk who, while not proprietors of the world, think themselves proprietors of revolutionary truth.

The revolution in Grenada resulted, in its final moment, from an almost Quixotic geste on the part of its leader, a still-young, ardent leader, one who had great confidence in his people.

Taking advantage of the absence of the head of the government, Bishop and a dozen companions attacked a police station. It surrendered without resistance. With the weapons captured there, they were able to arm other militants, then still others. Meanwhile, government forces joined the movement. And the entire government establishment had collapsed as if it had been run over by a steamroller. It was a revolution that had been waiting to happen. Without the malaise of the popular masses, without their hope and their readiness for change, the "wild idea" of Bishop and his companions might not have gotten by the second obstacle.

History does not surrender or bow docilely to the arrogant will of the voluntarist. Social transformations occur upon a coinciding of the popular will, the presence of a leadership blessed with discernment, and the propitious historical moment. Thus, a popular movement seized power with a minimum of social cost. Ruling interests did not even have time to react. The island was preparing to walk in a different direction. A different government was attempting to change the face of the country.

My first visit to the island had been arranged a month before, in Managua, Nicaragua, where I had gone at the invitation of Fernando Cardenal, then Literacy Crusade Coordinator and later education minister. It was in Managua, where I gave the crusade a bit of

myself, as well, and my understanding of education, that my friend
Arturo Ornelles, who had worked with me in São Tomé, in Africa,
and who was then working in the Education Sector of the Organization of American States, informed me of the Grenadan ministry of
education's interest that I should visit that country. It was up to me,
Arturo told me.

Arturo took charge of communicating to the government of Grenada that I had accepted the invitation, but that the minister would
have to request my trip to his country from the World Council of
Churches, in whose Education Division I was working. Everything
was in order, and in mid-December we arrived in Grenada, where
every indication was that only the power elite outside the government and their foreign masters radically opposed the country's new
political direction. What else could have been expected? They were
defending their class and race interests.

They must have been jubilant, then, when Mr. Bishop's assassination at the hands of the sectarian, authoritarian fanaticism of an
incompetent Left—occasioning such a strong reaction on the part
of Fidel Castro—further facilitated the already-easy invasion of the
island. And so the dreams of the popular majorities were demolished. Now they would continue to live their difficult life, perhaps
plunged once more into the fatalism in which there is no place
for utopia.

This was not the historical climate at the time of my two visits to
Grenada. On the contrary, a contagious joy was afoot. People spoke
with the hope of persons who were beginning to share in the re-
creation of their society.

Three meetings on the first visit left an indelible impression on
me. One consisted of an entire day of conversations with the minister
and various national teams, in which we discussed certain basic
aspects of the new education they were gradually attempting to put
in practice.

Together, we reflected on an education that, while respecting children's understanding of the world, would challenge them to think
critically. It would be an education in whose practice the teaching
of content would never be dichotomized from the teaching of precise
thinking. We spoke of an antidogmatic, antisuperficial thinking—a

critical thinking, which would constantly resist the temptation of pure improvisation.

Any effort in the direction of implementing the above considerations—that is, any attempt to put into practice an education that, first, while respecting educands' understanding of the world, will challenge them to think critically, and second, will refuse to separate the teaching of content from the teaching of thinking precisely—any such educational enterprise calls for the ongoing formation of the educators. Their scientific training, above all, calls for a serious, consistent effort to overcome the old authoritarian, elitist frameworks, which linger, latent, in the persons in whom they "dwell" and are ever ready to be reactivated. And without the exercise of this attempt to surmount the old—an attempt that involves our subjectivity, and implies the acknowledgment of its importance, a subjectivity so disdained and belittled by the dogmatism that reduces it to a mere reflex of objectivity—no attempt at changing the school by steering it in a democratic direction will likely carry the day.

The two principles I have just stated can actually base an entire transformation of the school, and of the educational practice within it. Starting with these two points, I told the educators in our meetings, it would be possible for us to proceed to develop any number of dimensions, with innovations in curricular organization, with a new relationship between educators and educands, with new human relations in the school (administration, teachers, maintenance, security), new relations between the school and families, new relations with the neighborhood the school is in.

It was appropriate that, in February of the following year, 1980, a National Leadership Training Seminar should be held, which would subsequently develop into dozens of training meetings all over the island.

Invited to the February seminar, which had been set up by the Education Sector of the Organization of American States—the agency in which Arturo worked, as I have already mentioned—were Brazilian sociologist, now professor at the Federal University of Pernambuco, João Bosco Pinto, Chilean educational sociologist Professor Marcela Gajardo, who was unable to attend, myself, and naturally, Arturo Ornelles.

The second meeting that impressed me so much on my first visit to Grenada was the one I had with administrators of the ministry of education. The minstry set aside a morning for our dialogue, to which all were invited, including clerks, chauffeurs, secretaries of the various departments, and typists.

"I am convinced," the minister told me, in requesting the meeting, "that we'll never manage to change, to redirect, pedagogical policy, and place it in the democratic perspective we're striving for, unless we can count on the participation of all of the sectors that, in one way or another, make up the ministry of education. Nor shall we be able to do anything without the cooperation of the educands, their families, their communities."

This was actually the first time a new administration that was gradually taking things in hand had invited me to speak to its educational personnel on the importance of our school tasks, whether our own particular job be to sweep the classroom floor or to construct educational theory. Nor did I practice any demagogy in my approach, any more than I do today.

Reactions ranged from stunned surprise on some faces, to great curiosity and an ebullient eagerness to learn more in the expressions worn by the majority.

One of the conclusions my auditors came to as they sat there with the minister was that meetings like the one we were holding ought to be held on a systematic basis, although attendance would be optional.

The third meeting I was to hold was with Mr. Bishop himself. He received Arturo Ornelles and me, at the presidential residence, for nearly three hours. Our conversation was over fruit juice, and we had at our disposition, for tasting (or ravenous gulping), on a side table, a luscious tray of native fruits.

At the moment I write, and comb my memory, I wonder about two or three qualities of that person, so soon to be erased from the world that loved him, which touched Arturo and me in our conversation with him.

I think I might begin with his simplicity and lack of artificiality. It was the simplicity of a person who lived a life of consistency between what he said and what he did. He did not even need to make an effort to keep from falling into self-adulation. It was thus that, with simplicity, at times with the smile of a child, he spoke to us of the adventurous exploit (but not that of an adventurer) that he had undertaken, he and his companions, in search of the assumption of the power that he then sought to re-create.

He had a taste for freedom, and a respect for the freedom of others. He was determined to help his people help themselves, mobilize, organize, retrace the outlines of their society. He had a clear sense of historical opportunity—an opportunity that does not exist outside of ourselves, an opportunity that makes its appearance in a certain compartment of time, waiting for us to pursue it, but an opportunity that is waiting precisely in the relationship between ourselves and time itself—an opportunity deep in the heart of events, in the interplay of contradictions. It is an opportunity that we ourselves create, right in history—in a history that punishes us both when we fail to take advantage of the opportunity, and when we simply invent it in our heads, without any foundation in social fabrics.

I remember his dialectical way of thinking (not a way of *speaking about dialectics*). The impression I have now, in recalling the meeting, is that Bishop thought dialectically so spontaneously and habitually that there was no separation in him between discourse and practice. Hence, for example, the understanding he revealed in conversation of the importance of subjectivity in history, which led him to recognize the role of education before and after the production, or better, the effort to produce, a new power.

Perhaps this was one of the points, developed in the political practices of his government, that provoked the "mechanists," as I call them, who are so very undialectical and who turned against him.

At one moment in my conversation, Bishop asked me something that revealed his great relish for democracy, and revealed the remarkable similarity between him and the great African leader Amílcar Cabral, about whose struggle we were enthusiastically speaking. Bishop asked me to devote some of my time to the military during my visit to the island. He said something like: "It would be very helpful if you discussed with them the frankly *civil* spirit with which, and with which alone, we can remake our society."

Even without expressing it in so many words, Bishop perceived that, at bottom, in the democratic reinvention of society, the military fit in only when they know their function in the service of civil society. The military fit into civil society, not the other way around.

And of course this was one of the things I stressed in my conversation with the military. It provoked certain silences, perhaps in an expression of disapproval.

Of my meetings, the one with the military was the one that impressed me the least. Before, I had met with some higher-ranking officers, in Lima, and in Lisbon, after the so-called Carnation Revolution. I had had three hours of conversation with majors and colonels from the various branches. They were a youthful folk, weary of an unjust, impossible war in Africa.

What was happening, really, was that the Portuguese colonial armed forces, even in the mid-1970s, enervated by a war in which they had gradually come to perceive the absurdity of the process, were having to face off with Africans with whom just the reverse was happening: they were growing in the conviction of the ethical and historical correctness of their struggle.

My encounter with the Portuguese military, who had thus been "conscientized" by the African war—a meeting arranged by a major who told me he had read *Pedagogy of the Oppressed* over and over (over and over in secret, obviously) and had used it on the underground assignments he carried out with other members of the military—revealed to me, among other things, this obvious basic point: the agents of war are not only the highly technical instruments employed, invaluable though they be; nor are they only men and women. The agents of war are men, women, and instruments.

For the success of the fight, the ethical awareness and political awareness of the fighters is of paramount importance. Technology is at times replaced by the weaker side's power of invention, which emerges from a strength they possess that is lacking to the mighty: their ethical and historical conviction that their fight is legitimate.

This is what happened in Vietnam, as well, where a highly advanced North American technology yielded to a *will to be* on the part of the Vietnamese, and to their artful inventiveness, that of the weaker side.

So this is what happened in Grenada, itself, where a lack of ethical and historical conviction on the part of the side possessing the weapons gave way to the force of a courage armed with the ethics and the history with which Bishop and his companions came to power.

In February 1980 we returned to Grenada, Arturo and I, along with João Bosco Pinto, who was making his first trip there.

First off, we had a meeting with the national planning committee for the seminar, where we learned how the seminar would function, and what task would fall to each of us.

The intention of all of us, the national team's as well as our own, was to steer the labors of the seminar as much as possible in the direction of a unification of practice and theory. We therefore excluded, from the outset, a course consisting of "theoretical" discourses, however fine they might be, on theory and practice, school and community, the cultural identity of the educands, the relationship between educators and educands, or what it is to teach and what to learn. Or on the question of programmatic content and how to organize it. Or on an investigation of the milieu in which the school is located, or in which various schools in the same area are located. And so on.

Of course, we should have to create, imagine, hypothetical situations—authentic codifications—upon which we would ask the participants of the seminar, whom we would present with elements typifying the situation, to spend a given amount of time to write their analyses: in other words, to decode the codification.

On the basis of the example that I shall now give, we shall be able to imagine the others, for which, regrettably, none of us any longer has any documentation. Let me take the example of a sketch in which we could see a *school* typical of the island, with a given number of elements of its ambience included.

The coordinating committee asked the members of the seminar to:

A. Characterize, describe, what they saw in the picture, in purely narrative terms.

B. Describe and analyze a day's routine, not only of the school, but also of the area around the school.

C. Describe, this time more in detail—on the basis of experience, if they had had such experience, or else on the basis of what they had heard—relations between the teachers and students in such a school.

D. In case of a need to criticize the kind of relationship prevailing between teachers and students in the school, to try to identify the causes of that relationship, and to make suggestions as to how to improve it.

E. Answer the following question: what do you think is good or bad about a rural school in whose programmatic content there is nothing, or almost nothing, about rural life?

F. Answer this question: in your own practice, what is it, to you, to teach, and what is it, to you, to learn?

G. Answer this question: do you find that the role of the teacher is to mold students in accordance with some ideal model of men and women, or instead, to help them to grow, and to learn to be themselves? Defend your position.

As I say, there were other such investigatory projects. The participants had two-and-one half hours to answer, beginning at 8:00 A.M.

Beginning at 10:30, we read the answers. First, each of us individually read them. Next, we discussed the various reports among ourselves. Then, for part of the afternoon, we discussed their implicit or explicit theoretical, political, and methodological aspects with the entire group.

The dialogue we held with the national educators was a rich one. Their analysis and their positions stimulated our reaction. And we, the coordinators of the seminar, engaged in discussions about how we reacted to the reaction of the national educators.

Over the course of three days, while, from 8:00 to 10:30 A.M., the participants answered the questions proposed to them, we met with various cabinet members (the ministers of agriculture, health, and planning) and conversed with them about the possibility and need of a common effort in which the efforts of their ministries would be combined with those of the ministry of education—or better, the possibility and need to have the ministry of education, in planning its policy, do that planning in light of what those of agriculture, health, and planning had in mind for the country.

I remember that, in our second and last meeting with Mr. Bishop, we spoke of this need of a comprehensive view of the country—the importance of an interconnection among the various sectors of the government, with a view to an adequate balance between the means and ends of each respective ministry, as well as an adequate communication among them all. We spoke of the question of ethics in addressing the public welfare, and of the candor with which the government, regardless of the breadth or depth of its activity, from a police department in a remote corner of the island to the prime minister's cabinet, should say or do things. Everything should be out in the open. Everything should be explained. We spoke of the pedagogical nature of the act of governing, of its mission of formation and of offering an example, which requires utter seriousness on the part of those who govern. There is no such thing as an authentic, legitimate, credible government if its discourse is not confirmed by its practice, if it practices political patronage and the pork barrel, if it is severe only with the opposition and kind and gentle with its coreligionists. If you give in once, twice, three times to the shoddy ethics of the mighty—or even of your "friends," who are exerting pressure on you—the floodgates will open. From now on there will be only scandal upon scandal, and connivance with scandals ends by anesthetizing its agents and generates a climate typical of the "democratization of shamelessness."

As I sit here recalling these twelve-year-old things I am thinking about what we are experiencing today in Brazil. The avalanche of scandals at the highest levels of power become an example for the simple citizenry and the people.

Everything becomes possible: deceit, betrayal, lying, stealing, falsifying, kidnapping, calumny, murder, assault, threats, destruction, taking "thirty pieces of silver," buying bicycles as if they were going to open bicycle rental shops all over the country. We must put a stop to everything being possible.

The solution, obviously, is not in a hypocritical puritanism, but in a conscious, explicit relish for purity.

"I'd like to talk with you a bit, sir," said a young man with a

Portuguese accent, phoning me one Sunday morning in Geneva in the spring of 1971.

I quickly consulted Elza, and with her consent asked him to come over for breakfast. I was then to spend the afternoon working on an upcoming interview for a European periodical. And so, inviting him to come for 11:00 A.M., I told him in the same breath that at 2:30 I was going to have to start a job with a Monday morning deadline.

In Geneva, everything runs on time. Even the buses run on time. The 10:04 bus actually comes at 10:04. And if it doesn't, it would be no surprise if the people of the neighborhood received a courteous letter from the Department of Public Transportation asking forgiveness and promising that it won't happen again.

And so it was not long after the phone call that the doorbell rang, and the young man, indeed a Portuguese, had arrived. Uncomfortable, and speaking rapidly, the boy swallowed his syllables, and slurred some vowels in the words of his structure of thought, playing them differently from the way we in Brazil make them "dance" in our thought structure. It was just what we Brazilians and Portuguese find so annoying in conversation with each other. It is not precisely the tighter rhythm of Portuguese speech that annoys us, and our more open rhythm that annoys them. It is the syntax. Nor is it the semantics inextricably imbedded in the syntax. It is the syntax itself, the thought structure. This is what annoys us both.

In 1969, two years before that morning in Geneva when I conversed with the uneasy young man, I had received, in the United States, a series of little notes, several of them written on the same sheet of paper, from Portuguese who had only recently learned to read and write. They had been sent by peasants of a rural area near Coimbra. They were writing to me to express their gratitude for what I had done for them, to tell me of their friendship, and to invite me, when political conditions should permit, to come and visit them, so that I might receive their embraces and hear of their fondness for me.

A young American was the bearer of the messages, and she brought me one more thing along with them—a banner, or pennant. The motto on the pennant, by the way, is worth pondering: "There are people who can make flowers grow where it had seemed impossible." Yes, they might have thought they had been born to a sure fate, under the sign of an inability to read *words*, and had been convinced of this. But they had learned to read words. And so the reason must have been outside themselves! In their teachers and in me. Of course, had they failed, the reason would have had to be inside themselves.

I answered all of those who had written to me by penning little cards, in a simple, though never simplistic, language, and addressing them in care of Maria de Lourdes Pintacilgo, who within a few years would become prime minister of Portugal, and who at the time, together with Tereza Santa Clara, was heading the efforts of a group of excellent folk working in the area of popular education. The literacy campaign in that rural area near Coimbra was only a small part of what was being accomplished by that dedicated, competent, loving, and discerning Grail team.

At one point in our conversation, that Sunday morning on which I report here, the young Portuguese gentleman referred directly to the work at Coimbra. "Does Paulo Freire know how a group of Catholic women have perverted his ideas in the countryside around Coimbra?"

"What I know of the work done in Coimbra doesn't seem to me to be a distortion of my proposals. By all indications, it was simply what could concretely be done," I said, and I went on: "Under what regime, under what police observation do you think those young women were working in Coimbra?"

But without answering my questions, the young man insisted that "they had not associated the literacy campaign with the political struggle against Salazar. They were just nice little Catholic girls. They had no understanding of the class struggle as the thrust of history," he concluded, triumphantly.

Three years had passed since the *conscientização* of the Portuguese colonial armed forces. The Carnation Revolution had erupted. A new government was in place, and had initiated the process of democratizing Portugal and decolonizing the Africa once misnamed "Portuguese."

Hope reigned. Spirits forbidden to so much as speak shouted and sang. Minds prohibited from thinking discoursed, and burst the bonds that had held them.

I visited Portugal at the invitation of the new government, in which the university had joined, and I spoke to teachers and students. I visited Coimbra, and its university. And of course, led by the same loving, dedicated young women who had believed in God and in the need to change the world in behalf of the outcast and had done such wonderful service in the environs of the city, I visited the peasants who, in 1969, had written me those cards that spoke of their brotherly and sisterly love. I embraced them all, lovingly. Our personhoods were, as it were, inscribed on one another's hearts, and our affectionate discourse expressed a mutual gratitude. Theirs to me. Mine to them all.

It was that morning in Coimbra, out in the country, that I learned of the little rural community that, along with a small number of others, had given such complete support to the revolutionary government at one of the moments when the Right was flailing about in all its frenzy. One of the more daring of the elderly peasants taking the literacy course with the young women of the Grail got up early one particular morning, and, before anyone else was awake, went around collecting all the Fascist propaganda that had been distributed during the night in her little village. The whole village refused to support the rightist demonstration to which they had been invited by these pamphlets!

No discourse on the class struggle had been necessary during the literacy course, however real that struggle might be, in order for her and her companions to perceive, once the right moment had come, the relationship between the reading of the word, the reading of the world, and above all, the transformation of the world!

The only sensible way for the Catholic girls to have done their work had been within the limits of good tactics. Any other approach would have been "reactionary."

News of the Carnation Revolution took me by surprise on a thirty-five-day visit to Australia, New Zealand, and some of the principal islands of the region. *Pedagogy of the Oppressed*, once more, was at the center of the frameworks of our meetings. Its publication by Penguin Books, as I have pointed out, enabled it to reach all of that world, along with India, and the misnamed "British" Africa.

Never have I accepted the denomination of British, French, or Portuguese Africa, not to mention the other "Africas." I have disputed with friends in the ministries of the Portuguese ex-colonies ("Portuguese ex-colonies," yes) a number of times, arguing against the designation of a "Portuguese-speaking Africa." I do not believe in the existence of such a thing, any more than in that of a "French-speaking" or "English-speaking" Africa. What we have is an Africa over which there hovered, in domination, colonial-style, the Portuguese *language*, the French *language*, the English *language*. That is another matter.

The big risk, or one of the big risks, of these Africas is that, partly out of nostalgia for the old colonial days—under the impulse of the ambivalent feeling the colonized have for the colonizers, one of repulsion and attraction at once, to which Memmi (Albert Memmi) refers—partly from necessity, partly under pressure, linguistic "ex-expressions" consisting of the old linguistic bonds would now deepen into an incarnation of a new kind of "language" or expression: the neocolonial. Not that I defend, for the various Africas, the absurdity, the impossibility, of an absolute breach with the past, which basically remains untransformed, and a renunciation of the positive factors in the cultural influences of old Europe. What I defend and recommend is a radical breach with colonialism, and an equally radical rejection of neocolonialism. I call for the defeat of the colonial bureaucracy, as I actually suggested to the governments of Angola, Bissau, and São Tomé and Príncipe; the defeat of the colonial school, the formulation of a cultural policy that would take seriously the question of the national languages, which the colonizers called, pejoratively, "dialects."

In fact, colonized persons and colonial nations never seal their liberation, conquer or reconquer their cultural identity, without assuming their language and discourse and being assumed by it.

That a Portuguese, a French, a British ex-colony not turn its back on these languages and these cultures, that they make use of them, that they study them, that they take advantage of their positive elements, is not only right and good, but altogether needful. The basic thing, however, is that the country that receives "foreign aid," in whatever form that aid be offered, technological or artistic, do so as an active, autonomous agent, and not as the passive object of the transfer effectuated by the other country. I was once told, perhaps by way of caricature, that a certain African country had received foreign aid (to be repaid, however) from the former Soviet Union, in the form of a snowplow, for clearing the streets after snowstorms! In this case, it was the Soviet Union that fluttered over this country of Africa!

But to get back to the trip to Australia, New Zealand, Papua New Guinea, and Fiji. I shall omit any commentaries on the beauty, in some cases the peerless beauty, of this region, and attempt to concentrate on one or other point of the theory of which I speak in *Pedagogy of the Oppressed,* a theory anchored in my own practice rather than in other persons' practices that I would have been able to explain theoretically. This was true, by and large, of everything I did on the journey, in discussion, research, negative criticism, concordant analysis, and requests for explanation.

In Australia, especially, I had the opportunity of associating with intellectuals, Marx's loyal allies, who precisely as his authentic followers had grasped the dialectical relationship between the world and consciousness, and had assimilated the theses defended in *Pedagogy of the Oppressed* rather than looking upon it as a volume of idealism. But I also dialogued with persons imprisoned in a dogmatism likewise of Marxist origin, who, while not precisely belittling consciousness, reduced it to a mere shadow of materiality. For those who thought in this way, mechanistically, *Pedagogy of the Oppressed* was a book of bourgeois idealism. Actually, however, one of the reasons why this book continues to be as much sought after as it was twenty-two years ago may be precisely because of content that led certain critics of that time to regard it as idealistic and bourgeois. I refer to the importance the book ascribes to consciousness, without, however, seeing consciousness as the arbitrary maker of the world. I refer to its recognition of the manifest importance of the individual, without ascribing to individuals as such a strength they do not have. I mean the weight, which the book likewise recognizes, in our life, individual and social, of feelings, passion, desires, fear, insight, the courage to love, to be angry. I mean the book's vehement defense of humanistic positions, but without ever sliding into sloppy sentimentalism. I mean its understanding of history, in whose intermingled context and motion it seeks to understand that of which it speaks. I mean its rejection of sectarian dogmatic opinions. I mean its relish for the ongoing struggle, which generates hope, and without which the struggle withers and dies. I mean *Pedagogy's* pervasive opposition, so "early on," to the neoliberals, who fear the *dream,* not the impossible—since the impossible should not even be dreamt of, while the dream makes things possible—in the name of facile adaptations to the catastrophes of the capitalist world.

Many in the 1970s, sometimes in a letter addressed to me, said: "I desiderate the Marxist presence in your analyses, or your ignorance of the fact that 'the class struggle is the driving force of history.' But I think" (and these persons were the most sensible of the lot!) "that we can get something out of what you are doing and saying by 'rewriting' you in a Marxist vein." And many of the men and women who thus expressed themselves are to be found today, sadly, in the ranks of the "pragmatic realists," although at least they acknowledge the social classes when they walk through the hills, gullies, slums, *callampas,* and streets of Latin America.

And so I traveled through much of Australia. I held discussions with factory workers, with "aborigines," as they are called (I was received by one of their groups at a special meeting). I held debates with university professors and students, and with religious groups, Protestant and Catholic. In the religious groups, whether Catholic or Protestant, the launching pad was the Theology of Liberation, both the importance of that theology, and the defeat it proposed of *accommodation* and *immobilism* through acceptance of the deep meaning of the presence of man and woman in history, in the world—a world ever to be re-created on pain of having, not a *world,* but a mere *platform* to set things on.

In New Zealand, I held more discussions about *Pedagogy of the Oppressed,* with groups like those in Australia and emphasizing one aspect or other of the book. I was impressed by my discussions with indigenous leaders—with their insight, their awarness of their position of subjection and their rejection of that position, their thirst for the struggle, their nonconformity. Today, the Maori population of one-hundred-thousand, who are bilingual, have the option of studying their own language in the schools.*

My trip through Papua New Guinea was a hasty one. The island

The Cambridge Encyclopedia of Language, ed. (Cambridge: Cambridge University Press, 1987).

was preparing to gain its autonomy, take itself in hand, within a few months, no longer to be a "protectorate" of Australia, which it had been since the end of World War II.

One of the meetings I set up was with a group of young politicos who bade fair to play a salient role among the leaders of the process of assumption of the reins of national government. Our meeting was a lengthy one, concentrating on problems of development and education, education and democracy. Primary, secondary, and university education. Cultural identity. Language, ideology, social classes.

That evening I shared in a discussion at the university, whose topics, as might have been expected, included doubts and criticisms about certain elements in *Pedagogy of the Oppressed.*

Some of the criticisms repeated others I had heard previously, in Australia.

Along with certain merits of the book, the "idealistic" stamp of my humanism was emphasized, for example—the "vagueness," to which I have referred in the present book, in my concept of "oppressed," or in my concept of "people."

I rejected that sort of criticism, of course, just as I do today. But our debates never lost the tone of a dialogue, never became polemical. The persons who dissented from my positions obviously meant me no harm. Their criticisms did not feed on some uncontainable rage against me. Thus, even in the case of diametrically opposed positions, in Australia or in New Zealand, the respectful relationship that prevailed between those who disagreed with me and myself was never lost. The same thing had occurred between North American scholar Chester Bowers and me at the University of Oregon, at a debate in the presence of sixty members of a seminar, in July 1987.

CHAPTER

7

We disagreed almost across the board, for an hour and a half, but without having to offend or abuse each other. We simply argued for our respective, mutually contradictory positions. We did not have to distort anything in each other's thinking.

The last stop on my long trip was Fiji. Two key events made my journey to such distant corners of the world well worth the while. One was a meeting at the University of the South Pacific, at which the students dealt with me in such a tone of intimacy that it was as if I were their teacher there, and lived there with them in their campus dorms. So familiar were they with my books, thanks to their translation into English.

Still today, I enjoy, genuinely enjoy, the recollection of the evening of that meeting. The huge auditorium, recently dedicated, was crammed to the rafters, with people spilling out into the university gardens, somewhat similarly to what happened this past April (1992) at the State University of Santa Cruz at Itabuna, in Bahia.

On both occasions, in the 1970s in Fiji and more recently in Itabuna, loudspeakers had to be installed facing the gardens of both universities, and the meeting delayed until they were in place.

Obviously we could not have the dialogue that we should have liked to have. On both occasions I simply spoke to the students. In Fiji in the 1970s I spoke about certain matters discussed in *Pedagogy of the Oppressed,* one of the textbooks they used in their courses. In the 1990s, in Itabuna, my material was from the present book, in which I am revisiting and reliving *Pedagogy of the Oppressed*.

Let the reader not puzzle long over why I set these two meetings in contiguity here, despite their distance in time and space. They had an element of similarity. The participants of both, students of some twenty years ago from the islands of the South Pacific, and students of today in Itabuna, Bahia, were impelled by like motives: they were on fire with a love of freedom, and had found a point of reference in *Pedagogy of the Oppressed*.

The second event was the homage offered me by the native community of a village deep in a beautiful, thick wood.

It was a festival at which politics, religion, and siblingship mingled.

The leaders and other members of the community were abreast of what I was doing and what I was writing about. Some of them had even read *Pedagogy of the Oppressed*. And so they welcomed me as an intellectual committed to the same cause that mobilized them and stirred them to the struggle. They insisted on stressing this aspect, just as had the natives of Australia, called aborigines, in receiving me with such intimacy, deep in the heart of their own culture.

It was as if, in the spirit and the rituals of their traditions, they had been bestowing an honorary doctorate on me.

For that matter, this becomes one of the reasons why, not out of arrogance, but out of a legitimate sense of satisfaction, I have accepted the homage of the intellectuals of the academies, and the intellectuals of field and factory.

I have no reason, in the name of some false modesty, to hide, on one hand, the fact that I am offered these homages, or on the other, the wholesome fact that I welcome them—that they gladden me, and comfort and encourage me.

The deeply meaningful ritual with which the solemnity or festival proceeded was simple and lighthearted. Yet it touched me deeply. Ultimately, the symbolic act of the ceremony, as I understood it (neither was it explained to me, nor do I think it ought to have been), suggested to me that, though a stranger, and unendowed with certain qualities or certain basic prerequisites, I was nevertheless being invited to "enter" into the spirit of the culture, of its values, of its siblingship. To this purpose, however, I had to "suffer" or undergo experiences calculated to result in my capacity to "communicate" with the loveliness and "ethnicity" of that culture.

It was significant, for example, that, at the beginning of the ceremony, basically one of purification, I might not *speak*. I was forbidden the right to the *word*—which is fundamental, indispensable, for communion. But not just any word can *seal* communion. Hence my silence until certain things should occur during the ceremony that would *reestablish* my word. Hence also the designation, by the priest, of an "orator" to speak in my name. Unless I could speak, in the intimacy or heart of the culture—even before my own word should be *reestablished*—it would be impossible for me to "suffer" the experience of the reestablishment of my word in absolute silence. The word that was lent to me by my representative had the function of mediating the reconquest of my own.

Only in the course of the ceremonial process, after the official speech of a delegate of the group, whose discourse was not translated for me, possibly a discourse of requirements being made of me, to which my "representative" responded, and only after taking, from the same "chalice" as he, the purifying drink, without manifesting any reluctance, was I finally ascribed the right to speak in the intimacy of his world.

My discourse was then the discourse of a quasi-sibling: a formal discourse that conformed to the rules, to the ethico-religious exigencies of the culture.

I now spoke a few words, in English, with a French Catholic priest who had been in Fiji for twenty years as my simultaneous translator, even though nearly everyone present understood English. I told of my joy and sense of honor at having become able to speak after such a long period of silence. My speech, I added, had been augmented by a meaning that it had not had before. Now my speech had been legitimated in a different culture, in which *communion* was not only among men and women and gods and ancestors, but also among all the other expressions of life. Now the universe of communion included the trees, the animals, the beasts, the birds, the very earth, the rivers, the seas: life in plenitude.

There were days—my days in all that part of the Pacific, and not only in Australia or New Zealand or Papua New Ginea or Fiji—

when I was torn inwardly in so many directions. I felt pulled toward the astonishing beauty of nature, of human creation; toward the feeling for life, and love for the earth; toward the populations called aborigines; and I was overwhelmed anew by a wickedness I already knew—the wickedness of racial and class discrimination. Race and class discrimination is an agressive, ostentatious discrimination, at times. At times, it is covert, instead. But wicked it always is.

I have saved, purposely, a bit of commentary on my last visit to Chile and my first visit to Argentina, for the end. It was in June 1973, while the Popular Unity regime was in power, that I most recently visited Chile, a few months before the violence of the coup burst over the heads of all. It was waiting in the wings, though, that was plain to see. My first visit to Argentina, in November 1973, would be separated from the next by a long interval, on account of the coup that resulted in the banishment of the books of Marx, Darcy Ribiero, and myself.

When I read the decree published in the press I could scarcely resist sending a telegram to the general who had appointed himself president to thank him for the excellent company in which he had placed me.

My trip to Chile in June 1973, regardless of the angle from which I observe it, and far as I am from it today, was one of the most unforgettable I have ever made.

I shall concentrate on two moments that I experienced then, in the extraordinary climate of the struggle of the political ideologies, in the class confrontation that reached such levels of finesse on the part of the dominant classes and was such a powerful learning process for the popular classes. It was apropos of this era that I heard from a worker that he had learned more in one week than in all his life up until then. What the young worker was ultimately referring to was the process of his apprenticeship in the class struggle. He had been serving on a committee of workers who were trying to understand the reasons why, suddenly, countless articles had begun to be absent from the Chilean market—rubber nipples that go on baby bottles, chickens, basic medicines, and so on.

Fathers and mothers spent sleepless nights, their children crying, on account of the shortage of rubber nipples. If you could find one rubber nipple in the pharmacies of Santiago it was a miracle.

"Good day, sir. Do you have any rubber nipples?"

"No, I'm very sorry. Its the fault of those who voted for Allende"—the little memorized ideological speech that was supposed to be recited those days, as I was told, in Santiago.

That is class struggle.

"Do you have a *pollo*—a chicken?"

"No. It's the fault of those who voted for Allende."

The dominant class had buried poultry by the thousands, reasoning that a temporary poultry-shortage was a small price to pay for a win tomorrow, without risk.

That is class struggle.

Some twenty years ago, the dominant class concealed merchandise, diverted products, and lied and said that it was the fault of those who had voted for Allende. Today, it pronounces a neoliberal discourse, in which, not only in Chile, but all over the world, it talks of the nonexistence of classes, and says that to protest the evil of capitalism is to return to the perilous, negative, destructive *dream* that has already done so much harm.

I hope that we progressives, who suffer, who lose companions, siblings, friends, in the perversity of all the coups we have had come crashing down on us, will be careful not to lend an ear to these falsehoods, which masquerade as postmodernity but are as hoary as the bullying and despotism of the mighty.

The first moment to which I should like to make reference is that of a meeting in which I participated with a large group of Marxist educators, who lodged criticisms identical with the "Marxist" criticisms to which I have already referred in this book. For example, they would cite my supposed failure to assign sufficient importance to the class struggle, or my "idealism," or the dialogue that, according to some of them, seemed to smack of "democratism" or humanism—as well as, once more, of the "idealism," with which *Pedagogy of the Oppressed* was alleged to be riddled.

It was a lively debate, and we went on for over two hours. It was recorded on tape to be printed as an issue of a Santiago educational periodical.

Unfortunately, I have lost track of my copy of the periodical, and so can now neither transcribe any of the things said, nor report more precisely on the topics addressed. But I can certainly declare the excellence of that encounter in terms of the seriousness with which we conducted our discussions.

I can see their faces now, even as I write, nineteen years to the month since that encounter, those debating companions of mine that evening in Santiago. I had been so full of hope that they had not let themselves so much as be tempted by the language of "pragmatic" accommodation to the world.

Before saying good-bye, and leaving the spacious hall, I asked my interlocutors to turn around and cast a critical glance at a poster they had been using for the literacy campaign. There were several posters hanging on the walls.

A middle-aged workman, sitting at a table, was having showered over his passive head, by a strong, determined hand—as if it were crumbling something between its fingers—pieces of words. The vigorous hand of the educator was sowing letters and syllables in the purely recipient head of the worker.

"This poster," I then told them, "was drawn by a progressive! That makes it completely inconsistent. Without so much as batting an eyelash, it goes ahead and expresses a barefaced authoritarian ideology. But besides that, it betrays a profound scientific ignorance of the nature of language.

"This is really the kind of poster that ought to be used by reactionaries, who, to their reactionism, join a crying ignorance of language, as I have just said."

Then there was another poster. It said: *Quem sabe, ensina a quem não sabe* (The one who knows teaches the one who knows not).

"But for the one who knows to be able to teach the one who knows not," I said then, and I repeat now, "first, the one who knows must know that he or she does not know all things; second, the one who knows not must know that he or she is not ignorant of everything. Without this dialectical understanding of knowledge and ignorance, it is impossible, in a progressive, democratic outlook, for the one who knows to teach the one who knows not."

The second specially exciting moment of that visit (a trip I have referred to earlier in this book) was the entire evening I spent, in the company of sociologist Jorge Fiori, in Población Nueba Habana—a "land invasion" that had begun to acquire the aspect of a *cidade livre,* a free city. I saw and felt, close up, the ability of the popular classes to organize and govern—the wisdom with which the *liderança* not only detected problems, but also discussed them with the whole population of the quasi *cidade*. No decisions were ever taken, in the collective life of the *"cidade,"* without first being submitted to discussion by all.

They believed in the democracy they were building together, in the "popular" law they had begun to codify, in the equally popular, progressive, democratic education they were in the course of shaping. They believed in the individual and social solidarity in which they felt and knew they were growing. And, on account of all of this, they also knew themselves to be, on the one hand, the agents of fright and fear in the dominant class, and on the other, the objects of that class's unbridled fury.

Nueba Habana was destroyed. Its leader was murdered in September 1973.

Its spirit of freedom, its sibling dream, its socialist ideal, live—perhaps, just possibly, biding their time against a possible return, by way of the defeat or rejection of the neoliberal "pragmatic" discourse.

In August 1973 I received a telephone call from Buenos Aires. It was from the chief of staff of Dr. Taiana, the Argentine minister of education. He told me that the minister himself wished to speak with me.

"Professor Freire," said Dr. Taiana, "we should be most pleased if you would accept our invitation to come to Buenos Aires as soon as you can. It would be ideal, for example, around the turn of the month."

I had already committed myself, for this same period, to certain meetings sponsored by the World Council of Churches that I could not afford to miss.

And so the visit was scheduled for November 1973—after the ministry had accepted certain conditions I laid down! Not working in the evening was one; some evenings, when possible, out listening to tango music was another.

The ministry complied. I worked hard in the daytime, but I went out to hear tango music two evenings, there in Buenos Aires!

On my way to Argentina, I stayed overnight with my dear friend Darcy Ribeiro, in Lima. We talked all night, such was our fondness for each other and our restless curiosity to know—the curiosity of those alone who, knowing that they know, know that they know little, and that they need and can know more. Not the curiosity of persons have who know themselves to be glutted with knowing.

Sitting in his pontifical-style armchair, with his legs tucked under him, Darcy talked about his work in Peru, his plans for books, his reflections in the areas of culture and education. He spoke, we spoke, also of our homesickness for Brazil. We saw once more what we had seen, and how we had seen what we had seen, in the days before the 1964 coup, when Darcy was President Goulart's[50] chief of staff and I was running the National Program for Adult Literacy.[51]

We spoke of Chile. Of his meetings with Allende, of the assassinated president's genuinely democratic mind and spirit. Of the coup in Chile that would have come even if the Left had not made the mistakes it had made. The fewer the mistakes, the sooner the coup would have come. In the last analysis, the reason for the coup was much more in the correct things the Left had done than in any mistakes it had made.

Our magnificent friend, Darcy's and mine, the great Peruvian— or rather, Latin American—philosopher Augusto Salazar Bonde, leader of Peru's great educational reform, whom Darcy and I, along with Ivan Illich, had helped out, picked me up at the airport. A week later, on my way back to Europe, I visited him in the hospital where he was to die within a few days. The cancer that had been killing him was still unrecognized, and was finally diagnosed only the evening before he died.

I remember, now, my conversations with philosopher Salazar in Cuernavaca, Mexico, sitting talking with Illich, or in Geneva in our home, or in Lima with his team. Always the serious, engaged, lucid thinker, Augusto was never an obscurer. He was always an unveiler.

When I met him, toward the end of 1969 in Cuernavaca, he had read a series of my texts, among them some that had been incorporated into *Pedagogy of the Oppressed* and that had been published by the Center for Intercultural Formation, at Cuernavaca, which Illich directed.

From Augusto I heard some of the analyses in function of which it seemed to him that *Pedagogy of the Oppressed,* then in process of being translated into English, would not be a book of merely transitory interest. "*Pedagogy of the Oppressed* is not a 'conjunctural' book," he told me one day, meaning not an "occasional" one, not a composition occasioned by the fortuitous conjunction of concrete phenomena that might not be repeated, or might recur only rarely.

On my way from the Lima airport, in the car with Augusto, I had a painful presentiment that my friend was nearing the end. I did not say anything to him, although something told me that he knew he was dying. My suspicions grew when he began to tell me about a book he was working on. He told me he was so concerned about whether he would have time to get it written that one day he decided to dictate portions of it onto a tape as he drove his car from one place to another. "I give the tapes to the secretary every day," he said.

I do not know whether my friend managed to record his book—finish it.

I was glad to have seen him on my way to Argentina, and then, for the last time, on the way back. I only regret that I was unable to talk with him about what I had seen—all I had seen and heard in Argentina: a cultural revolution almost without a power base. A cultural revolution being mounted by a government that was powerless in so many respects. A project in the field of systematic education, and one of huge wealth and creativity. An experiment that moved Darcy Ribeiro to say, excitedly, "Please, pay attention to what you're doing!"

My week in Buenos Aires was divided thus: two four-hour meetings with the rectors of all of the country's public universities; an all-day meeting with the ministry's various technical teams; a meeting with a popular group in a slum on the outskirts of Buenos Aires; and finally, an evening with political activists, at which we discussed what was happening in the country.

I was actually surprised at the innovative élan with which the universities were hurling themselves into the effort of their own re-creation. In all aspects of the experiment, there was something worth watching in each of them. Instruction and research both strove to avoid any dichotomy between them, as it ultimately harms them both. Another effort was in the area of "extension." In fact, although not all of the universities included extension projects in their renewal, most of them did. And instead of limiting this effort to simply doing social work in popular areas, the universities were beginning to encounter social movements, popular groups. And this encounter sometimes occurred at the university itself, not only in the popular areas. I remember discussing, at some length, not only the political problem, but the epistemological question it involved.

More than ever before, political decision making, in a progressive mold, ought to be extended into populism, so that a university would place itself in the service of popular interests, as well. This would imply, as well, in practice, a critical comprehension of how university arts and sciences ought to be related with the consciousness of the popular classes: that is, a critical comprehension of the interrelations of popular knowledge, common sense, and scientific cognition.

I had no doubt then, any more than I do today, that, when we think in critical terms of the university and the popular classes, in no way are we admitting that the university should close the door on an altogether-rigorous concern for research and instruction.

It does not pertain to the nature of a university's relationship with or commitment to the popular classes to tolerate a want of rigor, or any incompetence. On the contrary, the university that fails to strive for greater rigor, more seriousness, in its research activities as in the area of instruction—which are never dichotomizable, true—cannot seriously approach the popular classes or make a commitment to them.

At bottom, the university ought to revolve around two basic concerns, from which others derive and which have to do with the circle of knowledge. The circle of knowledge has but two moments, in permanent relationship with each other: the moment of the cognition of existing, already-produced, knowledge, and the moment of our own production of new knowledge. While insisting on the impossibility of mechanically separating either moment from the other—both are moments of the same circle. I think it is important to bring out the fact that the moment of our cognition of existing knowledge is by and large the moment of instruction, the moment of the teaching and learning of content; while the other, the moment of the production of new knowledge, is, in the main, that of research. But actually, all instruction involves research, and all research involves instruction. There is no genuine instruction in whose process no research is performed by way of question, investigation, curiosity, creativity; just as there is no research in the course of which researchers do not learn—after all, by coming to know, they learn, and after having learned something, they communicate it, they teach.

The role of any university, progressive or conservative, is to immerse itself, utterly seriously, in the moments of this circle. The role of a university is to teach, to train, to research. What distinguishes a conservative university from another, a progressive one, must never be the fact that the one teaches and does research and the other does nothing.

The universities with whose rectors I worked with for eight hours in Buenos Aires in 1973 held this same conviction. None of them was making any attempt to reduce the self-democratization of the university to a simplistic approach to knowledge. This is not what they were concerned about. What they were concerned about was to diminish the distance between the university and what was done there, and the popular classes, without the loss of seriousness and rigor.

Another matter, to which the rectors and their advisers likewise gave attention, in the area of instruction, was the quest for an interdisciplinary understanding of teaching, instead of merely a disciplinary one.

Various academic departments sought to work in this way in an attempt to overcome the compartmentalization of views to which we subject reality, and in which, not infrequently, we become lost.

However, not everything was coming up roses. Inevitably, there were reactions on the part of sectarians—ideologues of Left and Right alike, so deeply rooted in their truth that they never admitted anything that might shake it—a Left and a Right equally endowed with a capacity for hatred of anything different, intolerant persons, private proprietors of a truth not lightly to be doubted, let alone denied.

It was a fine thing, however fragile and threatened, that process I experienced so intensely over the course of a week, and I let no single meeting go by without expressing my concerns and suggesting tactics—tactics that would be consistent with the progressive strategic dream that animated the other participants, of course. It would be necessary (as I always told them, while they sat with frightened eyes, listening to my warnings, which seemed to them so unfounded) to be astute—wise as serpents. Some of them did not understand, and even reacted with annoyance when I told them it seemed to me that there was a big difference between what they were doing in the country, on the level of education, of culture, of the popular movement, of discourse, and the real power bases of their government. Not that they ought to limit themselves to doing just *something*. No, they ought to do a great deal. Only, they had better keep their eyes peeled when it came to the discrepancy just cited.

It did not seem to me that the fine-tuned sensitivity and knowledge of a good political analyst was needed to sniff the coup in the air, while I was "knocked for a loop" by the June 1973 "street corner coup" in Chile.

For example, in one of the meetings I had with the ministry technologists, someone from the police got in, and even asked me some rather provocative questions. After two sessions, one of the educators, a bit surprised, and disgusted, communicated the fact to me. I spoke to the coordinator, who replied that this would have no consequences. The educators with whom I was conversing were not discussing anything not public. Still, the presence of the police official meant more than how he might be able to use what he heard us say: his presence betrayed the imbalance between power and the government. Finally: true, this was an official meeting, sponsored by the government and convoked by the minister of education; yet, the repressive organs held the real power, and had infiltrated the meeting to do some "policing." It was as if—in fact it was actually the case—the reactionary forces running the country had, out of purely tactical considerations, permitted Peron's return, but meanwhile kept a very close eye on his government.

I think I should not be off the mark if, now, so long afterward, I were to say that, in none of the workshops in which I participated, not even in the one I held with the political activists, did anyone agree with my observations. Sometimes, like the Chileans in the early months of the Christian Democratic government, they said I was still showing the scars of the trauma I had sustained on the occasion of the 1964 Brazilian military coup.

The further they went with their programs, either in the universities or in the popular regions, in various areas of endeavor, practically all of these programs being in response to, and stimulating, popular curiosity, the more enraged the watchful forces of the coup became as they prepared the final debacle.

I expressed, in my conversations, my serious concern for my hearers in terms of sheer survival—at least in the case of some of them, those whose political participation might be, or might have been, major, or more in view, those whose practice had closer visible ties with the popular classes, or those whose picture the repressive service might have elected to paint in stronger colors.

Regrettably, my warnings were only too well-founded. The coup came after Peron's death. It was violent and wicked. Some of my friends who had not seen any basis for my analyses had to leave the country in hasty secrecy, while others, unfortunately, disappeared forever.

To them, and to all of the men and women in Latin America, in the Caribbean, in Africa, who have fallen in the just fight, I offer my respectful and loving homage, in this *Pedagogy of Hope.*

And now I shall bring my book to a conclusion, with a succinct report of the visit my spouse Nita and I paid to El Salvador in July of 1992.

In El Salvador, the peasant men and women who had been struggling, all through these years—with weapons in their hands and, at the same time, with curious eyes for sentences and words, as they read and reread the world, as they fought to make that world less ugly and less unjust by learning to read and write words—had invited me to celebrate with them, in hope, an interval of peace in the war. They wished to tell me of what they were doing, and show me what they were doing. It was their way of rendering me homage.

They were joined by their teachers, some of the *lideranças* in the battle, and the National University of El Salvador, which bestowed on me its doctorate *honoris causa*.

Pedagogy of the Oppressed was once more the nucleus around which our discussions revolved. Its basic theses were even more current and vital now than they had been at the time of its first editions in the 1970s. Not only had these peasant strugglers become familiar with adult literacy campaigns since then, as these campaigns were being conducted in the guerrilla encampments, but they saw *Pedagogy* itself, across the board, as a book of great import precisely for the historical moment in which they were living. I might put it this way: *Pedagogy of the Oppressed* was here the heart and soul of the literacy campaign being waged in favor of a reading of the world and a reading of the word—a reading that was at once a reading of context and a reading of text, a practice and a theory in dialectical oneness.

It is even possible that what Nita and I saw in El Salvador—first, guerrilla wars fusing militants together in their very differences, in function of their strategic objectives, militants who had matured in the crucible of suffering (radicals and not sectarians, then, educators with open, critically optimistic eyes); second, the Right, while unsatisfied, nevertheless more or less well behaved; third, the needed presence and example of the United Nations, ensuring the peace accord—it is even possible that all of this might collapse, be undone, and that would be profoundly regrettable, from the viewpoint of how much all this is coming to mean for current history.

What cannot be denied is that there is something relatively unprecedented in this experiment: Right and Left making mutual concessions in order to assure peace and thereby diminish the social cost—the suffering that overwhelmingly and almost exclusively befalls the popular classes and then extends to broad middle sectors of society, and even, less rigorously and in a different way, the dominant classes.

It could seem that the concessions being made by the dominant classes are indicative of a greater detachment on their part. After all, by continuing to fight they would suffer less than the popular classes. Indeed, it could seem that, in making their concessions, the dominant classes are demonstrating a spirit of magnanimity. After all, they have reasons for confidence in their strength, which, enhanced by help from the outside, from the North, would crush the guerrillas, so that the dominant classes would have complete power over the country.

I do not believe, however, in the magnanimity of the dominant classes as such. The existence of magnanimous *individuals* is possible, and demonstrable—among members of the dominant classes—but not of the dominant classes as a class.

Historical conditions have simply placed that class today in a position in which the peace accord has become a moment in the strug-

gle, for them as for the popular classes under arms. It is a moment
in the struggle, not the end of the struggle. The popular forces need
to be—and I am sure that they are, to judge by what I heard from
some of their leaders—on the alert, at the ready, eyes wide open,
ready for anything. They must not "doze off," as if nothing could
happen while they "sleep." They must not demobilize, fail to keep
prepared, under pain of being crushed.

At all events, this way of confronting the truce (nor is it a truce
that is always explicit on the part of the parties to the conflict)—
truce as a moment in the struggle, as an attempt at building or
inventing a peace from which might result a different, democratic
experiment—reveals or proclaims a new historical phase. But this
is not a "new history," without social classes, without the struggle
between them, without ideology, as if, suddenly, by some sleight of
hand, the social classes, their conflicts, their ideologies, had suddenly been swished away by the sleeves of some great magician's
black cloak.

Such things do not occur, of course, especially in the domain of
politics, except as engendered in the interplay of tactics in which
two sides, in function of their respective strategic positions, measure
their own stride against the steps taken by the other side. At bottom,
the antagonists regard their reciprocal concessions as lesser evils,
which could one day, in retrospect, for one side or the other, be
seen to have been victories.

If it had already been difficult, some years before, for the Left to
take power with impunity, never mind the means by which it had
done so, as in Chile, Nicaragua, or Grenada, now, after the decline
of "realistic socialism"—which is not socialism, let me repeat—when
conservatism had become even more bold the world over—then the
limits on the Left, for the short term, have shrunken still further.

Realistically, then, to strike a peace in El Salvador, despite its
obvious limitations, and despite, at times, larger concessions than
one could have hoped to have to make, is the best way, because it
is the only way, to make advances. It is the best way for the people
to assert themselves, to win a voice, a presence, in the reinvention
of their society, it is the best path to the lessening of injustice. For
that matter, it is the best way of creating, and gradually consolidating, a democratic lifestyle, in which a process might appear that

would even enable those accustomed to holding all power in their hands to learn that what seems to them to be a threat to their privileges—understood by them, of course, as inalienable rights— is only the implementation of the rights of those who have come to be forbidden to exercise them. A learning process might appear whereby the powerful would learn that their privileges, such as that of exploiting the weak, prohibiting the weak from being, denying them hope, are immoral, and as such need to be eradicated. It might be a learning process, at the same time, for the crushed, the forbidden-to-be, the rejected, that would teach them that, through serious, just, determined, untiring struggle, it is possible to remake the world. The oppressed may learn that hope born in the creative unrest of the battle, will continue to have meaning when, and only when, it can in its own turn give birth to new struggles on other levels.

And finally, it may be learned that, in a new democratic process, it is possible gradually to expand the space for pacts between the classes, and gradually consolidate a dialogue among the different— in other words, gradually to deepen radical positions and overcome sectarian ones.

In no way, however, does this mean, for a society with this sort of living experience of democracy, the inauguration of a history without social classes, without ideology, as a certain pragmatically postmodern discourse proclaims. In fact, the truth is just the opposite, or nearly the opposite. Postmodernity, as I see it, has a different, substantially democratic, way of dealing with conflict, working out its ideology, struggling for the ongoing and ever more decisive defeat of injustice, and arriving at a democratic socialism. There is a postmodernity of the Right; but there is a postmodernity of the Left, as well, nor does the latter—as is almost always insinuated, if not insisted—regard postmodernity as an altogether special time that has suppressed social classes, ideologies, Left and Right, dreams, and utopias. And one of the basic elements of the postmodernity of the Left is the reinvention of power—and not its mere acquisition, as with modernity.

This postmodern moment that we are living in the 1990s is not a time so utterly special that it knows no more social classes—not in Switzerland any more than in Brazil, and certainly not in El

Salvador. In fact, this is why one of the learning processes that a progressive postmodernity calls upon us to accept is the process of our apprehension that the total victory of the revolution in the present does not guarantee its existence in the future. A revolution can perish at the very height of its power, which it has simply acquired, and not reinvented, not re-created. In that case, it is lost on account of the excessive arrogance of its certitudes, and the inevitable lack of humility that such certitudes entail: it is lost by virtue of the authoritarian exercise of its power. It is lost by virtue of its modernity.

Concessions, then, are the best way of *coming to win*, only if, sooner or later, they actually *win the fight* that is never over and done. Winning the fight is a process of which it can never be said, "We've won, period." When this point is absolutized, the revolution is paralyzed.

We visited various regions of the country, and participated in regional education seminars in two of them. We paid a visit to a lovely clearing in the forest, a kind of theatrical stage on which the guerrillas met, then as today, to engage in discussion, dreaming, self-appraisal, recreation.

We attended a "culture circle" session at which armed activists were learning to read and write, learning to read words while doing a rereading of the world. The process of writing and reading the word, which is what they were doing in the course of their understanding of discourse, emerged from, or was part of, a larger, more meaningful process—that of the taking up of their citizenship, the taking of history into their hands. This is what I have always been for, this is why I have always fought for literacy compaigns that, being so acutely aware of the social nature of of the acquisition of language, I have never dichotomized from the political process of the battle for citizenship. What I have never been for is a "neutral" approach to literacy, a sheer shower of syllables, which, to boot, would start right out with the language of the educators rather than with that of the educands. We conversed with the combatants, and with their *comandante*, in a climate of hope.

In just such a climate of hope we spent nearly an entire day in a kind of new city, peopled by exiles who had managed to survive in a neighboring country.

From the peak of an elevation, we descried a whole world to be built differently.[52]

We took lunch with the leader of the brand-new city-in-the-middle-of-nowhere, and he spoke to us of what this return to their country was coming to mean for all of them, men and women, what it meant to them to participate in the transformations that would be needed in order for El Salvador to change its "face," and gradually become a less-wicked, less-unjust society, little by little more decent, more human and humane.

This dream—as far as we could gather from our conversations, and by reading the wonderful book by Ana Guadalupe Martinez,* one of the leaders of the Frente Farabundo Martí para la Liberación Nacional, the Farabundo Martí National Liberation Front or FMLN, as well as on the visit we made to Radio Venceremos (We shall prevail)—this dream is the utopia for which these Salvadoran militants had begun to struggle from the outset. But they had set out for the clash and the fray without ever scorning education and its importance for the battle itself. As far as was possible, they were avoiding both the illusions of an idealism that ascribes a power to education that it does not have, and the mechanistic objectivism that denies any value to education until after there is a revolution. I do not know that I have ever found, in popular groups, a stronger expression of a critical confidence in educational practice. The same must be said of their *lideranças*.

I cannot refrain from transcribing here the dedication I read on a piece of artwork on the occasion of my visit to the FMLN headquarters:

Paulo Freire

With your education for liberation, you have contributed to the very struggle of the Salvadoran people for social justice.

With gratitude and respect,

FMLN, July 1992

---

*Ana Guadalupe Martinez, *Las cárceres clandestinas* (San Salvador: Central American University, 1992).

The harshest difficulties, the wants and needs of the people, the ebb and flow of the process that depends on so many different factors for its solidification—none of this diminished in us, in Nita and me, the hope with which we came to El Salvador, with which we lived a week in El Salvador, and with which we left El Salvador—

—The same hope with which I bring to its conclusion this *Pedagogy of Hope*.

Afterword

Even before he had finished writing this book, Paulo Freire felt that certain points would require clarification—matters he was touching on only lightly, or perhaps doing no more than mentioning, without expansion, because considering them in depth would mean straying too far from the focus of the book's thematic interest. And so he has asked me to compose explanatory notes.

It has been an immense joy for me to collaborate in a work of his, especially as it has meant writing about things I relish so much and have come to be so involved in, so passionately involved in, lo, these fifteen years and more: namely, the "fabrics" of the history of Brazilian education.

Some of the notes may be extensive. I do go on. Others may seem superfluous to the Brazilian reader, but will be helpful to persons whose language is among those into which this book is already in the process of being translated. Persons, places, and things with which we are familiar here may be far less well-known to readers of other cultures and contexts, men and women of foreign lands. It could scarcely be otherwise, and I am sure that this state of the facts calls for a detailed explanation of certain things.

I became more and more intensely involved in my notes every time I picked up this book, once again to immerse myself in it. I found myself reliving moments of my childhood, when I knew Paulo as a student at Oswaldo Cruz Boarding School. Later, in my youth, he was my "Portuguese teacher," my language teacher. After I married Raul, I lived in São Paulo, where I would see him in my parents' home, in Recife, and follow his work in the creation and application of the Paulo Freire Literacy Method.

Then came the coup of 1964. From that time on, for a long while, I had only sporadic notice of him, in Chile, in the United States, and in Geneva, and of his pedagogical work, which was gaining in criticality and extension.

I read him for the first time in Spanish. It was a strange experience. It made me think: "So Brazilian, so Northeastern, so Pernambucan, so 'Recifian' a person—all the ways in which I have known him—and here I am reading him in a foreign language." It was a strange thing, and I was surprised and frightened. But then, with the ears of my imagination, I would hear him, in that familiar voice, repeating the text in Portuguese, with his gentle tones, powerful conviction, and ingenious creativity. And these were Northeastern qualities.

Finally there came his stories, so well told in the present volume, of the relationship he established, through the intermediary of *Pedagogy of the Oppressed*, with his hearers and readers in the world outside. These things seemed less easy for me to grasp. But this was only seeming, since, after all, I had been able to understand his relationships, these experiences of his, here in São Paulo when I discussed *Pedagogy of the Oppressed* with my colleagues in the teaching profession. Our discussions awakened among us, too, reflections, conclusions, and hesitations analogous to those he recounts in the present book, as he communicates to us the feedback he has received from various groups on the five continents.

Even without a face-to-face dialogue, then, there was a point in common between Paulo and me, and now, as I compose these notes, I feel I have become familiar with it. I am no longer a stranger to the things, events, and persons of which he speaks. And this, entirely apart from the fact that, over the last five years, I have indeed been physically present to, and experienced, these persons and things, in Paulo's actual company, in Brazil and abroad.

Writing these notes about the streets of Recife, about my father, Aluizio, about Oswaldo Cruz Boarding school, about Ariano and Taperoá, or about what *manha* means, or about President Goulart—all of this has been fascinating to me, as has been, as well, the task of describing and analyzing what the pedagogical thought of Paulo

Freire has meant for the history of education since the Second National Congress of Adult Education—or the Workers Party administration of São Paulo today and his incumbency as Municipal Secretary of Education—or the emotion-charged experience in political pedagogy that was ours—Paulo's and mine—in the form of the visit we paid to the new city of Segundo Montes in El Salvador.

Composing these notes was no mechanical, or "neutral" task, then. No, there is no such thing here, and it would be impossible for me anyway—the way I am, the way I am involved in things and understand the world. These notes are charged with living experience, with my grasp of the history of Brazilian education, and with my rebellion against the elitist, discriminatory authoritarianism of the colonial tradition and the Brazilian slavocracy, still alive and well among us.

I am fed up with bans and prohibitions: bans on the body, which produce, generation after generation, not only Brazilian illiteracy (according to the thesis I maintain), but an *ideology* of ban on the body, which gives us our "street children," our misery and hunger, our unemployment and prostitution, and, under the military dictatorship, the exile and death of countless Brazilians. The ban on Paulo Freire's body (along with his ideas), which was forbidden, for fifteen long years, in Brazil. The ban, the prohibition, imposed on him and on so many other Brazilians—which, by way of paradoxical reaction, led him to write *Pedagogy of the Oppressed,* the book that disallows all of the ban forms reproduced in Brazil down through the centuries and indicates the possibility of persons' liberation. And it is all brought to completion in the present *Pedagogy of Hope.*

These are the things that have stimulated me in writing these notes. And so I have committed to these notes my emotions, my knowledge of the history of Brazilian education—and especially, my reading of the world, whose orientation is in terms of this triangle: prohibition, liberation, and hope.

ANA MARIA ARAÚJO FREIRE

Notes

1. One of the most important of Freire's categories, the inspirer of such powerful reflections in *Pedagogy of the Oppressed* and *Pedagogy of Hope*, is the concept of "untested feasibility." Little discussed, and, I daresay, little studied, this category embraces a whole belief in the "possible dream," and in the utopia that will come once those who make their own history wish it so. These hopes are so characteristic of Freire.

   For Freire, human beings, as beings endowed with consciousness, have at least some awareness of their conditioning and their freedom. They meet with obstacles in their personal and social lives, and they see them as obstructions to be overcome. Freire calls these obstructions or barriers "limit situations."

   Men and women take a number of different attitudes toward these "limit situations." They may perceive the barriers in question as obstacles that *cannot* be removed. Or they may perceive them as obstacles they do *not wish* to remove. Or they may perceive them as obstacles they know exist and need to be broken through. In this last case, they devote themselves to overcoming them.

   Here, there has been a critical perception of the "limit situation." And so the persons who have understood it seek to act: they are challenged, and feel themselves challenged, to solve these problems of the society in which they live, in the best possible manner, and in an atmosphere of hope and confidence. To this end, these persons have separated themselves, epistemologically, taken their distance from, that which was objectively "unsettling" and "encumbering" to them, and have objectified it. Only when they have understood it in depth, in its essence, detaching it from its contingent factuality, from its sheer concrete "being there," can it be seen as a problem. As something "perceived" and "detached" from daily life, it becomes the "detached-and-perceived," or the "perceived detached." As such, it cannot, it must not, abide. Thus it comes to be a problem-topic—a topic that ought to be, must be, confronted. It ought to be, needs to be, discussed and overcome.

To the actions required for breaking through "limit situations," Freire gives the name, "limit acts." The name suggests the direction of these "acts": the defeat and rejection of the *given*, of a docile, passive acceptance of what is "there," with the attendant implication of a determinate posture vis-à-vis the world.

"Limit situations," then, imply the existence of men and women directly or indirectly served by them, the dominant; and of men and women whose affairs are "denied" and "curbed," the oppressed.

The former see the problem topics in their concealment by "limit situations," and hence regard them as historical determinants against which there is no recourse—situations to which one must simply adapt. The latter, when they clearly perceive these challenging societal topics no longer in disguise, no longer in their concealment by "limit situations"—when these problems come to be something "detached and perceived"—feel a call to mobilize, to act, and to uncover some "untested feasibility."

These latter are those who feel it incumbent upon them to burst through the barrier in question. How? By solving, dissolving, through action accompanied by reflection, these obstacles to the liberty of the oppressed. By removing the "barrier between being [o ser] and being-moreso [o ser-mais]," Freire's dream so dear. Of course, Freire represents the political will of all women and men who, *as* he or *with* him, have come to be workers for the liberation of men and women independently of race, religion, sex, and class.

The "untested feasible" then, when all is said and done, is something the utopian dreamer knows exists, but knows that it will be attained only through a practice of liberation—which can be implemented by way of Freire's theory of dialogical action, or, of course (since a practice of liberation does not necessarily make an explicit appeal to that theory), by way of some other theory bearing on the same ends.

Thus, the "untested feasible" is an untested thing, an unprecedented thing, something not yet clearly known and experienced, but dreamed of. And when it becomes something "detached and perceived" by those who think utopian wise, then they know that the problem is no longer the sheer seed of a dream. They know the dream can become reality.

Thus, when conscious beings will reflect and act for the overthrow of the "limit situations," which have left them—along with nearly everyone else—limited to being-in-a-lesser-way, to *being-less so*, then the untested feasible is no longer merely itself, but has become the concretization of that which within it had previously been infeasible.

We have these obstacles, therefore, in our reality, these barriers or boundaries, these "limit situations," which, once they are "detached and perceived," have not prevented some persons from dreaming the dream, nonetheless prohibit the majority from realizing the humanization and concretization of *o ser-mais*, being-in-a-larger way, being-moreso.

2. Colégio Oswaldo Cruz was in operation, under the direction of Aluizio Pessoa de Araújo, from 1923 to 1956, when, to his regret, and that of all who knew the results he obtained, and who had benefited from contact with him, the school was shut down. Beyond any doubt, it had been one of the most important educational activities in the history of education in the Northeast—indeed, we might say, with all justice and realism, in the history of Brazilian education.

Known for its strict ethics, and the excellence of its instruction, Recife's Oswaldo Cruz (which had no connection with the school of that name in São Paulo), drew its student body not only from Recife and Pernambuco, from practically the whole Brazilian Northeast, over an area stretching from Maranhão to Sergipe—from practically the whole Brazilian Northeast—who sought an education there on the basis of their confidence in its principles and educational practices.

As director (as well as Latin, Portuguese, and French teacher), Aluizio associated experienced professionals with himself from the various fields of knowledge. Yet he always welcomed the contribution of young, new teachers, as well. Paulo Freire is one of many examples. It was at Oswaldo Cruz that Paulo began his work as a teacher of Portuguese. Aluizio's criterion for the selection of teachers was ever their professional competency, plus their serious dedication to the act of educating.

Most of the professors of the faculties of nearly all of the departments that merged in 1946 to form the first Federal University of the State of Pernambuco, were chosen from among the teachers at Colégio Oswaldo Cruz.

An utterly committed educator, Aluizio built his Colégio into what for the time was an innovative and progressive educational institution. He introduced coeducation as early as 1924. It was likewise at this boarding school that students from other religious backgrounds, especially Jewish (Jews had no school of their own in Recife until the 1940s), received their moral and academic formation.

Colégio Oswaldo Cruz had three science laboratories—for biology, physics, and chemistry, respectively, housed in three amphitheaters the like of which many schools and colleges in the country still today may only dream. Its collection of historical and geographical maps, and its library, were up to date and of a high quality. There were bands, orchestras, choral groups, and, for the girls, ballet halls. Its students established student guilds and other organizations, and published newspapers and magazines. Examples of the latter would be the *Sylogeu* and the *Arrecifes*.

Students and teachers who had studied at Colégio Oswaldo Cruz in Recife included nationally and even internationally recognized scientists, jurists, artists, and politicians like (to name only some of the most outstanding) José Leite Lopes, Mario Schemberg, Ricardo Ferreira, Newton Maia, Moacir de Albuquerque, Claudio Souto, Ariano Suassuna, Walter Azoubel, Pelópidas Silveira, Amaro Quintas, Dácio Rabelo, Abelardo and Aderbal Jurema, Egídio Ferreira Lima, Hervásio de Carvalho, Fernando Lira, Vasconcelos Sobrinho, Odorico Tavares, Evandro Gueiros, Dorany Sampaio, Etelvino Lins, Armando Monteiro, Jr., Francisco Brenand, Lucílio Varejão, Sr., Jr., Ricardo Palmeira, Mario Sete and his sons Hoel and Hilton, Valdemar Valente, Manoel Correia de Andrade, Albino Fernandes Vital—and as we have seen, both in the text and in these notes, the author of this book—individuals representing the most varied ideological vectors, but all of them persons of solid training and professional competence.

Colégio Oswaldo Cruz, in the person of its director, had no fear of breaking with the elitist, authoritarian traditions of Brazilian society. Those who passed its portals knew no discrimination of class, race, religion, or gender.

3. Writing about one's own father is not an easy job. But when you feel, when you know, that, throughout the nearly eighty-three years of his life, your father was a living example of the human qualities of generosity, solidarity, and humility, without any sacrifice of his dignity, it becomes a pleasant, gladsome, and rewarding experience to speak of him.

Said the daily newspaper of Aluizio's father, Antonio Miguel de Araújo, a physician:

> He was born at 4:00 A.M. on Wednesday, December 29, 1897. He was baptized February 21, 1898, by Father Marçal . . . (surname illegible), the godparents being Urbano de Andrade Lima and his wife, Dona [Madame] Anna Clara Lyra Lima.

Aluizio Pessoa de Araújo, born in Timbaúba, died in Recife November 1, 1979.

The Pernambucan educator received his academic and religious training in the (secular) Seminário de Olinda. After completion of the "major courses," to his parents' sorrow, he cut short his secular formation and went to Rome to prepare for the priesthood.

A few years later, on June 25, 1925, Aluizio married Francisca de Albuquerque, known as Genove, who had been his executive assistant ever since the opening of the (then) Ginásio (Gymnasium) Oswaldo Cruz. They became the parents of nine children, and had the joy of celebrating their fiftieth wedding anniversary, although it had to be without one of their children, Paulo de Tarso.

The fact of having broken off his priestly studies and married instead was never an obstacle, in Aluizio, to a life ruled by the norms and principles of the Roman Catholic Church. On the contrary, he was now led to a more profound piety—a more authentic religiousness as the guideline of his private and professional life, which he lived by living his faith and prioritizing those special qualities of his, generosity and solidarity. Over and above this, his earnest commitment to ethics and humanism led him to pursue an educational practice of extreme liberality with all men and women who sought, needed, and desired to study. And he did it with humility.

From the 1920s right up to the early 1950s, as Recife had so few public (and therefore free) secondary schools, what Aluizio really did as Director and proprietor of the COC, as his boarding school was known, was to make his private institution for all intents and purposes a public one. Without ever having access to public funds, he granted scholarships, in his own educational establishment, to many a young person in need.

And when he granted them, he granted them. Never did he permit his scholarship students to repay, in any way, shape, or form, what he had bestowed on them out of his personal generosity and in virtue of his social awareness of the fact that education was everyone's right.

He never let these principles slip from his grasp. He was ever convinced that this was his "vocation" in the world.

4. The secondary course was the target of legislative material from the outset of Getúlio Vargas's administration. This material took the form of two decrees—dated April 1931, and April 1932, respectively—the latter confirming and consolidating the systematization and manner of organization the former had prescribed for this branch of instruction, the secondary level.

Throughout Brazilian historical tradition, legislation concerning the schools had been handed down almost exclusively by way of acts of the executive power, bypassing the prescribed initiatives of the legislative branch or of civil society. This reform of the early 1930s, then, raised eyebrows—all the more so, inasmuch as, after losing the elections, Vargas had taken power, in November 1930, by means of revolutionary forces that rejected, more than anything else, the hegemony of the coffee, São Paulo, and mining aristocracy that had ruled the country throughout almost the whole republican era.

Technically, it is true, this educational reform on the part of Vargas and his education minister of that time, Francisco Campos, was innovative. But, while a new departure in terms of method, it was flawed politically, and this flawed it through and through. It had not managed to escape the weight of tradition. It was excessively authoritian and centralized, and toadied to the elitist tastes and tone of the commanding minority of our society.

The provisions of Vargas's original educational reform prevailed until 1942, throughout his incumbency, except for the period from 1937 on, when it was replaced by another, even more antidemocratic set of prescriptions.

Secondary instruction was of a traditionally academic mold, and offered no professional or technical training. It was conceived merely as a bridge to higher education—quite a paradox in a country that was seeking to industrialize and had such a need for doing so. The secondary level was the branch of instruction enjoying the greatest prestige, and prerogatives thereunto accruing, in political society, as well as in the middle and upper echelons of civil society, where the still prevailing elitist dreams implanted by the Jesuits in the sixteenth century, with their style of education (in subjects called the "humanities"), lived on.

The secondary course systematized in 1932, to which Freire refers, set up two instructional "cycles." The First Cycle, called the Fundamental Cycle, was a five-school-year course, and enrolled pupils of both sexes beginning at the age of eleven, upon successful completion of quite a rigorious admissions examination covering carefully selected material. The Second Cycle, which was "college preparatory," was two school years long, and was called the Complementary Cycle. Successful completion of the Fundamental Cycle was a prerequisite for enrollment in the Complementary Cycle.

The Complementary Cycle was subdivided into three "sessions," in function of the particular "major" the individual high-schooler proposed to pursue at the university after successful completion of this Second Cycle. The three sessions, in both public and private high schools, all to be modeled on Colégio Pedro II—the official model for *all* secondary-education institutions in the country—comprised curricula in, respectively, pre-law, premedicine, and preengineering.

As there was as yet no "normal" training for teachers at this time—university-level courses in education—all students inclining to a formation in the area of the human sciences, or envisaging a career in secondary education, were required to complete the "Pre-Law Secondary Cycle," after which they would matriculate in a School of Law.

This is what Freire did. Having no clear idea, as yet, when he enrolled in the Recife Faculty of Law, in 1943, of becoming an educator, let alone in 1941 when he began prelaw, still, he felt and knew that he wanted to be as close as possible to human problems.

5. The SESI—Serviço Social da Indústria—was created by Law Decree 9403 of incumbent President of the Republic Eurico Gaspar Dutra, June 25, 1946.

As it endowed the National Confederation of Industry with particular powers, enjoining upon it the responsibility of creating, organizing, and directing the new service, the legal act sets forth certain considerations in justification of the measure being taken.

Succinctly, the following considerations had led the Executive power to enact the decretal: "The difficulties created for the social and economic life of the country by the burdens of the postwar period." After all, it was the duty, while not the exclusive duty, of the state to "foster and stimulate cooperation among classes by way of initiatives tending to promote the welfare of working men and their families," as well as to foster the requisite conditions for an "improvement in the pattern of life." A further consideration was the availability of the National Confederation of Industry as an entity among the producing classes for "offering social assistance, as well as better housing, better nutritional and hygienic conditions for workers, and indeed, the development of a spirit of solidarity between employees and employers," along with the fact that "this program, as an incentive to a sense and spirit of social justice among classes, will greatly contribute to the elimination from among us elements favorable to the germination of divisive influences prejudicial to the interests of the collectivity."

We see a portrait of the country. It will be interesting to analyze this material, and point out what the "letter of the law" does not say, that the spirit of the decree surely contains.

First, the act is unacceptable by reason of its very form.

It comes from the top down, down from the executive branch. Furthermore, it is even more authoritarian than a simple decree would have been: it is what is called a *law* decree, that is, a decree that the chief of the executive branch, in this case the president of the republic, issues with the force of law, thereby arrogating to himself functions proper to the legislative branch and exercising them as if they were his own.

Like other Brazilian presidents, Dutra used this mechanism in a manner so bare-facedly partial to Brazilian centralist authoritarianism that, happily, it has now been written out of existence in our bureaucratic apparatus of state.

The document in question speaks of difficulties arising in the postwar era. Brazil could have emerged from the war years awash in wealth. After all, it had been among the countries that supplied stockpiles of various products essential to a war effort.

Other considerations advanced in the document betray a terror of "communism." They translate a fear that, one day, some Brazilian regime might be antagonistic to Northern capitalism, which was ordering all the witch hunts for "communists." They camouflage the class struggle. At all costs, a clear awareness of the existence and nature of the class struggle must be prevented.

It "asks" a calm, passive acceptance of the crying discrepancies in material conditions between owners and employees. "Assistance" is offered, in lieu of honest confrontation.

Freire took a job with this government. On the face of it, that could seem a contradiction. But he learned, in this job. After all, he was dealing with working families of factory, farm, and fishing coast, and—most of all— he was doing so in a context of the relations imposed by management on labor. Thus was he enabled to formulate a pedagogical thinking that would be stamped with those salient characteristics of dialogue, criticality, and social transformation with which we become so familiar in this book.

6. The Recife Law Faculty, today a department of the Federal University of Pernambuco, was always one of the political battlegrounds of the Brazilian scene. Many a new idea sprang into being there.

Created along with the São Francisco Square school of São Paulo on August 11, 1827, shortly after Brazil's declaration of independence from Portugal, this school of law, which initially operated in São Bento Convent in Olinda, was not established merely as a training ground for individuals who would come to compose the national juridical apparatus. It was the alumni of these two schools who, initially, actually forged the Brazilian apparatus of state.

7. Freire had to leave Brazil and request political asylum when only forty-three years of age. He was obliged to live outside his native land, far from his nearest and dearest, for more than fifteen years.

During his time of exile, he lost his mother and many of his friends. Among the latter were countless political activists who had been in charge of the "culture circles," or monitors of the National Literacy Program. They were not to be spared the tortures and persecutions of the coming years of military dictatorship.

Thus, paradoxically and ironically, Freire's departure from our midst at the moment in which he was acting and producing so effectively, efficiently, and enthusiastically, occurred by reason of precisely these qualities in him.

His "sin" was to have taught literacy for the sake of *conscientização* and political participation. For him, the purpose of literacy was to help the people to emerge from their situation of domination and exploitation. Once politicized by the act of reading the word, they could reread, critically, the world. Such was Freire's understanding of adult education. His widely used "Paulo Freire Literacy Method" was based on these ideas, so that it conveyed the reality of the unjust, discriminatory society we had built—a reality that needed to be transformed.

The program on the drawing boards would have brought this to so many who had been denied the right to schooling. It was wiped out by the military coup of 1964.

In the gruesome spirit of McCarthyism, and of the National Security Doctrine, inspired in the North, that had installed itself in Brazil, the military officers who had seized power destroyed or otherwise neutralized everything they could get their hands on that they understood to be "subversive."

In this "new" reading of the world—old in its tactics of punishment, abuse, and prohibition—there was no room for Freire.

He who so loved his country and his people was deprived of *being-in* his country and *being-with* his people.

8. The State of Pernambuco is one of the smaller political units of the federation. Its territory is a narrow strip of land extending from the Atlantic Ocean to the border of the State of Piauí, and lying between longitude 35° and 41° west, and latitude 7° and 10° south.

In terms of rainfall, humidity, vegetation, and temperature, it is considered to be divided into three "zones." Beginning on the coast: the Zona da Mata ("Wooded Zone"), Zona do Agreste ("Agrarian, Farming, Rural"), and Zona do Sertão ("Hinterland," the desert region).

The first, where you can still see a little of the Atlantic Forest that covered it at the time of the Portuguese invasion of American lands in 1500, has torrential rainfall, blistering temperatures, and high humidity. Even today it is the zone of the canebrakes, in the Portuguese tradition that made the region that nation's most abundant source of wealth in the sixteenth century.

It was the Portuguese colonial adventure that occasioned the deforestation of so much of this zone. Slave labor drove the mills, and felled the trees to make room for the brakes, and now sugar (until then thought of as a "spice") could pour into the welcoming arms of European markets, thus sealing the fate of this zone—ecological destruction.

As we move a few kilometers away from the maritime strand, climatic conditions modify, with sparser vegetation and diminishing rainfall, all the way to the border of the Zona de Sertão.

Vegetation in the Sertão is limited exclusively to cactaceous plants, especially the *mandacaru* or Peru cereus, and *xiquexique*, other cacti, yielding what we call a *caatinga*—the stunted, spare forests we have in the Northeast. Daytime temperatures soar, under a blazing sun, in a blue, cloudless sky, and plummet at night.

There are no trees at all, and of course rainfall is a rarity. The frequent droughts of the Zona de Sertão may last months, even years.

The *secas*, as we call them—the droughts—leave the riverbeds empty and the populations hungering and thirsting. The soil that has served for "subsistence farming" splits agape, to receive the misery—the dead livestock and all the hopes—of a folk who now know they must migrate to the Southeast of the country or die.

9. The *jangada*, the little boat that dots the lovely seascape of Northeastern Brazil, is a catamaran used by small deep-sea fishers to make their living. At sunset, they sell the day's catch—all that they have harvested from the generous sea of tepid waters that wash the shore in that region of Brazil. Not that the catch is taken "for free." No, the risks are great, and the toil most arduous.

A fragile vessel, the *jangada* is constructed of a light, porous wood that floats so high in the water that the little craft will tend not to sink even if it is awash.

It is composed of five logs of *jangada* wood, each some four or five meters in length, joined together to form its ballast by several sticks of tough, hard wood running across them from one side of the one-and-one-half to two-meters-wide vessel to the other.

The *jangada* has a big cloth sail, traditionally white, which the wind "hits" to propel the raft over the water. It carries almost no paraphernalia other than the fishing trap and the sail—only a rustic wooden tiller, a creel (the *samburá*, a round wicker basket to hold the fish after they have been retrieved), and a wooden dipper used to keep the sail wet and *impermeável*, or "wind-proof." And an anchor—as rustic as everything and everyone else in the *jangada*, a stone tied to the end of a rope of *caroá* fibers that stops the *jangada* where the *jangadeiro* wants it to stop, wherever his intuition tells him that it will be here that he will find the riches of the sea that are the object of his quest.

10. The fishers of the Northeast call it *pescaria de ciência* (scientific fishing), their rudimentary elementary method of deep-sea navigation that consists of the following. The fishers select three points of reference. Two

of them will be, for instance, a hillock, or the steeple of a church—anything that stands out from the landscape at a distance. The third will be the edge of the coast itself, the waterline. These three points enable the fisher to head for the open sea on a course as nearly vertical as possible with the coastline, and several kilometers in distance, as he navigates with the naked eye, keeping equidistant from the two previously chosen inland points. Then, at this spot where he has come, from where everything on shore merges into a single, vague point, and where his intuition and sensitivity have told him, "Ah, this is it . . . this is a good place," he lowers his trap. Several days later, without having left any sign for himself (or for strangers) of how his creative wit has served him here, he sails to the same spot and draws in his net and his catch.

The "hand tool" employed amidst this *scientific cognition* of his (this concept of an isosceles triangle), the instrument applied between his two acts of "measuring" and determining the right point for gaining the fruits of the sea, is the *covo*, or wicker fish trap. Constructed of flexible, but tough forest vine, or *cipó*, the *covo* is a large box attached to a stone that drags it deep down into the water. The *covo* floats at this underwater point, which the fisher has selected, for the time needed to fill with the fish, prawn, and other "fruit" that enter there, never to leave again for the freedom of the immense sea waters.

The techniques are very rudimentary, of course. But they are the effort of common sense, of the reading of the world done by the humble folk of the seashore, to make of observation and experience the route to a knowledge analogous to our own scientific cognition.

Cognition like this "scientific fishing" is the object of study of UNICAMP ethnoscientist Marcio D'Olme Campos, who works among the fishers of São Paulo state, although in terms of different conceptions from those set forth here (see note 36).

11. *Caiçara* is the name we in the Brazilian Northeast give to a shelter built from fibers of the coconut trees growing along the ocean, which serve to protect fishing boats and their equipment. It is also a place where the fishers gather to talk and to rest between stints on the open sea.

12. When an "educator," parent or teacher, obliges a victim to extend his or her hands, palms up, and beats them, generally with a palm switch, the assailant inflicts more than pain. The stripes ("to pay you back," the child hears) nearly always swell up, in the aftermath of this disciplinary act, into enormous "cakes"—as the people call them, due to the fact that they rise like cakes in an oven.

13. The military governments of Brazil were headed by the following officers: General Humberto de Alencar Castelo Branco, from April 15,

1964, to March 15, 1967; from the latter date to August 31, 1968, when illness obliged him to resign, General Arthur da Costa e Silva; replacing him on that date, a military junta composed of General Aurélio Lyra Tavares, Brigadier General Marcio de Souza e Melo, and Admiral Augusto Rademaker Grunerwald, to October 30, 1969; Emílio Garrastazu Médici from that date to March 15, 1974; Ernesto Geisel from then to March 15, 1979; and João Batista Figueiredo, from this last date to March 15, 1985.

14. It will be well for us to indicate the current (September 1992) structure of education in Brazil since the enactment of the new Law of Directives for and Foundations of National Education by the National Congress. Drafted and implemented in 1971, during the harshest times of the military dictatorship, the created three scholastic levels were the First Degree, lasting eight school years, and comprising the old primary school and gymnasium curriculum; the Second Degree, of three or four years, depending on the branch of courses in which the student is enrolled; and the Third Degree, known as the "upper" level, the university level, offering curricula of three to six years' duration.

In Brazilian historical tradition, regular instruction included elementary or primary instruction, the middle level (secondary, commercial, normal, agricultural, industrial, and nautical), of which six branches only the first-named, the secondary, was not geared to training in a particular trade, but was college preparatory; and the upper level, which we cannot call the university level, because the oldest institution of that level of instruction among us recognized as such is the University of São Paulo, created by the government of São Paulo State in 1934.

The primary schools to which Freire refers were those that, of course, offered the first level of instruction, and officially were supposed to educate all children between seven and ten years of age.

15. "Meridionate them" [suleá-los]. Paulo Freire has used the term sulear-se—which does not actually exist in dictionaries of the Portuguese language—to call readers' attention to the ideological connotation of the terms orientar-se, to "orientate oneself" (lit., point oneself to the east, get one's bearings from the east), orientação (orientation)," nortear-se (a synonym for orientar-se, but in terms of the north rather than the east), and suchlike derivatives of the Portuguese words for "east" and "north."

The North is the First World. The North is on top, in the upper part of the world. The North lets knowledge "trickle down" to us in the Southern Hemisphere, where we "swallow it without checking it against local context" (cf. Márcio D'Olme Campos, "A Arte de Sulear-se," in Interação Museu-Comunidade pela Educação Ambiental, Manual de Apoio ao Curso *de Extensão Universitária,* ed. Teresa Scheiner [Rio de Janeiro: Uni-Rio / Tacnet Cultural, 1991], pp. 59–61).

The first thinker to alert Freire to the ideology implicit in terms like these, calculated to mark different levels of "civilization" and "culture" between the Northern and Southern Hemispheres, between the "creative" hemisphere and the "imitative" one (and mark them quite to the positivist taste), was the physicist we have just cited, Márcio Campos, who is currently working in ethnoscience, ethnoastronomy, and "ambiential education."

Let me quote the words with which Campos himself, in the book just cited, sets forth his conception and denunciation of the pretended intrinsic superiority of intelligence and creative power of the men and women of the North:

> Universal history, and geography, as understood by our Western society in its scientific tradition, mark out certain spaces and times, periods and eras, on the basis of internalistic, indeed ideological reference points very much to the taste of the central countries of the planet.
>
> Many are the examples of this state of affairs, which is imposed on the education of the peripheral countries—that is, the countries of the Third World—as a perfectly casual, textbook kind of thing, a matter of simple information.
>
> In our instructional materials, we find the earth represented on globes having the north pole at the top. Maps and their legends likewise respect this convention, which the Northern Hemisphere finds so appropriate, and are displayed in a vertical plane (on a wall) instead of a horizontal plane (on the floor or on a table). Thus, folks in Rio are heard to say that they are going "up" to Recife; and for all anyone knows they might think there is a north on every mountain peak since "north is on top."
>
> In questions of spatial orientation, especially with respect to the cardinal points of the compass, the problems are equally grave. The "practical" rules taught here are practical only for persons situated in the Northern Hemisphere, who, in their particular situation, will want to *septentrionate* (*north*-ate) themselves so to speak, by analogy with the word *orientate* (*east*-ate), meaning getting one's bearings from the east.
>
> The imposition of these conventions on our hemisphere establishes confusion with respect to the concepts of above and below, north and south, and, above all, principal and secondary, and upper and lower.
>
> At any local reference point of observation, the rising sun, appearing in the direction of the east, founds an *orient*ation. In the Northern Hemisphere, the polestar, Polaris, the North Star, founds a *septentrion*ation. In the Southern Hemisphere, the Southern Cross is the perfectly adequate basis for a *meridion*ation (or *south*-ation).
>
> Despite all this, the practical rule that continues to be taught in our schools is the rule of the north: that is, you mentally place yourself with

the rising sun to the east on your right, with the west on your left, the north straight ahead "up there," and the south behind you, "down here." This thoroughly flawed practical rule provides a corporeal schema that, at night, leaves us with our back to the Southern Cross, the fundamental constellation for the act of *meridion*ation. Would it not be better for us to position ourselves with the east on our left? [Emphasis added]

Having cited this lengthy, but indispensable, passage, I should like to call attention to a few words in it that, few as they are, nevertheless say a great deal, and say it very powerfully. They are not abstract words; rather, they imply a particular behavior, and an attitude adopted by the person who exhibits the behavior. A person practicing this behavior and adopting this attitude does so because he or she has acquired them concretely.

Let us carry Professor Campos's observations and denunciations a bit further, then. Let us ask ourselves, with the purpose of stimulating our own reflection: To be "left with our back to the Southern Cross"—to turn our back on, to turn around so that we are "left with our back to," the Southern Cross, which is the cross on our flag, the symbol of Brazil, a reference point for us—will this not betoken an attitude of indifference, contempt, disdain, for our own capabilities to construct, locally, a knowledge that would be ours, and would bear on things local, things concretely ours? Why is this? How has it arisen and perpetuated itself among us? In favor of whom? In favor of what? Against what? Against whom, this manner of reading the world?

Would not that "thoroughly flawed practical rule" be one more form of alienation infecting our signs and symbols, by way of a knowledge developed to the point of producing a cognition that *turns its back* on itself, and turns, with open heart, gluttonous mouth, and head as hollow as a pot (waiting to be filled by signs and symbols from elsewhere), so that we end up as a continent of knowledge developed and produced by men and women of the North, the "summit," the "upper part," the "top"?

16. General Eurico Gaspar Dutra was President of the Republic from January 31, 1946, to January 31, 1951, in the period immediately following the dictatorship of Getúlio Vargas—which the general, alongside so many civilians and other military had helped to build from 1930 onward, when the cowboy politician began his struggle for the power that he finally won and held onto for fifteen years.

In October 1945 Dutra was one of the dictator's overthrowers. As soon as he was elected president, he initiated, ironically enough, the period we refer to as that of our Brazilian "redemocratization."

17. Vasco da Gama is an overcrowded "popular" or lower-class neighborhood of the then peripheral zone of Recife.

18. In the Northeast, we use the word here translated "yard" [*oitão*] to designate the stretch of ground running along the side of a house, between the house and the wall of the property on which it has been built. Or the area running along the side of any building.

For example, when we say "no oitão da igreja" (in the *oitão* of the church), we are referring to the little stretch of ground running along the sides of the church, not the front churchyard or any yard that may lie behind the church.

A house with *oitões livres*, then, as the Portuguese reads, is one that has been built in such dimensions as to leave a space—not necessarily a very big space, although it could be a *quintal*, or real yard, too—between the house and the wall at the edge of the property on which the house has been erected.

19. In the 1950s, "Arno-brand appliances" were the symbol of the purchasing power of the Northeastern middle class, which in those postwar years was very limited, especially by comparison with that of its equivalent in the United States or many European countries—or, for that matter, with that of southeastern or southern Brazil itself.

This "poor" middle class of the Northeast of those days sought to salvage some prestige, and respect for its purchasing power, by purchasing and using at home a line of name-brand electrical appliances produced in Brazil under the trademark Arno. Anyone who could afford an Arno blender, vacuum cleaner, or egg-beater—and when they could, they were careful not to hide the fact!—felt and esteemed themselves to be privileged members of the modest Northeastern middle class.

20. Jaboatão, a city just eighteen kilometers from Recife (and merging with its outskirts today) was felt in the 1930s to be lying quite a distance from the Pernambucan capital, due to the precarious conditions of access to it—almost exclusively by train, on the British-owned Great Western Railway.

It was there that the Freire family moved in the hope of better days to come, having been plunged into poverty, like so many other Brazilian families, by the New York stock market crash of 1929.

It was from Jabotão too, that, after having lost her husband in 1934, Tudinha Freire "traveled" daily to Recife in hopes of obtaining scholarship money for her son Paul. Each evening that she returned with her "I didn't get it," her cadet seemed to see his chances of a university education slip further away.

Desperate, Tudinha made one last attempt, and early in 1937, received a yes from Aluízio Pessoa de Araújo.

Chancing to pass along Dom Bosco Street, she noticed a sign, on the building at number 1013, which read, "Ginásio Oswaldo Cruz" (Oswaldo Cruz gymnasium, or secondary school). Only in the 1940s was the institution renamed Colégio Oswaldo Cruz (Oswaldo Cruz boarding school). She entered the building and asked to speak with the director. And Tudinha's request was promptly granted—on one sole condition, "that your son, my newest pupil, likes to study."

It was in Jaboatão, where he lived from the age of eleven to twenty, that Paulo became acquainted with a world of difficulty, in which one lived on scant financial resources. There were the difficulties arising from his mother's untimely widowhood, when society was much less open to a woman's working outside the home than it is today. And there were the difficulties he felt personally, "skinny, bony little kid" that he was, in fending off the hostility of a world that had such little sympathy for the weak and impoverished.

But it was also in Jaboatão that he learned to play soccer, which was an exciting experience for him. And it was there that he swam in the Jaboatão River, where he watched poor women, squatting, and washing and beating against the rocks either their own families' clothes or those of more wealthy families, for whom they worked. It was there, again, that he learned to sing and whistle—things he still loves to do today to relieve the weariness that comes from intellectual activity, or from the tensions of everyday life. He learned to dialogue in his "circle of friends," and learned sexual appreciation for, "falling in love with" and loving, women. Finally, it was there in Jaboatão that he learned and assimilated—with a passion!—his studies of both the popular and the cultivated syntax of the Portuguese language.

Jaboatão, then, was the space–time of a learning process, and of intense difficulties and joys in life—all of which taught him to strike a harmonious balance between having and not having, being and not being, capability and incapability, liking and not liking. Thus was Freire molded in the discipline of hope.

21. I should like to call the reader's attention to the names of Recife streets. They are picturesque, regional, lovely, romantic names, nor have they gone unnoticed by intellectuals, poets, and sociologists (for example, Gilberto Freire).

The names are not always cheerful ones, but they almost always contain a preposition, and tell a little story. We may read them on the blue, white-lettered signs of centuries-old Recife: Rua das Crioulas (Street of the Native Women), Rua da Saudade (Street of the Longing, for home), Rua do Sol and Rua da Aurora (Street of the Sun and Street of the Dawn; these are the streets running along the Capibaribe River in the middle of town, one along the west bank, the other along the east bank), Rua das Graças

(Thanksgiving Street), Rua da Amizade (Friendship Street), Rua dos Miracles (Street of the Miracles), Corredor do Bispo (Bishop's Way), Rua das Florentinas (Street of the Florentine Women), Praça do Chora Menino (Square of the Little-Boy-Weeping), Rua dos Sete Pecados (Street of the Seven Sins) or Rua do Hospício (Hospice Street), Rua dos Martirios (Street of the Martyrs), Beco da Facada (Stab Alley), Rua dos Afogados (Street of the Drowned), and so many others.

Rua da Imperatriz (Empress Street), so familiar to all Recifians, which runs from the intersection of Rua da Matriz (Womb) with Rua do Hospício, across Ponte da Boa Vista (Bellevue Bridge, we might say) and becomes Rua Nova (New Street) is actually—something few of us know—Rua da Imperatriz Teresa Cristina, named in homage to the consort of the second and last Emperor of Brazil, Dom Pedro II.

22. *Massapé*, or *massapê*, according to the "Aurélio" (Aurélio Buarque de Holanda Ferreira, *Novo dicionário da língua portuguesa* [Rio de Janeiro: Nova Fronteira, n.d.], derives most probably from the words *massa*, "mass" or "dough," and *pé*, "foot." If this is its etymology, this clay would receive its name from the powerful clutch it applies to the feet of anyone attempting to walk in it. Peculiar to the Brazilian Northeast, *massapé* is calcareous, almost always black, and ideal for sugar-cane cultivation" (Aurelio, p. 902).

23. A *pinico* or *penico* is a chamber pot, a small vessel used in a bedroom at night as a urinal before homes had modern bathrooms with flush toilets.

The popular strata use the expression *pinico do mundo* (the world's chamber pot) by analogy for regions of Brazil of extremely high annual rainfall.

24. A *badoque* or *bodoque* is a slingshot—a crude, homemade weapon frequently built by children and consisting of a forked stick fitted with a rather broad rubber band between the prongs. The elastic strip is drawn like a bowstring, then released to launch a small stone from the center of the strip. It is used as a toy, or, especially among the poorer populations of the rural zones, for hunting birds for food.

25. The use of the word "archeology," here, is obviously metaphorical—as, for that matter, it is so typically of the Freirean taste for figurative language. The term is used by analogy with its literal meaning. Freire is speaking here of the archeology he is practicing upon the emotions of his past. Reliving these emotions, he executes an analysis that searches, that veritably "digs" into the particular emotions that have caused him to suffer, to fall into depression.

This archeology, then, is not the one French philosopher Michel Foucault is referring to when he uses the term.

26. Anyone from the Northeast of Brazil—or of Africa, Freire adds—knows the scent of earth.

In Recife, to whose soil the educator is referring, when the hot, humid topsoil is rain-soaked, it exudes a strong scent of moisture and heat, reminiscent of the scent exhaling from a woman's body—or a man's, for that matter—when stimulated by the sensuality of tropical climes.

27. Freire had been friends with Paulo de Tarso Santos ever since the latter had invited him to head a national literacy program.

The 1961 Law of Directives for and Foundations of National Education, with its decentralizing tendencies, had a certain inhibiting influence on campaigns of national scope. But one evening President João Goulart attended a literacy course graduation, in Angicos, Rio Grande do Norte. There he had the opportunity to observe how well Freire's team worked. And so he conceived the notion of breaking with the new orientation in educational policy and assigning all initiatives in educational practice to the responsibility of federal agencies alone.

With the government taking this decision, the sensitivity of Paulo de Tarso, now minister of education—known today, as well, for the beauty and expressiveness of his painting, to be seen where Brasília stands as a symbol of the early, rebellious years of the 1960s—led him to create the Programa Nacional de Alfabetização, the National Literacy Program.

It fell to Freire, then, to coordinate that program, which was supposed to teach five million Brazilians to read and write in two years. Every indication was that this would bring about a shift in the balance of political power—as indeed was the intention of the approach being used. After all, the Paulo Freire Method now being officially implemented sought not to impart literacy mechanically, but to politicize the persons learning to read and write.

With this societal swerve to the left in prospect, the conservative elite, enlisting the support of certain sectors of the middle class, proclaimed the Paulo Freire Method, now being officially implemented, "highly subversive." And of course it was, although not from the perspective of the dominated.

The dominant, ignoring the real needs of the people, which called for greater seriousness in the business of education, were in dismay—at the method, its author, and Goulart's populist government itself.

With the military coup of April 1, 1964, one of whose main targets was to keep the people from acquiring use of the written language, the program was quashed, and its mentors persecuted. The method had failed to retain the alienated and alienating characteristics of earlier literacy campaigns.

For many of Freire's associates, then, as for himself, the choice was prison and torture, or exile.

28. *Cidade-dormitório* (bedroom city) is a Brazilianism denoting municipalities most of whose families have their breadwinner going to work every day in another town, generally to neighboring cities that are larger or whose employment opportunities are more abundant. These working people return from their distant tasks so late each day that it is already time to retire for the night.

Freire has obviously used the term as a metaphor, meaning that, at that moment of which he speaks, intellectuals were scurrying to Santiago from various parts of the world, seeking to enhance their own politicization, and to discuss "Latin Americanness" and the Christian Democracy of Chile.

29. *Manha* (wiles, craftiness) expresses a certain quite Brazilian behavior in which, unwilling or unable to confront another person, or some bothersome or difficult situation, a person attempts to camouflage the fact or situation with the strategem or artifice of idle gossip, or noncommittal, casual chatter that is neither positive nor negative with respect to the matter under discussion. The purpose of the "wily one" is to stall for time, and thereby manage to draw some advantage for himself or herself without being explicit about that intent. The person exercising *manha* plays with words—and often enough, plays make-believe with his or her own person— in a superficial, false engagement that seeks to escape the reality of the situation.

In Freire's understanding, *manha* is all of this, and one thing more: a necessary defense tactic in the cultural and political resistance of the oppressed.

30. Josué de Castro, a celebrated Pernambucan physician, after careful research of the diets of the Northeastern populations, has drawn up what came to be called the crab diet. The name comes from the fact that the crab is the typical crustacean of the lands of the mangroves, and one of the most important sources of nutrition for the most impoverished strata of the population of these areas. It is found in abundance where it likes to live best, alongside the palafittes, the pile structures built over the sloughs where the mangroves grow, and its meat is of high nutritional value.

Castro's most important book, known throughout the world, is *Geografia da fome* (Geography of hunger). Shockingly realistic, it paints the portrait of the hunger and the struggle for survival of the populations in the Brazilian Northeast to whom survival is forbidden.

31. Minas Gerais (General Mines) is one of the federated units or states of Brazil, and is located in the Southeast (latitude 14°–22°, longitude 41°– 51°). Its name derives from the fact that, within its present territory, toward

the middle of the eighteenth century, the great gold deposits were discovered, as well as, later, those of many other precious metals.

32. PUC-SP is the familiar abbreviation, amoung us Brazilians, for the Pontifícia Universidade Católica de São Paulo: São Paulo Pontifical Catholic University.

33. What we call a *favela*, in Brazil, here translated "slum," is an agglomeration of shacks inhabited by the poor and originally constructed of discarded building materials, old lumber, sheets of zinc, scrap iron, and so on. Until very recently, *favelas* were entirely without running water, electricity, sewer systems, refuse collection, or public transportation.

The first *favelas* were erected toward the end of the last century, by communities of emancipated slaves. Unemployed, possessing no tools or skills, they invaded the hilly areas of the large cities, at first, to settle there. Later, abandoned in the streets, they wandered to the inner city for survival.

Many of the *favelas* that swell the large Brazilian cities are no longer among the hills (which have become the bourgeoisie's favorite place to live). Now they are to be seen along streets or streams, as well, or on private urban terrain they have occupied in their "invasion of the land," or under viaducts—indeed, in any abandoned area in which they find it possible to install themselves, in small or large family groups, and gain a feeling of being closer to employment and/or civilization.

Brazil's largest *favelas* are to be found scattered across the hills of Rio de Janeiro, where the first emanicipated slaves came in large numbers. The Roçinha *favela* counts more than 500,000 inhabitants. Despite the huge number of shacks, and the promiscuity that translates their inhabitants' abandonment by society, even the denizens of the *favelas* are gaining politicization, often enough with the assistance of pastoral teams of the Catholic Church, and are beginning to organize in neighborhood associations that vindicate their right to public services.

In the Roçinha *favela*, as in so many others, violence and hostility is on the increase—in response, it seems to me, to the centuries-old exclusion from social life of those Brazilians who have been obliged merely to "mark off the days of their lives."

Such is the revenge wrought by the oppressed on their oppressors. Today we are paying the price: in our *favelas* we have one of our most serious social problems, and it calls for urgent, definitive solutions.

Among the solutions would be agrarian reform. Brazil is just as colonial today as it was in the sixteenth century, when it was divided into huge estates called *latifúndios*—the hereditary "captaincies"—in the naive hope entertained by Portugal that these "lands that grow anything you plant" could become a populated, productive region.

The immense *latifúndios*, barren and uninhabited, each the private domain of a single family, are preventing the creation in our country—which is one of the few modern capitalist nations in the world, and, incredibly, the eighth economic power worldwide—of a more humane, more rational distribution of these vast expanses (not that such a distribution has ever been seriously attempted).

In reality, the authorities today, especially the mayors, have to deal with these clandestine clusters of shacks, the eyesore of nearly all of the large cities of Brazil. City hall is faced with the task of providing decent living conditions for the persons who are obliged to live there.

A determined political will must strike an alliance with technological solutions. Given Brazil's current economicosocial structure, it will be impossible to do away with the thousands of *favelas* scattered across the country.

In the city of São Paulo, the current municipal adminstration is attempting to improve the conditions of the *favelas*—but only of those that have sprung up on terrain solid enough to bear the physical weight of a large number of homes and persons. *Favelas* that have been erected on terrain vulnerable to landslides and caveins are discouraged. The *favelas* are no longer the stopping-off place once used by the migrants on their way to establish themselves in the economic life of this metropolis.

As we all know today, politicians and plain citizens alike, the *favela* is the only available space in the city of São Paulo for working families that have arrived in recent years. Saturated and swollen by a population overflow (the census says around 10 million, but the actual population is over 12 million) the city is simply out of room. And so the newcomers have been obliged to go to live among the destitute, outcast, old residents of the *favelas*, who were condemned to live in them more than a century ago.

The *favelados*, the *favela* people, of the city of São Paulo have mounted a campaign for the legalization of their homes and, and of their occupation of the land on which these homes stand. Nowadays most of the dwellings are of brick or cement block, and are roofed with tiles. Countless are the societies of "Friends of the Neighborhoods" who set up adult literacy programs in collaboration with the Municipal Secretariate of Education, and at the same time lobby municipal authorities with a view to obtaining other public services.

The goal of the *favelados*, then, is to make their de facto possession of their homes a de jure ownership. They feel that this would make it possible to urbanize the *favelas*, and thus improve their public services. A large number of São Paulo *favelas* now have water, electricity, and in some cases, a sewer system.

The São Paulo municipal budget is the third largest governmental budget in the country (after the federal budget and that of the state of which it is the capital, São Paulo State). São Paulo is a dynamic pole of the national economy and the cultural center of the nation. Paradoxically, it is also home to a population, according to city hall records (1992), of some one million *favelados*, in 1,790 *favelas*.

34. Like the *favelas*, the *cortiços* (beehives) represent more than just a housing problem. They are symptomatic of even broader and more serious social problems.

Cortiços are houses inhabited by a number of families at once, each family leasing some little part of the house or building in order to make their home there. They may lease them from the owners themselves, or (more commonly) from intermediaries who sublet them.

The first *cortiços* were old mansions, standing in the center of town, where affluent families once lived. The latter, obliged to move to a better neighborhood far removed from the great problems of the inner city, where violence now reigns, have abandoned their antique dwellings with their numberless rooms of all sizes to the lower or very-low-middle classes to make their homes in. Today the *cortiços* have spread practically all over the city, and consist, often enough, of far more modest houses than those noble old mansions.

Promiscuity is rampant, of course, as are the great risks generated by the absence of hygienic living conditions, and the precarious physical condition of both the aristocratic old mansions and the new *cortiços*.

Estimates by the municipal housing secretariat, SEHAB-HABI, indicate, for São Paulo, in 1992, 88,200 "beehive" homes, housing a total of three million persons.

Sometimes a family does not even have an entire apartment to itself. It may share it with other families, occupying it in eight- or twelve-hour shifts, especially in the inner city, where the "beehive clientele" is to be found.

The city of São Paulo, like nearly all large Brazilian cities, has part of its population living in these conditions, imposed on them by an unjust distribution of the national income.

35. The upper-middle and upper-class neighborhoods of the city of São Paulo known as the Gardens, which were originally divided into Jardim América, Jardim Europa, and Jardim Paulista (Garden America, Garden Europe, Garden São Paulo), today form a single whole. Their long, tree-lined boulevards, with their trees, sidewalks, lawns, and gardens, are lined with great, lovely, well-constructed houses set amidst huge, flowery gar-

dens, and apartment buildings where good taste, comfort, and luxury are in abundance.

The Gardens are at the opposite extreme from the *favelas* and the *cortiços*.

36. Ethnoscience is the name used for their practice by the team of Unicamp researchers (of the University of Campinas, at Campinas in São Paulo state) to which Márcio Campos belongs. These investigators ply their various sciences under a common "ethnoscientific" umbrella. What they have in common is that they do precisely an ethnography of the cognition and technology (hence an "ethnotechnology") of various distinct cultural contexts. Ethnoscience, then, is an academic science practiced upon another science, that of another culture. Its practitioners study, for example, various native groups of the territory of Brazil, as well as the *caiçaras* (here denoting the coastal dwellers themselves) of São Paulo State, and thereby create a body of knowledge that articulates the science and technology of these peoples with the culture that is theirs as well.

The focus of these scientists' research is on how these peoples, who live by fishing, gathering, farming, and hunting, construct their knowledge and develop their techniques of production and extraction. This knowledge and these techniques are based on observations, perceptions, and experiences, which in turn are systematized by these peoples, thus coming to form, in the understanding of the ethnoscientists, genuine scientific knowledge.

More conservative academicians regard this knowledge as no more than a kind of common sense, and hence prescientific knowledge. The ethnoscientists reject this interpretation, arguing that, on the contrary, the cognition of these peoples is authentically scientific, in a sense analogous to the scientific character of the cognition systematized in universities. The two "productions of knowledge" differ only in their argumentation, premises, methodology, and consequently, in their distinct manners—both valid—of reading the world. Whereupon, from these distinct readings of the world, distinct cognitions constantly emerge whose vehicle is an awareness of the historical situation—not the prehistorical—of each individual, and every people.

Accordingly, ethnoscientists defend, from their scholarly position in the broader world, the preservation not only of our planet's biological diversity, but of its sociocultural diversity as well. Indeed, the latter supports the former, which in turn is overwhelmingly composed, by reason of their geographical predominance, of the peoples of the tropical forests.

37. Freire calls Rio de Janeiro simply "Rio," which is how we usually refer to the city. Celebrated for its matchless beauty, bounded by the sea,

the mountains, the forests, and a lagoon, Rio is one of the most important cities of the country from a politico-economico-cultural viewpoint. It had been the capital of Brazil ever since the colonial period, all through the shift of the dynamic economic pole from the Northeast, with its sugar production, to the Southeast with the initiation of the "mining cycle," when, in 1960, the seat of government of the union was transferred to Brasília, that creation of the courage of President Juscelino Kubitscheck combined with the talents of Oscar Niemeyer and Lúcio Costa.

During one period of the military regime, Rio de Janeiro, the "Wonder City" (as we Brazilians all style it in homage, when we are not "singing" its actual name), was a city-state, known as Guanabara.

38. Ariano Suassuna, today a member of the Brazilian Academy of Letters, and a brilliant alumnus of Colégio Oswaldo Cruz, was born in Taperoá, in the very center of the state of Paraíba, in the hinterland or desert region, not far from the Serra da Borborema.

For all his funny name and pale skin, Ariano is one of those Northeasterners who are glad to be alive, who are caught up in a "taste" for being. He is a lover of the heat, the rocks, the dry soil, the scrubby vegetation— but especially, of the wisdom and shrewdness of his native region.

His works deal with the uncultured—the illiterate or semiliterate. They tell of the dry earth, and the austere men and strong women who forge their personhhoods in the fire of aggressiveness. They are tales of persons with calloused hands, and feet discalced by poverty and split by the dryness of their bony, skinny bodies, which, for days and years, have been out in the merciless glare of the sun. They expound the naughty wiles and talent for deception by which these men and women keep at arm's length from oppression and the oppressor.

Ariano's tales, recounted in the ingenuous speech of the personages of his *Autos* (Acts, that is, officially documented actions of a solemn personage), in a popular lingo, and in the context and situations that so well characterize the Brazilian Northeast, have burst the barriers of that region to conquer the nation and the world, ever since the publication of a work he composed while still very young, his finest and best loved, the *Auto da Compadecida* (Act of the compassionate woman).

39. Freire uses the expression *interdição do corpo* (interdiction of the body) in quotation marks because he is referring to a category that I am exploring in my research on the history of Brazilian illiteracy.

I have learned through my investigations that the Jesuit-style domination employed to subdue the Indian, the colonist, or the black, at the beginning of Brazilian colonization, and render them docile, with a view to swelling the coffers of the Portuguese crown (and later that of the Society of Jesus itself, which had come here with the official mission of "instructing and catechizing the Indian") was so efficient that the dominant class adopted it as one of the mechanisms it applied in order to reproduce the society of the few who have knowledge and power, and the many who remain excluded and prohibited from being, knowing, and "being able."

I have dubbed this ideology the "ideology of the interdict of the body," letting *corpo* (body) stand, as we do in our language, for the person as the self. The reason I have called it this is that it explains the phenomenon of absence from the privileged space of the school in terms of the intrinsic inferiority, the incompetency, of those who do not occupy that space. Thus it camouflages (as does any dominant ideological discourse, being the voice of the dominant class) the authentic reasons for these prohibitions. The actual reasons for these interdictions, and for this ideological discourse, stand in dialectical relationship with the political and economic context of our society, by virtue of the manner in which that society produces its existence.

A social organization such as ours, which was always colonial, even after political autonomy (1822), and which still preserves the telltale signs of a colonial society—a society molded concretely and historically of values, behaviors, hierarchies, and preconceptions whose guidelines are discrimination, authoritarianism, and elitism—will necessarily be founded on prohibitions and interdicts.

Thus, from the dawn of Brazilian history down to our very day, these prohibitions have managed to reserve Brazilian illiteracy for the strata of lesser social value. Included today are, especially, black women and men, and white women of the popular strata.

The Jesuits' reading of the world, during the period of their missionary work in Brazil (1549–1759), which was inaugurated under the regime of King John III, exaggerated the extent of incest, nudity, and cannibalism as practiced here—natives' ways of being—and introduced the notion of sin, inculcating an internalized spirit of obedience, subservience, submission, hierarchy, imitation, example, and Christian devotion—European values—which counterbalanced the notion of sin in a dynamic tension. This is the origin of what I have come to call the ideology of the "interdict of the body." (Cf. Ana Maria Araújo Freire, *Analfabetismo no Brazil*, cited in Paulo Freire's text, above.)

40. "Brazil's slavocratic past" is still extensively present, in the aristocratic discrimination among the various social classes, and in race and sex discrimination (although no longer in discrimination based on religion, which still prevailed among us until a few decades ago).

Brazil comes to be considered by the "culture of the North," which is the culture that allows its knowledge to "drain" down the throats of us dwellers of the Southern Hemisphere—one of the territories discovered by the white, civilized European.

In 1500, Brazil was indeed "conquered" by Portugal, and the victors hung their flag between the altars and masses of the Catholic fathers and the naked Indians, who by now had been stripped of their taboos and their alleged "art of oppressing and exploiting."

There was created, then, in these American lands, a colony, which would have the function of producing whatever the world division of labor were to require of it.

Thus, if it was economically inviable to go to the Orient in quest of spices, the latter would have to be extracted here (in the Amazon region) or produced here (in the Northeast).

With the selection of what was to be produced in the immense expanses of fertile lands (sugar), with Holland's capacity to produce the machinery needed in the manufacture of this consumer product in such demand in Europe, and with Portugal's experience, meager but adequate, in that manufacture, only one problem remained. Who would work on the cane plantations, and who would mill the cane in the machines? And who would stir the hot syrup in the caldrons with wooden sticks from the Atlantic Rain Forest, then dense and luxuriant in the Brazilian Northeast, while it thickened?

The solution was found in black slavery. Thus, the colonizers went in quest of the citizens of Africa, purchasing them—as cogs in the wheels of the sugar machines—from the Dutch, who for a time plied the black slave trade between Africa and Brazil. From 1534 to 1888, when slavery was abolished, thousands of blacks entered Brazil—an estimated average of five thousand souls per year. (I have said "souls," since the Jesuits who came here in 1549 regarded the blacks as creatures without souls.)

Despite the fact that they were the "engine master's" heaviest investment, in this colonial enterprise, the slaves were not on that account handled with care.

It is recorded by our historians that the useful life span of this black "coal" that fueled the sugar production of the first Brazilian centuries was, on the average, seven years of slave labor.

Women, less used for the heaviest work, were house slaves, many of them, performing domestic service in the great houses—those in which the lord and his family resided.

It was common, in the era of a slavocratic economy in Brazil, for a white man to "mate" with his black slave women, whether merely to "possess" many women, or to enlarge the most valuable element in the legacy they would hand on—their slaves—by way of their own descendants.

Thus, a society formed in Brazil that, beginning as elitist and authoritarian, became discriminatory as well, losing all or nearly all respect for person-to-person relationships—especially, I reassert with the author, for relationships between different sexes, races, and classes, and above all between wealthy whites over poor blacks.

41. *Quilombo*, in its acceptation in this text, has a strong political connotation. A *quilombo* is a place where the black slaves of Brazil took refuge, building there, together, in complete solidarity and community, an all but self-sustaining city. Thus, they founded a genuine culture of resistance to the barbarizing oppression of slavery.

Décio Freitas, ranking scholar of the black question among us, declares, in his *Palmares: a guerra dos escravos* (Palmares: the slaves' war): "As long as there was slavery in Brazil, the slaves revolted, and expressed their revolt in armed protests whose repetition is unparalleled in the history of any other country of the New World" (p. 11).

I must warn that official historiography omits such an interpretation. It denies its realism. It has "reasons" for not understanding and not accepting the incontestable factuality of the political and revolutionary content of the slave revolts.

These specious objections only betray an authoritarian, discriminatory rot or rancidity that the blacks, ever the vanquished of our history, have been obliged to accept in silence.

Today, black movements, still timid, are appearing here and there in our country. Under the leadership of certain black men and women, some blacks are coming to accept their blackness and to value it. Thus they are forging a new time and a new space for the black race in Brazil. Without ever ceasing to be Brazilians, in heart and mind, these men and women are purposely accentuating the cultural marks of their African heritage. The silence of centuries is at last finding a voice, as Brazilian blacks begin to assume themselves historically—take responsibility for an autonomy in the conduct of their own concrete history.

The slave rebels of the sixteenth century rebelled not only in order to preserve their African heritages; they likewise struggled, for over a century, against slavery as a system, of which they were the greatest victims whether they had a clear and critical awareness of it or not.

The black republic of Palmares, the most important of the *quilombos*, established in the South of the Captaincy of Pernambuco, was an example of a productive economy and exemplary social organization of blacks who had risen against the slavocratic labor regime on which, along with the *latifúndio* and the sugar monoculture, the colonial economy rested.

Freitas ends his bruising, beautiful, and highly significant study on the black insurrections, whose life was from the late sixteenth to the late seventeenth century in the Northeast—the most economically dynamic region of Brazil in colonial times, thanks to its sugar production—with these words:

> Every *quilombo* that appeared on the summit of a wooded ridge constituted an obscure little epic. Evaluated as a whole, and in historical perspective, the *quilombos* assume the dimension of a *great* epic.
>
> They did not achieve success in their attempts to transform society, but they did exhibit the specificate predicate of the epic: the heroic action through which human beings assert themselves as such, independently of success or failure. These rustic black republics manifested the dream of a social order founded on an equality of siblingship, and are therefore integral to the revolutionary tradition of the Brazilian people.
>
> Palmares was the most eloquent manifestation of the antislavery discourse of Brazilian blacks throughout nearly three centuries of slavery. The resolution taken at Serra da Barriga to die rather than accept reenslavement expresses the essence of the message that the Palmares blacks send from the depths of their night. After all—to cite the Hegelian reflection—"The master is master only in virtue of the fact that he possesses a slave that recognizes him as such" (Décio Freitas, *Palmares: a guerra dos escravos*, 2nd ed. [Rio de Janeiro: Graal, 1978], p. 210).

42. The authoritarian discriminations of Brazilian society ultimately proclaim the illiterate incapable of thinking, deciding, or choosing, so that they ought not to be accorded the right to vote. Indeed, we hear, anyone elected by the illiterate would also be uncultivated, and equally "harmful to the nation."

Those who think in this way ignore the fact that the illiterate are precisely illiterate with respect to reading and writing, not orally, and that the reading of the world precedes the reading of the word, as we learn from Freire himself.

Our historical tradition, arising as it does from the slave mode of production prevailing in colonial times, molds us to an authoritarian, elitist, discriminatory society, as I have asserted in several of these notes to Freire's book.

In the Brazilian Empire, only "good men" voted—that is, male property owners. The first republican constitution, of 1891, having excluded the illiterate (along with beggars, women, and the noncommissioned military) from voting, dialectically perpetuated an inexperience with democracy, and within that, an inexperience with choosing and voting. Women voted and could be elected to office only from 1933 on.

Only with the 1985 elections did the illiterate win their suffrage. They might vote if they wished: they were not, however, obliged to do so, as were all literate citizens of Brazil, native or naturalized, from the age of eighteen.

Beginning with the 1989 elections, the right to vote was extended to young persons from the age of sixteen up—provided, of course, they knew how to read and write.

In the presence of this historical tradition of "aristocratic, elitist rancidity," one readily appreciates the dismay, rejection, and fear prevailing, in any phase of the electoral process, in a Brazilian election.

43. Luiza Erundina is Mayor of São Paulo, and the "Petist" administration is the government she as a member of the Petist party has formed for the management of that immense city. The word *Petist* derives from the protogram for Partido dos Trabalhadores, Workers Party: *PT*, pronounced "pay-tay."

The *PT* is both a new political party, and a novel one in terms of its orientating ideologies. It maintains a doughty, committed militancy, with the result that the degree of its intervention and participation in the national political scene (and not only in that of municipalities where it has had its candidates elected to the prefecture) waxes by the day.

44. To the extent permitted by the Constitution, the Municipal Education Secretariate of São Paulo prioritizes primary instruction: eight school years, maintained in 355 schools. It also conducts a secondary school, and many (324) nursery schools. It maintains no institution of higher education, and only five "special education" schools, which are exclusively for the hearing-impaired and comprise both the primary and secondary levels.

In Brazil, the federal, state, and municipal governments all maintain free instruction, in accordance with the wherewithal and priorities of each, on the higher, secondary, and primary levels.

I speak of priorities because there is nothing to prevent (and it actually occurs) a state of the federation from maintaining primary and secondary schools (São Paulo State is the best example), or a municipality from offering instruction at all three levels: higher, secondary, and primary. The federal union itself only very rarely offers instruction below the university level.

Let us observe that this official instructional network—regular, and in various special purpose modalities, *supletivo* (supplementary)—is further complemented by private systems, which also offer instruction on the three levels instituted in the country.

These private establishments are monitored and financed by the various

234 · PAULO FREIRE

government offices for education on all three levels of government, besides being subject, of course, to the principles, objectives, and finalities imposed by the Law of Directives for and Foundations of National Education, which sets standards for all Brazilian schooling.

45. The authoritarian, centralizing power tradition so familiar to Brazilian society has of course extended itself to all facets of that society. Education could scarcely have expected to be an exception.

In 1961 we saw the first law voted by the National Congress for the three levels of instruction. From 1822 to 1961, all matters concerning education had been determined by decrees and "law decrees," with the exception of two pieces of legislation that instituted, in 1827, the "law courses" and the "schools of primary letters" in Brazil. Up until 1961, then, the disciplines and their curricula, their objectives, their standards, and especially their content—or their programs, since content was more commonly referred to up until then—were determined by legally binding regulations of various kinds issued by the Minister of Education with the endorsement of the President of the Republic.

Only with the enactment of the 1961 Law of Directives for and Foundations of National Education did local officials and the instructional institutions themselves receive official authority to engage in determinative deliberations on instructional matters. Heretofore local discussion had been permitted only by way of exception and/or solely within the letter of the law.

This experiment in the democratization of instruction, unprecedented in extent and depth, was initiated during the democratic administration of Mayor Luiza Erundina, thanks to the administrative skills, authority, and competence—professional, pedagogical, and political—of Paulo Freire.

The arduous, difficult task in question, to be performed without the old authoritarian, interdicting "rancidities," but also without going to the other extreme of permissiveness and "spontaneism"—constant concerns of Freire—was carried out, with enthusiastic concurrence on the part of all involved, in Paulo's tenure from January 1, 1989, to May 27, 1991, as Municipal Secretary of Education.

Thus, the content of the courses pursued by the students of the São Paulo city schools, which have taken with alacrity to the new democratic experience of self-management, takes its point of departure in community needs and experience, which latter are thereupon subjected to cognitive exploration by teachers specializing in the various fields of knowledge, all working simultaneously.

An interdisciplinary approach to studies, and the choice of themes to be investigated, as part of the democratization of instruction, have yielded excellent results in terms of the acquisition of knowledge in itself scientific but based on a starting point in the commonsense knowledge that the children bring with them to school. In fact, the children come to perceive (and this is basic for their formation) the unity prevailing in the plurality of things, as well as the importance of a minute interpretation of each of the various parts of the universe within the totality.

During his term as head of the São Paulo Municipal Education Secretariat, through the implementation of an authentically democratic approach to management, Freire has demonstrated that decentralization is not only possible, but desirable. A democratic decentralization is found to occasion the active reinforcement of decisions that need to be taken in function of the desires and needs of the various communities, and in terms of the social classes of each, throughout the immense metropolis that is the city of São Paulo.

Delegating his authority to the secretariat's technological teams, Freire encouraged the formation of a number of deliberative bodies whose purpose would be to address various matters impinging on the main core of the act of educating, the act performed by that municipal organ that is the school.

These bodies are made up of pupils, teachers, directors or principals, superintendents, counselors, and mothers and fathers, together with all of the support personnel in the schools—in other words, everyone involved in the educational process.

46. Freire could have cited a work he had already written, before 1960 (the date of the text at hand), as evidence of his concern for content from his earliest writings onward.

I refer to the "Theme Three Report" he developed, which was presented by the Pernambuco Commission, and then included as well in the Second National Congress of Adult Education, held in Rio de Janiero, July 6–16, 1958.

I recently read a paper in the Mining Symposium on the Thought of Paulo Freire held in Poços de Caldas, September 3–6, 1992. I showed that, by way of that 1958 composition, Freire marked his entry into the history of Brazilian education. The revolutionary thesis he presented at that adult-education congress was that important.

That Report of Freire, I am certain, was the seed of all of his other, later works; but it had a value in itself, as well.

I also declared, there at the beautiful little spa near the hydromines of Minas Gerais State, that, in my view, when he published *Pedagogy of the Oppressed* in 1970—ironically in English in the United States rather than in his native Portuguese—he established his place in the universal history of education.

That book, which became revolutionary the moment it came into the hands of its first readers, is revolutionary, first, by virtue of the manner in which its author had come to understand the pedagogical relationship between human beings and the world. And it is revolutionary in that it opens up to those human beings the opportunity they have for liberation for them all, once they take up their histories for reflection—"detach" their problems and confront them. Thus, the once seemingly unfeasible becomes, through the dream, "untested feasibility": the dreamers of the dream—the oppressed—liberate themselves and their oppressors alike (see note 1, above).

The problem themes to be studied, to be reflected on, and to be conquered by each society, will obviously consist in the experiential content of the lives of those men and women who, in communion, exercise a praxis of liberation.

Now, with *Pedagogy of Hope*, Freire expounds and plumbs his favorite analytical themes more maturely. Objectively, after all, these themes need to be analyzed as elements of the body of a critical, liberative pedagogy. And in this new book we are led to understand the author's pedagogical thinking even better, through the critical seriousness, humanistic objectivity, and engaged subjectivity which, in all of his works, are always wedded to a creative innovation. Thus, Freire bequeaths us not only *Pedagogy of Hope*, but a pedagogy of hope steeped in "dialogicity," utopia, and the human liberation.

But let us return to the Theme Three Report, whose subject, as proposed by the Ministry of Education, which scheduled and sponsored the event, was: "The Education of Adults and Marginal Populations: *Favelas, Mocambos*, "Beehives," Foreign Enclaves, and So On." In an altogether new pedagogical language, most progressive and innovative for the era, Paulo Freire proposed that the education of adults in the zones of the *mocambos* (shacks hidden in the woods, constructed of thatched Brazil satintail and clay and covered with dried coconut straw) ought to be based on students' awareness of the reality of their everyday lives, and must never be reduced to simple mechanical, uncommitted literacy. The content, then, ought to arise out of that experience and that reality.

In the body of his address, Freire spoke of the importance of the programs of the literacy courses, as content was more commonly called in those days. I shall transcribe here a part of his "Conclusions and Recommendations," which constitute a synthesis of his whole discourse, and thereby not only provide us with a condensation of his ideas, but indicate solutions as well.

The programmatic content, then, which ought to be democratically selected by the parties participating in the act of educating for literacy, within a broader proposal, of educating, was specified as follows:

> E. That the *program* of these courses—always in conformity with local, regional, and national reality—be developed *with the participation of the educands* in some of its aspects, at least in flexible concerns admitting of adjustment:
>
> 1. Hygienic, moral, religious, recreational, and economic aspects of life in the local area
> 2. Aspects of regional and national life, especially when they bear on the development of the country
> 3. Development and utilization of local democratic leadership
> · 4. Creation of new attitudes toward the family, neighbors living close by, the broader neighborhood, and the municipality. These attitudes ought to be based on a spirit of solidarity and understanding. [Emphasis added.]

As early as the 1950s, then, Freire was building a dialectical relationship among three elements: literacy education, study content, and the political act of educating, with this third element "imbedding" the other two.

47. *Bate-papo* (chewing the rag, chewing the fat) is a Brazilian colloquialism denoting a noncommittal, amiable, desultory, or even inconsistent conversation.

48. As a work of basic importance for the rifts in countless societies of our time, *Pedagogy of the Oppressed* has been subjected to embargos and interdicts in various parts of the world.

This was the case, for instance, in the 1970s in Portugal, Spain, and Latin America, where extremely authoritarian government actions bereft of all popular legitimation proscribed *Pedagogy of the Oppressed* as "tares"; weeds sown amidst good wheat.

I have in my files a dossier on the interdict imposed in Portugal on this work of Freire's, where institutions languished under the Salazar yoke up to the Carnation Revolution in 1974.

These documents, of which I shall now present a summary analysis, show that, on February 21, 1973, the Office of Information Services, an organ of the Secretariate of State for Information and Tourism, in its *Ofício* (Order) no. 56-DGI/S, "respectfully besought" the Director General of Security, "for the welfare of the Portuguese nation," to "be at pains that the publication" of *Pedagogy of the Oppressed*, by Paulo Freire, published by João Barrote, be "distrained" or seized, inasmuch as the Information

Office had ascertained that the work in question was "a book of political theory, and experiment in the *mentalização* [*mentalization*, an attempt to instill a particular mentality, to brainwash] of the people with a view to inciting a social revolution."

The document concedes that *Pedagogy of the Oppressed* is not "necessarily" a work "of a Marxist nature," but insists that this work of Freire exhibits "a great deal of [Marxist] influence."

Portuguese authorities likewise "understood" that, as the edition was a limited one, and the language of the book "inaccessible," the danger within the Portuguese nation itself was not great. They overlooked the fact that underground copies were being circulated; nor can the language limitation have been very considerable, as we may gather from the testimony of Portuguese subjects in the African colonies, whose experiences and sufferings enabled them to understand Freire's language and proposals altogether adequately.

49. Thiago de Melo, the Amazonian poet who sings the praises of the Amazon River—"Water's Native Country"—with such beauty and creativity, lives today by the water's edge, twenty-four hours from Manaus by boat.

He lives *on*, he lives *with*, he lives *from*, he lives *for* that *rio-mar*, that "ocean of a river," that he so loves—as he loves the Amazon rain forest, which is just as full of surprises.

Amidst the flora and fauna, the *pororoca* (din of the river waters crashing into the Atlantic), flooded forests, and copper-colored *caboclas* (mixed-race Indian-and-white men and women) in that extraordinary, exuberant, and exotic scenario, Thiago de Melo lives his life, awash in that world of millions of lives.

Decades ago, in the 1960s, while serving as a Brazilian cultural attaché in Chile, he hosted a group of Brazilians in his home—almost all of them exiled from the country next door—and invited Paulo Freire to explain the approach the latter had been using in his adult-literacy programs in Brazil. Afterwards, Thiago composed one of his most intensely moving poems.

He had not been able to sleep after the meeting. Freire's concept of adult education had been too exciting, too astonishing for him. The next morning, on that summer's day of 1964, in solidarity with the numberless folk of his race and kind who were then prevented from reading the word, he composed his "Cançao para os poemas da alegria" (Ballad for the poems of gladness). It appears as an appendix in Paulo Freire's *Educação como prática da liberadade* (Brazilian edition).

He composed it in order that his glad wonderment at the creation of the method, mingled with his sorrowing wonderment that Freire could have been considered subversive, might proclaim the wonderment of hope.

50. Brazilian President João Belchior Marques Goulart took power as head of state on September 7, 1961, after a surprising turn of events had brought him hurrying back from China to Brasília, capital of Brazil and seat of government of the union.

As vice-president-elect, he had had to cut short his official visit to China in order to be sworn in as president of the Republic, following the unexpected resignation of Jânio Quadros, a mere seven months after the latter had taken office amidst great hope and enthusiasm on the part of the Brazilian people who had elected him.

Goulart, another of our populist rulers, erroneously regarded as a Communist, was under the watchful eye of the military, the dominant Brazilian class, and the Northern "owners of the world," throughout his incumbency.

His indecisive measures for a grassroots reform, necessary though they were for the country—and in the interest of the subordinate strata and therefore of progressive sectors—left those of the political Left almost as dissatisfied as those of the Right, who considered that President Goulart had gone too far in his concessions to "those people."

Strikes, including by navy personnel and sergeants of the national army; the emergence of peasant organizations, especially the peasant leagues; educational and popular cultural movements; attempts at a land reform to deal with the *latifúndios improdutivos*, or enormous unproductive land tracts; social legislation in behalf of farm workers; tactless, inflammatory speeches by members of his administration, some of them delivered from the public reviewing stands of the streets; a National Adult Literacy Program that responded to the interests of the social strata excluded from the schools for centuries; the public apology of the agricultural minister, Carvalho Pinto, which did manage to subdue some of the wrath of the right—along with other considerations—unleashed the military coup. Mounted in the name of the *subversion* (?) of *inflation* (100 percent a year then; now 1000 percent!), and *corruption* (!!!), the coup signaled the beginning of a strangling of the Brazilian people and nation that went on from April 1, 1964, to March 15, 1985.

51. For the National Literacy Program, see notes 7, 27, 49, above.

52. This "city" is called Segundo Montes, and is named for one of the Jesuits murdered in San Salvador a few years ago by the forces of established power.

The residents of this locality recounted to us that they themselves had had to seek refuge in Honduras, for long years, having fled the massacres perpetrated by the national army against women, children, and men not all of whom were engaged in the revolutionary struggle. This is how it was in Perquin, where more than two thousand simple peasants were crammed onto a little piece of ground and murdered, as an example and warning to all: Desist from the struggle or die. Desist from the struggle to *be-moreso*, from the battle for more being.

The survivors had then made their way, in anguish and distress, to the neighboring country. Now, in the company of gentle, peaceable United Nations troops—for they had come on a mission of peace—these same survivors, ten years older, had trudged for days upon end, traversing mountains and valleys, in anxiety and affliction, returning to their country to rebuild it.

They had returned to their Province—Morazón—not far from where they had come. But now they abandoned their former, blood-drenched locality for another point—a place where, between the forests and the mountain winds, they might build a place of life, and not of death. Thus arose the town of Segundo Montes.

They plant crops, breed barnyard animals, discuss their social organization, sing their songs, provide literacy courses for their adults, and educate their children. They are women and men who, reading the world with humanity and justice, are creating a different world, and they keep their eyes on Segundo Montes, "the Father."

That Jesuit and five of his companions were roused in the middle of the night to suffer the agony of knowing they were being lined up to be "executed."

As the order had been given to leave no witnesses, the woman who did the domestic work in the Padres' house, like her fifteen-year-old daughter, found no mercy.

This massacre, an inhuman tactic if there ever was one, had been premeditated by the forces in power as a form of intimidation. After all, the murder of Archbishop Romeo, shot dead as he celebrated mass in San Salvador Cathedral, had not sufficed.

The rightist government hoped that, with the massacre of the Jesuits, all the guerrilla forces of the left would surrender. Instead, they grew stronger still.

Segundo Montes, native of Spain, martyr of El Salvador, lives on. He lives in the *Viva!* his people shout every few minutes in praise of those to whom they would do homage. And he lives in their longing, in their irrepressible desire for the education of which they have such need and which they love, as they cry out, in a chorus that rings like thunder: "Viva la educatión popular!"